PRAISE FOR
The Peak in the Middle: Developing Mathematically Gifted Students in the Middle Grades...

The Peak in the Middle appears against the backdrop of NCTM's recent calls for coherence and focus in mathematics education. This new book highlights similarities as well as differences between gifted and other students. All students need opportunities to reason about and make sense of significant mathematics. But as gifted students engage in solving rich problems, their rapid grasp of ideas and processes sets them apart, underscoring their need for special accommodations. The possibilities include differentiated instruction, early exposure to algebra and geometry, and math-focused extracurricular activities. The authors offer many ideas about the advantages and drawbacks of different accommodations, challenges in articulation, issues of equity, and other countries' approaches—all with an eye to keeping our mathematically talented middle school students engaged and interested in mathematics. We cannot afford to lose these students at a time in their lives when they are developing interests and understanding that will guide their decisions for a lifetime.

Hank Kepner
President, National Council of Teachers of Mathematics

Students arrive at middle school with widely varying math experiences, abilities, and interests. With the current emphasis on reaching grade-level standards, how do we accommodate highly able and highly motivated students? How can we adapt instruction so that all students learn to the best of their abilities? *The Peak in the Middle* provides the rationale for offering advanced mathematical content in the middle grades as well as the practical information that school leaders need to develop procedures for assessing promising math students, selecting program options for their schools, making student placement decisions, and implementing appropriate professional development. In addition, *The Peak in the Middle* contains valuable information to assist educators in creating a responsive and challenging mathematics experience inside and outside of school. Finally, the authors offer suggestions to promote continuous progress in mathematics without undue repetition or gaps in instruction. To ensure that our most advanced math students have a high-level, creative, and appropriate mathematics education, educators will find practical guidance and much to consider in this well-balanced publication.

Ann Robinson
President, National Association for Gifted Children
Director, Center for Gifted Education
University of Arkansas at Little Rock

While specifically addressing the needs of academically gifted middle school students, *The Peak in the Middle* offers insight and practical advice to fully engage the general young adolescent population in learning math. The editors have tapped a wide range of expertise on developmentally responsive approaches to identifying needs, grouping students, appropriate curriculum, teaching approaches, articulation, and a look at the global perspective. This book is a must-read for educators working to implement *This We Believe*, the position paper of National Middle School Association, in math classrooms. It offers explanations of logical, practical ways to maximize learning by appropriately challenging students who might otherwise fall below the radar by simply meeting routine expectations or "tuning out." Policy issues, teacher support, and real-world models further provide the foundation for meeting the needs of mathematically able students who thrive on complexity.

Cathie Thibodeau
President, NMSA Board of Trustees
National Middle School Association

D1314682

THE PEAK
IN THE MIDDLE

THE PEAK IN THE MIDDLE

Developing Mathematically Gifted Students in the Middle Grades

Edited by

Mark Saul
Bronxville Schools (retired)
Bronxville, New York

Susan Assouline
University of Iowa
Iowa City, Iowa

Linda Jensen Sheffield
Northern Kentucky University
Highland Heights, Kentucky

 NATIONAL COUNCIL OF TEACHERS OF MATHEMATICS

 NATIONAL ASSOCIATION FOR Gifted Children

 NMSA.

Copyright © 2010 by
THE NATIONAL COUNCIL OF TEACHERS OF MATHEMATICS, INC.
1906 Association Drive, Reston, VA 20191-1502
(703) 620-9840; (800) 235-7566; www.nctm.org
All rights reserved

Published simultaneously by the National Council of Teachers of Mathematics, by the National
Association of Gifted Children, 1707 L Street, N.W., Suite 550, Washington, DC 20036, www.nagc.org,
and by National Middle School Association, 4151 Executive Parkway, Suite 300, Westerville, OH 43081,
www.nmsa.org.

Library of Congress Cataloging-in-Publication Data

The peak in the middle : developing mathematically gifted students in the middle grades /
edited by Mark Saul, Susan Assouline, Linda Jensen Sheffield.
　　p. cm.
　ISBN 978-0-87353-634-9
　1. Mathematics—Study and teaching (Middle school) 2. Gifted children—Education.
3. Middle school education. I. Saul, Mark E. II. Assouline, Susan G. (Susan Goodsell),
1953- III. Sheffield, Linda Jensen, 1949-

QA11.2.P43 2010
　372.7—dc22

　　　　　　　　　　　　　2010007354

Printed in the United States of America

Table of Contents

Preface ix

Chapter 1

Philosophy and Policies to Guide Middle School Mathematics
Instruction: Issues of Identification, Acceleration, and Grouping 1

Tamra Stambaugh
Vanderbilt University, Nashville, Tennessee

Camilla P. Benbow
Vanderbilt University, Nashville, Tennessee

Chapter 2

Program Models: Matching the Program to the Abilities, Needs,
and Interests of Mathematically Talented Students 29

Ann Lupkowski-Shoplik
Carnegie Mellon University, Pittsburgh, Pennsylvania

Chapter 3

Using Curriculum to Develop Mathematical Promise in the Middle Grades 51

M. Katherine Gavin
University of Connecticut, Storrs, Connecticut

Linda Jensen Sheffield
Northern Kentucky University, Highland Heights, Kentucky

Chapter 4

Preparing Teachers for Mathematically Talented Middle School
Students 77

Carole Greenes
Arizona State University, Tempe, Arizona

Dawn Teuscher
Arizona State University, Tempe, Arizona

Troy P. Regis
International School Bangkok, Bangkok, Thailand

Chapter 5

Extracurricular Opportunities for Mathematically Gifted Middle
School Students 93

Richard Rusczyk
Art of Problem Solving, Inc., Alpine, California

Chapter 6
Articulation 115

Janet Lynne Tassell
Western Kentucky University, Bowling Green, Kentucky

Rebecca Ruth Stobaugh
Western Kentucky University, Bowling Green, Kentucky

Beth Duvall Fleming
Western Kentucky University, Bowling Green, Kentucky

Chloe R. Harper
Western Kentucky University, Bowling Green, Kentucky

Chapter 7
Middle School Geometry: A Case Study 133

John Benson
Evanston Township High School, Evanston, Illinois

Chapter 8
Equity 155

Max Warshauer
Texas State University, San Marcos, Texas

Terry McCabe
Texas State University, San Marcos, Texas

M. Alejandra Sorto
Texas State University, San Marcos, Texas

Sharon Strickland
Texas State University, San Marcos, Texas

Hiroko Warshauer
Texas State University, San Marcos, Texas

Alex White
Texas State University, San Marcos, Texas

Chapter 9
**Inspiring and Developing Student Interest: Several Examples
from Foreign Schools** 171

Alexander Karp
Columbia University, New York, New York

Afterword 186

Preface

EACH STAGE OF LIFE BRINGS ITS CHALLENGES. Early adolescence is a stage of life that presents children with some of the most difficult tasks in personal development at a time when they may not yet have developed the resources to meet those challenges. These years challenge children to examine their self-definition before they fully understand those around them, to find a place among peers while those same peers are finding their own places, to distance themselves from their families while still accepting their families' support. For many young people, these years are the most confusing time in their lives.

The difficulties faced by children with intellectual gifts can be subtle or hidden. Their success in the usual academic curriculum can mask problems they have in fitting in with their peers or in relating to adults. Indeed, academic success can itself be a problem: gifted students may become bored with work they have already mastered and may yearn for more exciting material even as they are praised for earning good grades.

The middle school movement was born of a recognition of the particular difficulties that students face at this time in their lives. But no institution is a perfect match for the individuals it serves, and middle schools—as well as other educational institutions—sometimes have trouble serving their gifted students. Happily, the middle school is an institution that is still developing. Its traditions are young and its methods often untried. Middle schools are constantly fine-tuning their efforts on behalf of all their students, including gifted students.

We offer this book of essays as support for middle school teachers, principals, supervisors, and administrators who are engaged in just this sort of fine-tuning. The authors bring a variety of backgrounds and perspectives. Some are academic researchers, others working teachers. Still others are outside the usual academic or educational institutions that support but also confine us in our work.

Chapter 1, on policy and philosophy, offers what is perhaps the book's widest-angled lens on the subject. Chapter 2 instantiates many of the general points made in chapter 1 by describing and classifying specific models of programs for this audience. Chapter 3 focuses in on still more detail, discussing specific issues connected with curriculum for middle school students with high ability in mathematics.

But curriculum in itself is meaningless until implemented by teachers. Chapter 4 discusses the knowledge and skills that middle school teachers need in their work with mathematically gifted students. The points raised are applicable both to preservice education of teachers and to in-service professional development.

Not every opportunity for gifted children arises in the classroom, and not every opportunity comes through the classroom teacher. Chapter 5 offers examples of materials and programs that can supplement and enrich classroom experiences. Teachers and administrators should be aware of these possibilities and how they articulate with more formal experiences in supporting the growth of mathematically promising children.

Articulation is an issue on many levels. Chapter 6 examines various types of articulation from issues within the classroom to those on the national level, and several in between. Chapter 7 offers a look at a working classroom in an example by a master teacher of how to articulate the program of a high school with the goals of a middle school whose students it will serve.

The last two chapters of the book return to a wider perspective. Chapter 8, on equity, addresses a topic of paramount importance. This topic must be discussed with respect to any educational initiative at all, but it has particular nuances in work with gifted students. Chapter 9, on international models, offers a rare look outside the American educational system at possibilities and opportunities offered in selected countries around the world.

Readers of these essays may sometimes find themselves wondering how they relate to the specific issue at hand. Many of the points raised are as valid for general students as for gifted students. Many relate equally well to high school or elementary school as to middle school. And many apply across the curriculum—not just to mathematics. This phenomenon is inevitable: gifted education is a part of education, and good teaching or good curriculum for gifted students must include elements that are important for all students. Part of the message of these essays is to underscore the particular meaning for mathematically gifted middle school students of basic principles of general education.

Readers will find different points of view and different levels of advice and information in different essays. Some of the information in one essay may be repeated, with a slightly different meaning, in another.

And inevitably, readers will find that something has been left out. For example, this volume does not provide specific technical information about identification or assessment. There is abundant literature on this subject. A technical background in, say, testing or psychometrics is not assumed of the reader. However, the references given will lead readers to more detailed discussions of any particular topic.

Another important omission—and for the same reason—is specific content. Very little actual mathematics appears in this book, simply because the field is too wide to cover in a small volume. Again, readers are invited to pursue their interests through an examination of the materials referred to in the essays.

This invitation comes with a caveat, however: the essays' references to other materials appear for the readers' information only, and their inclusion does not imply endorsement by NCTM or the editors. In fact, the same is true of all the opinions expressed in the essays. They are the work of experts in the field, but it is a large and growing field. There are other opinions to be held—perhaps even by our readers themselves.

In fact, we invite you to form your own opinion, whether or not it agrees with those expressed in these essays. That is, we hope that the essays here will stimulate your interest in the large, growing, and fascinating field of education for mathematically gifted middle school children.

Philosophy and Policies to Guide Middle School Mathematics Instruction: Issues of Identification, Acceleration, and Grouping

Tamra Stambaugh and Camilla P. Benbow

◆ Policy for mathematically gifted middle school students should rely on research evidence that supports best practice for this population.

◆ Policy should provide multiple opportunities for access to accelerated coursework that incorporates more depth and complexity as well as multiple ways of accelerating the curriculum according to the student's level of ability and motivation.

◆ Overwhelming evidence supports policy that recognizes the need for flexible, homogeneous grouping for targeted instruction with a curriculum matched to a student's aptitude in mathematics.

◆ Policy should include mechanisms to identify students who are ready for accelerated coursework in mathematics. The identification process should include multiple opportunities for assessment and the use of a variety of identification tools that are fair, reliable, and valid for advanced learners, including out-of-level assessments.

◆ Policy at all levels should include a professional development component for teachers of advanced and gifted students in mathematics.

Students arrive at middle school with different skills and knowledge as well as capacities for benefiting from the opportunities provided by schools; these differences persist throughout schooling (Benbow and Stanley 1996). This conclusion has been documented widely in the literature, going back as far as Learned and Wood (1938). Learned and Wood were among the first to empirically show the wide range in knowledge among students in the same grade. For example, inspection of their graphs reveals that approximately 10 percent of high school seniors had more scientific knowledge than the average college senior. Such individual differences in knowledge and skills are evident even before entry into kindergarten, are reflected by the variance of test scores, and persist in every grade thereafter (Paterson 1957; Pressey 1949; Seashore 1922; Terman 1954; Tyler 1965; Willerman 1979). Moreover, differences occur in rates of learning. The thirteen-year-olds who are in the top 1 percent of ability, for example, can assimilate, in three weeks of intensive schooling, a full year of high school biology, chemistry, Latin, physics, or math (e.g., Lynch 1992; Stanley and Stanley 1986; VanTassel-Baska 1983). Those who are in the top 1 in 10,000 in ability can accomplish even more in this time frame. Furthermore, highly mathematically able students, with their exceptionally strong short-term working memories (Dark and Benbow 1990, 1991, 1994), enjoy abstract, unstructured problems and thrive on complexity, traits that are different from those that are called for in the learning environment that is typical in the "regular" classroom.

At the other end of the spectrum are students who need a volume of intensive work and structured support and scaffolding over a long period of time to master basic skills in reading and mathematics. A challenge in teaching, then, is to be responsive to these individual differences so that all students make progress and are allowed to achieve their potential (National Research Council 2000, 2002; Stanley 2000). Particularly challenging for teachers are those students who are so advanced or so seriously struggling that the typical age-grade curriculum becomes inappropriate. In the case of the advanced student, major adjustment is required if we are to teach them only what they already do not know (Stanley 2000).

Philosophical and Empirical Underpinnings

It is generally agreed that good teaching is responsive to individual differences, tailoring instruction to meet the needs of individual learners (Janos and Robinson 1985). In the case of gifted students, who are advanced in their skill and concept attainment and can learn new material at a much more rapid rate than their age-mates (e.g., Lynch 1992; Stanley and Stanley 1986; VanTassel-Baska 1983), it is the professional opinion of those in gifted education that such students need a curriculum that is differentiated (by level, complexity, breadth, and depth), developmentally appropriate, and conducted at a more rapid rate (Van Tassel-Baska 1998). This is typically accomplished to some degree through a combination of—

- accelerating or adjusting the pace *and* complexity of the curriculum to avoid repetitious learning;

- grouping students homogeneously for the purpose of skill development based on a group's ability, interest, and motivation;

- providing enrichment, including material beyond what is typically offered in a regular school curriculum; and

- individualizing or tailoring a curriculum to meet the needs of unique individuals best served by specialized plans.

Differentiation is a concept in need of some "unpacking." Beyond what was stated above, it encompasses the continued development of exceptional talent within a content domain (Bloom 1985; National Research Council 2000). Students who possess the ability, interest, and motivation to perform in a particular area should be provided with opportunities to work at their own pace and ability level prior to matriculation in college. Yet, what is needed at one stage of development is different from what is needed at another. Providing an enriched opportunity is not simply a matter of taking the complex task of, for example, a professional, breaking it down, and "doing" it earlier. Indeed, Sosniak (1985) has described the transitions and needs of talented individuals at various stages of development and dubs the adolescent stage as one of rigorous practice in a talent area. She explains that in the elementary years students home in on their interests through exposure to a variety of opportunities, so exposure to a wide range of disciplines becomes important. By adolescence, gifted students are—or should be—involved in a regimen of in-depth practice and application in their areas of interest and ability, spending many hours focusing on their craft (Sosniak 1985). The term *practice* needs some clarification. It does not simply imply that students work at a faster pace or engage in rote recitation. A student who has appropriately mastered a problem-solving strategy or skill should encounter a new set of complex mathematical problems so that growth is continual.

Achievement at an advanced level, however, is only one of many factors to be considered. Educators must also consider student interest as part of the equation. Lubinski and colleagues (2001) documented the fact that exceptional graduate students in mathematics and the sciences identified their passion during their elementary years and then worked hard through adolescence, developing their talents in their chosen domain. Early focus and hard work seemed to be crucial to the development of students' mathematical abilities based on their early interest in the field, as did their teacher's ability to cultivate their talent. Csikszentmihalyi, Rathunde, and Whalen (1993) found that one of the most important aspects of a child's development was the role of the teacher during critical periods. They describe the resulting challenge to teachers:

> From the start and throughout the teaching career, professional development should incorporate time for the nurture of those [student] interests that attract teachers to their specialty in the first place. It is by keeping their own interests alive and by challenging their own abilities that teachers most often inspire the young to express their unique talent. The same strategy, we might add, is the best buffer against the everyday pressures and frustrations that so frequently exhaust even the most efficient classroom managers." (Csikszentmihalyi, Rathunde, and Whalen 1993, p. 191)

As teachers develop their own cognition and talents in the field, they are more able to cultivate the talents of their most precocious students.

Individual differences among students are well documented in the literature, and the need to be responsive is well articulated. Nevertheless, the philosophical underpinnings and subsequent instructional practices of middle school teachers do not necessarily coincide with research-based practices that acknowledge individual differences or the development of domain-specific differences—especially for mathematically gifted adolescents (Tomlinson 1995; Callahan and Moon 2007). Two primary factors contribute to this disconnect. First, few teachers are adequately prepared to teach mathematics. Also, very few teachers have had appropriate training to work effectively with gifted learners. Fewer than 40 percent of educators have participated in professional development opportunities or enrolled in courses pertinent to the education of gifted students (Archambault et al. 1993). Therefore, many myths are perpetuated about giftedness in general, with no opportunity to dispel them. So, it is not surprising that when Moon, Tomlinson, and Callahan (1995) surveyed hundreds of middle school teachers and principals, they found that approximately half of the principals believed that their teachers were ill prepared to teach the gifted. Only 22 percent of teachers who are teaching mathematics at the middle school level majored in the subject, and fewer than half possess a teaching certificate in mathematics (Loveless 2002), making it difficult for them to provide content expertise to advanced students—a situation that naturally inhibits student learning (National Research Council 2000).

Second, many philosophical differences separate middle school educators and educators of the gifted (Tomlinson 1995). Debate continues to erupt on issues such as excellence versus equity, inclusion versus exclusion, and limited access versus open access to accelerated courses. Positions in these debates are typically manifest in practices that implement decisions about ability grouping, how students are identified or selected for advanced coursework, and to what extent exposure to accelerated or enriched coursework in mathematics is encouraged. Fueling the debate in mathematics, in particular, is the national emphasis on increasing America's competitive edge in a "flat" world (Friedman 2005)—especially in mathematics and the sciences. For the United States to maintain its economic edge in a global society, policymakers emphasize increased resource investments in students who are capable of gaining an in-depth understanding of mathematics so that these highly capable students may use their knowledge and skills to further the national agenda. This result is especially important since the percentage of undergraduates who enroll in college-level mathematics courses continues to decline when compared with the percentage of students enrolled in college overall (Bressoud 2009). Bressoud (2009) hypothesizes that this downturn may be attributed to a disconnect between high school and undergraduate mathematics coursework as well as the approach that higher education professors take when teaching advanced mathematics.

Even though support of the national agenda is important, we also must remember that gifted and talented students have learning needs that require exposure to advanced curriculum and different instructional techniques earlier in their school career, especially if they are to succeed at the top levels (VanTassel-Baska and Stambaugh 2005). Wright, Horn, and Sanders (1997) found that talented students (defined as those in the top 20 percent) showed a pattern of underachievement over time when their pre- and post- standardized test results were compared each year from third through eighth grade. They attributed this finding to "a lack of opportunity [for gifted students] to proceed at [their] own pace; lack of challenging materials; lack of accelerated course offerings; and concentration of instruction on the average or below-average students." They continued, "This finding indicates that it cannot be assumed that higher-achieving students will make it on their own" (p. 66). When advanced students are provided with accelerated curriculum and individualized pacing beginning in middle school, they are more likely to enjoy advanced achievement in their field and to make more creative contributions over time, well beyond the middle school years (Park, Lubinski, and Benbow 2007).

Given the general acknowledgment of the importance of developing future innovators in science, technology, engineering, and mathematics (STEM) and the need for a differentiated curriculum for advanced learners, why does the debate continue at the middle school level? Why is there so much resistance? Wertheimer (1999), citing Ernest (1991), identifies five possible ideologies that inform and fuel the middle school mathematics debate. These are the ideologies of "the industrial trainer," "the technological pragmatist," "the old humanist," "the progressive educator," and the "public educator." These ideologies incorporate many unspoken ideas that educators have about teaching and learning as well as how best to acknowledge differing student abilities. Which of these ideologies educators adhere to drastically affects the pedagogical approaches, identification measures, grouping strategies, and curriculum selected for middle school mathematics instruction.

The "industrial trainer" ideology and the "technological pragmatist" ideology are similar in their approach. Those who subscribe to these philosophies believe that intelligence is fixed. They believe that only the top percentage of capable students should be selected and trained to serve the needs of the country—a position commonly held by policymakers. The "progressive educator," by contrast, believes that intelligence has a biological basis but also can be developed if students are exposed to appropriate educative experiences. This belief system emphasizes that all students should be permitted access to opportunities that help them reach their potential. It follows, then, that identification of talent would include a variety of measures. Those who believe in the "old humanist" ideology adhere to the notion that only a small portion of society is capable of learning sophisticated mathematics, and those persons should be selected and trained for careers in mathematics. The emphasis within this ideology is on the preservation of mathematical ideas instead of the individual student. Finally, the "public educator" ideology focuses on a malleable and environmental view of ability. This perspective contrasts with a more traditional approach that considers ability as fixed and hereditary. Those who subscribe to this philosophy believe that many disadvantaged students, if given access, could and would perform at higher levels than currently permitted by society. According to this ideology, it is the limitation of society and the unequal distribution of *opportunities*—not the variability in human ability—that is the primary force behind individual differences. If society found sufficient will and made sufficient investment to alter the environment to provide equal opportunities, then the achievement gap could be closed.

Each of these ideologies reflects a different focus (e.g., the individual, society, or the educational content) and view of talent and its identification. These varying belief systems are present within a school system either by choice or by policy endeavors, and educators should acknowledge and discuss them to move forward with the identification of talent and the provision of appropriate educational instruction for mathematically precocious students. When these underlying systems of belief are not acknowledged, they become the "elephants" in the classroom.

Identifying Mathematically Talented Middle School Students

Who receives placement in advanced mathematics courses is an issue of ongoing controversy—especially in this age of access and accountability. If a child is identified as gifted in second grade, should that child be placed in honors or advanced courses in the middle school? Past performance does, of course, predict future success, and needs to be considered. So, although early identification of talent is important (Bloom 1985; Csikszentmihalyi and Schneider 2001; Horowitz, Subotnik, and Matthews 2009), previous performance, motivation, and prior exposure to advanced material also are critical components that can shape the development of expertise in a specific content domain, and these should be factored into any decision-making process and subsequent placement (Horowitz, Subotnik, and Matthews 2009; Robinson, Shore, and Enersen 2007; Gagne 2009). Much research has shown that abilities are not fixed; they grow or diminish with experience. Hence, an early test score indicating high potential needs to be considered in the context of how that potential has been subsequently developed.

There are many other misconceptions about the identification of students for placement in mathematically accelerated courses. One erroneous notion is that exposure to honors-level mathematics is reserved exclusively for the gifted student. Whether enrollment in a particular honors class should be reserved in this way, however, depends on the curriculum and how advanced or challenging it is. The more complex and advanced the course is, the more talented the students need to be if they are to benefit from the experience.

Many educators are surprised to learn that interested and motivated mathematics students who are permitted access to advanced mathematics courses at the middle school level are more likely to perform at acceptable levels in those classes than students of equal ability who are placed in lower-level courses (Burris, Heubert, and Levin 2006; Levin 1988; Singham 2003). High expectations and challenge benefit students, and this fact is important to emphasize. Identification, then, should be designed so that a variety of students who are interested in and capable of learning sophisticated mathematical content at earlier ages have a chance to be included in a program of some kind. The programs might not all be the same, however, as that provided to the most highly mathematically gifted. One should not adjust the content or pace of a class for highly gifted students to accommodate those who cannot manage the more rigorous material that the course sets out to cover. When students are provided access to prealgebra and algebra in middle school, they are more likely to enroll in advanced math classes in high school (Burris, Heubert, and

Levin 2006; White et al. 1996; Mason et al. 1992). Thus, more students should be allowed access to these subjects in middle school than is currently the case, and identification mechanisms need to permit this outcome.

Moreover, giftedness encompasses wide ranges of abilities. In an age cohort, the profoundly gifted student is as different from the typically gifted student as the latter is from the typical, average student. Consequently, another erroneous belief is that all gifted students are the same, and their needs will be met by heterogeneous prealgebra and algebra courses in seventh and eighth grade, respectively. This is not true for all gifted students. Gifted students are not uniformly good at everything, and they exhibit distinct strengths and weaknesses (Achter et al. 1996). Thus, not surprisingly, after an exhaustive review of the literature, the National Mathematics Advisory Panel (2008) reported, "Mathematically gifted students with sufficient motivation appear to be able to learn mathematics much faster than students proceeding through the curriculum at a normal pace, with no harm to their learning, and should be allowed to do so" (p. 65).

In other words, there are certain students who, by the nature of their advanced mathematics ability, need exposure to even more sophisticated content and accelerated mathematics curriculum than heterogeneous courses in prealgebra and algebra in seventh and eighth grade can provide. Such students should be permitted access to the high school curriculum in middle school. These mathematically minded students are usually in the very top percentiles of their classes. They often think in ways that begin to approach the habits of mind of a practicing mathematician or expert (Sriraman 2004), and consequently, they need access to more challenging coursework long before even the top 5 percent of students are ready to engage in such material. The key word here is *challenging*. As previously discussed, challenging or accelerated curriculum does not necessarily involve moving students through a rote curriculum at a faster pace but exposing these students to more advanced problems not typically encountered or understood by others in their grade.

How does one identify such students? The talent search model is a testament to how research on the identification of highly gifted students is operationalized. Hundreds of studies over the past twenty-five years have documented the validity of out-of-level assessments for gifted learners (e.g., SAT, ACT, Explore), as well as the capability of students at the middle school level to perform as well as or better than college-bound seniors on measurements of mathematical ability (Benbow 1992; Olszeweski-Kubilius and Kulieke 2008; Olszeweski-Kubilius 1998; Stanley, Keating, and Fox 1974). Olszeweski-Kubilius and Kulieke (2008) present some of the most recent data collected from a talent search—namely, the Midwest Talent Search. The Midwest Talent Search, along with other talent search organizations across the nation, administers out-of-level assessments, such as the ACT or SAT, to eligible and interested sixth- through eighth-grade students who score in the top 5 percent on grade-level standardized assessments. Like many similar organizations, the Midwest Talent Search also administers the Explore test, a typical assessment for eighth graders, to participating third through sixth graders who score in the top 5 percent on standardized grade-level assessments. Table 1.1 shows the percentage of students from the Midwest Talent Search who scored above the mean for the typical eighth grader or college-bound senior on each assessment in mathematics. A wide range in performance among the gifted is obvious, emphasizing the fact that the most gifted students should be afforded rigorous mathematics *opportunities* at even earlier ages and that these opportunities should include more in-depth and complex instruction than the streamlined curriculum for the top 25 percent of students (e.g., an algebra 2 course that includes depth and complexity in the middle school).

Table 1.1. Comparison of Younger Students Scoring above the Mean for Older Students in Mathematics, 2005–2006

	Explore: Percent above Eighth Graders (SS = 14.4)	ACT: Percent above College Bound (SS = 20.7)	SAT Percent above College Bound (SS = 516)
Grade 3	13%		
Grade 4	34%		
Grade 5	60%		
Grade 6	85%	4%	17%
Grade 7		10%	25%
Grade 8		28%	43%

Data from "Midwest Academic Talent Search Statistical Summary," copyright 2006 by the Center for Talent Development, Northwestern University, Evanston, Illinois. Reprinted by permission.

Finally, educators cannot rely exclusively on one measure to inform student placement. The identification of mathematically precocious middle school students must include the use of multiple assessments (VanTassel-Baska 2008; Sheffield 1999; Webb 1993) that are reliable and valid (Callahan 2007). Too often, schools identify and place students in courses on the basis of teacher- or administrator-created assessments that are not statistically validated. A single test score could qualify a student for more advanced mathematics but should not be a sole determiner for excluding a student from advanced mathematics courses, just as a single teacher observation or lack of a strong recommendation should not keep a highly talented student out of an advanced course. Multiple measures (e.g., parent and teacher referrals, grades, test scores, student products, and measurements of such qualities as motivation on affective scales) should be examined in tandem to gain a complete picture of the student's mathematical abilities, motivation, and subsequent mathematics placement (Robinson, Shore, and Enersen 2007). For this model to function well, however, we must see placement in advanced subject matter as a form of "tryout," as is customary in athletics. If the student does not perform, he or she needs to be placed in a setting that offers additional support and appropriate curricular scaffolding. When managed in this way, the use of multiple assessments promotes equity and access by allowing twice-exceptional students, underachieving students (Robinson, Shore, and Enersen 2007), and students of poverty (VanTassel-Baska and Stambaugh 2005) alternative options for showing their talents. "It [the use of multiple assessment criteria] serves social justice by increasing the possibility of recognition to poor, minority, and other systematically different groups of children" (Robinson, Shore, and Enersen 2007, p. 241).

Persistence and motivation are also key considerations in identifying highly gifted students, especially in mathematics (Sheffield 1999). In a study of high achievers across the content areas, Bloom (1985) found that persistence in solving difficult problems was a key factor that separated those students who succeeded at high levels from those who did not. Persistence and motivation are also important factors to consider in determining who is provided access to the most advanced courses. These themes of motivation, persistence, and interest are also prevalent in the underachievement literature (Siegle and McCoach 2009), suggesting a notable caveat to the National Math Panel's (2008) recommendation regarding the acceleration of mathematically gifted students. When assessing motivation or persistence, educators must not exclude seemingly unmotivated students who do not complete mundane or rote tasks with accuracy. Many gifted students are perceived to lack motivation if they are unchallenged (Clark 2006; VanTassel-Baska and Stambaugh 2005; Niehart et al. 2002). However, when presented with appropriately challenging mathematical problems, most seemingly unmotivated gifted students will rise to the task if they feel supported by their environment to perform, are interested in the content, and possess a strong sense of efficacy (Siegle and McCoach 2009). Table 1.2 displays sample identification options and course placements for students who are identified as mathematically gifted at corresponding levels of ability and talent. These sample interventions allow for deeper investigations, creating and solving mathematical tasks in a variety of ways, applying mathematics to engineering and other areas, as well as opportunities for appreciating the beauty of mathematics itself. Moreover, the suggested placements are contingent on adequate results from multiple assessment options such as those listed, and in most cases, students should successfully meet the criteria for three of the five options to qualify for advanced coursework (VanTassel-Baska 2008). (There are some—but very few—exceptionally talented students who qualify simply by the power of their abilities.)

Table 1.2. Recommended Identification Options and Corresponding Mathematics Interventions

	Top 25%	Top 10%	Top 1% to 5%
Identification options	State and national achievement tests in mathematics Motivation/persistence scale or observation when solving difficult problems Portfolio Teacher recommendation Grades in previous math courses	State and national achievement tests in mathematics Motivation/persistence scale or observation when solving difficult problems Portfolio Teacher recommendation Grades in previous math courses	Out-of-level assessments (ACT, SAT, Explore) Motivation/persistence scale or observation when solving difficult problems Portfolio Teacher recommendation Grades in previous math courses
Possible intervention	Prealgebra* – 7th grade Algebra* – 8th grade Extracurricular math competitions, clubs	Prealgebra* – 6th grade Algebra* – 7th grade Algebra 2* – 8th grade Extracurricular math competitions, mentorships, internships, clubs	Accelerated individualized mathematics Extracurricular math competitions, mentorships, internships, clubs Intense, accelerated talent search summer/extra-curricular programs Advanced Placement and International Baccalaureate options earlier

*NCTM recommends that mathematics instruction for all students address the content outlined in *Curriculum Focal Points for Prekindergarten through Grade 8 Mathematics: A Quest for Coherence* (NCTM 2006) and *Principles and Standards for School Mathematics* (NCTM 2000). Therefore, some middle school students with high ability in mathematics also might benefit from a telescoped middle school curriculum that helps them develop a deep understanding of all topics identified for grades 6–8.

Accelerated Curriculum

We have discussed several issues that have policy implications for identifying mathematically talented students for placement in advanced or enriching classes or experiences. We now move to discussing the evidence supporting possible policy recommendations for ways to develop the mathematical talent that has been identified. We begin with acceleration, the option that has been the most widely studied but least implemented or accepted (Colangelo, Assouline, and Gross 2004). Southern and Jones (2004) identified eighteen forms of acceleration. The National Association for Gifted Children (NAGC) position statement on acceleration defines the term in the following way:

> Acceleration practices involve allowing a student to move through traditional educational organizations more rapidly, based on readiness and motivation. Research documents the potential academic benefits and positive outcomes of all forms of appropriately implemented acceleration strategies for intellectually gifted and academically talented learners. These research-based best practices include grade skipping, telescoping, early entrance into kindergarten or college, credit by examination, and acceleration in content areas through such programs as Advanced Placement and International Baccalaureate at the high school level. Instructional adaptations in the classroom such as compacting, which allows for more economic use of learning time in a specific subject, are also a desirable and best practice for talented students. (NAGC 2009, p. 1)

As explained in the NAGC definition, single-subject acceleration, or individualized acceleration in a content area, is one promising way of adapting the instructional experiences to the needs of gifted students (Southern and Jones 2004), especially those advanced in mathematics (Benbow and Stanley 1996). The curriculum is adjusted to meet the needs of the individual learner, or, rather, the individual is placed in the curriculum at the approximate level of his or her functioning. Some call this "placement according to competence" or "developmental placement" (Benbow and Stanley 1996). Acceleration may include enabling a student to—

- encounter subject matter content earlier (e.g., algebra in seventh grade) or at a faster pace;

- engage in self-paced learning or with a compact curriculum;

- participate in Advanced Placement programs as a freshman or sophomore (i.e., college-level classes in high school);

- take college classes while in high school;

- skip grades and graduate early from high school and subsequently enter college early.

Whatever form acceleration takes, it provides a differentiated curriculum for gifted students by using curricula designed for older students. The opinion of most educators, however, is that good acceleration does not stop there (VanTassel-Baska 1998). It also explores topics more deeply, probes the interconnectedness of concepts, and adjusts the content to make it more complex and abstract. These characteristics of good acceleration can emerge in special accelerated classes for gifted students or in the regular classroom with a truly excellent teacher.

Several points need to be considered when assessing the value and use of acceleration for gifted students and, thus, the implications for policy. First, acceleration, beyond self-paced learning or offering algebra to eighth graders, is reserved for the highly gifted (typically, the top 1 percent). Second, because of the social and academic disruptions that it causes, acceleration is used only with students who want to accelerate (VanTassel-Baska 1998). A widely held opinion among professionals is that no matter how positive the effects of acceleration could be, it is inadvisable to accelerate a child who offers significant resistance (Benbow 1998). Thus, this educational intervention is different from others (e.g., choosing a specific textbook or teaching method) because student choice is a factor in its use. It may be that those students who choose to accelerate are more academically motivated or desire academic challenges more than those who choose not to accelerate. Alternatively, those who choose not to accelerate may need or want to emphasize other, nonacademic, factors in structuring a satisfying life. That is, "accelerates" and "non-accelerates" may have different priorities in how they want to live their lives, and this choice is confounding when the aim is to assess effects related to acceleration itself. Thus, any recommendations about the use of acceleration pertain only to academically motivated students—the very ones with whom acceleration is to be used according to practice guidelines that have been developed on the basis of professional opinion.

Third, accelerating mathematically gifted students by placing them together for special classes creates a very different academic and social environment, which appears to be highly valued by and motivating for gifted students (Benbow, Lubinski, and Suchy 1996). Students who are exposed to acceleration in special classes benefit in more ways than just by having exposure to advanced mathematical content. Students report feeling affirmed and challenged in ways that the regular classroom does not and probably cannot do. Also, the nature of the discourse changes in the special classes, becoming much more high-level and intellectually challenging (Fuchs et al. 1998). Accelerated classes offer more than just content taught at a fast pace. Consequently, it is hard, if not impossible, to separate out the effects attributable only to the acceleration in these types of programs.

Studies on Acceleration

We highlight five studies specific to acceleration and mathematically gifted adolescents that we think are important to include in a chapter with a focus on recommendations for policy. These are studies by Brody and Benbow (1990), Ysseldyke and colleagues (2004), Ma (2005), Swiatek and Benbow (1991a), and Swiatek and Benbow (1991b). We selected these studies on the basis of methodological criteria for acceptability that were adopted by the National Math Panel as it developed its policy document and thus were included in the final report (National Mathematics Advisory Panel 2008).

Brody and Benbow (1990) investigated whether short-term, accelerative academic training had an effect on SAT scores of middle school students who were in the top 1 percent in ability. Program participants were enrolled in a fast-paced, three-week summer academic program that was focused on increasing their content knowledge in algebra. Their performance on the SAT was compared with that of a nonrandomized control group not participating in any accelerative learning experience during the summer but also in the top 1 percent in ability (with lower SAT-M scores initially but not SAT-V) or with that of students enrolled in other, nonmathematics accelerative classes in the academic summer program. The results from the ANCOVA, adjusting for relatively large initial differences in ability across groups, revealed that in-depth instruction over a short period of time in specific mathematical or verbal areas had little or no impact on SAT scores at the conclusion of the program.

Ysseldyke and colleagues (2004), in another quasi-experimental study, compared sixth-grade gifted students whose mathematics curriculum was differentiated and adjusted to the students' needs through an instructionally based curriculum management system called Accelerated Math (Renaissance Learning). This self-directed, four-month mathematics program provided assessment of skill level, tailoring of the instruction to match skill level, individual pacing and goal setting, ample practice, and immediate feedback to the student and teacher on performance outcomes. Groups were similar on the pretest, and the results were analyzed by ANCOVA with pretest scores as a covariate. No adjustment was made for nesting within classrooms and schools. The statistically insignificant effect size was .45. (According to Slavin [1991], as reported in Kulik [2004], an effect size of .25 is considered "educationally significant" [p. 14].)

Ma (2005), in a correlational study, compared the math achievement at the end of high school of students who were in the top 10 percent in ability and took formal algebra either in seventh or eighth grade—an increasing trend in the United States for capable students—and equally able students who took such algebra in ninth grade or beyond. Ma used a subsample of the Longitudinal Study of American Youth that was divided into gifted, honors, and regular students. For students in each category, Ma examined differences between students who took algebra 1 early (accelerated) and those who did not—a distinction mainly reflecting practices in different schools. Ma found relatively balanced numbers of accelerated versus not accelerated students among the gifted (46 percent) and honors (21 percent) students, but few "regular" students were accelerated in this way (4 percent), as would be expected. The mathematics achievement outcome variable, which captured performance on a combination of basic mathematical skills, algebra, geometry, and quantitative literacy items, was a growth curve of achievement measures from grade 7 to 12. This repeated-measures growth curve provided some control for time 1 pretest values. Additional control variables in an HLM regression model were student gender, SES, and various background characteristics, as well as a number of relevant school characteristics. Score differences favoring accelerates were small and not statistically significant. All accelerated students seemed to perform well on this test, however, even though reservations have been expressed about early learning of algebra (e.g., Prevost 1985).

Swiatek and Benbow (1991a), in a quasi-experimental study, assessed participants ten years after the completion of two homogeneously grouped and fast-paced mathematics classes. The students in these classes had learned algebra and in some cases all the content up through precalculus at a rapid rate. These classes were the model for the fast-paced programs that have sprung up across the country in the past thirty-five years and now serve more than 100,000 gifted students a year. The initial class was taught by an experienced math teacher at a pace dictated by the capacity for learning of the most able students in the class. Most students in the class completed four years of mathematics in fourteen months, and their standardized achievement test scores were well above the 90th percentile on relevant tests of mastery. A subgroup completed just two years of math in that time frame. They were less able initially and thus experienced difficulty in maintaining the pace of the faster-moving group. The study compared participants in the two fast-paced mathematics classes with students who had been matched on ability but did not attend and students who dropped out of the class. All were at least in the top 0.5 percent in ability, but motivational and other differences may have separated participants and non-participants. Another limitation was that the same teacher taught both classes, although reassuringly similar results in mathematics have been found with other teachers (e.g., Lunny 1983; Mezynski, Stanley, and McCoart 1983). At the end of high school, the participants scored higher on standardized mathematics achievement tests, such as the College Board Math Achievement Test, than the nonparticipants or dropouts, despite their younger age, and did not regret their acceleration (Benbow, Perkins, and Stanley 1983). Ten years after the initiation of the class, few statistically significant differences on academic achievement variables emerged between the participants and the comparison group, but they all tended to favor the participants (who also tended to be several years ahead in their educational progress and so were younger at time of comparison on specific variables than nonparticipants). The one statistical difference that was noticeable was the percentage of students at age 23 who were attending graduate school in applied mathematics, engineering, or computer science—50 percent of the participants versus 28 percent of the comparison group.

Swiatek and Benbow (1991b) conducted a correlational study that compared, in a ten-year follow-up, mathematically talented students (at least top 1 percent in ability) who had managed to accelerate their education so that they entered college at least one year early with equally able students who had not entered college early. This was a nonrandomized comparison, but the groups had been matched on gender and pretest SAT scores (within 10 points for math, 20 for verbal). The mathematics achievement outcomes were indirect— number of undergraduate mathematics courses taken, number of unrequired mathematics courses taken, mathematics major as an undergraduate or graduate student, and interest in, confidence about, and perceived ease with mathematics. The study found few statistically significant differences on the various achievement variables. However, in the aggregate, the differences favored accelerates, who, of course, also had the advantage of being advanced in their education.

In all of these studies, when psychosocial variables were measured, acceleration was not associated with poor psychosocial adjustment. This finding counters a fear that many have when considering acceleration (Benbow 1991).

Finally, it would be useful in this policy chapter to consider results from a meta-analysis of acceleration, even though those results are not limited to mathematics. Kulik and Kulik (1984) and Kulik (2004) reported in their meta-analyses that accelerated students performed as well as the older students with whom they were placed and, most interesting, were about one year ahead in achievement than their equally able non-accelerates of the same age. We can conclude, therefore, with some confidence, just as the National Math Panel (2008) did, that learning mathematics at an earlier age or at a faster pace than is typical benefits mathematically gifted students by allowing them to learn advanced mathematical concepts and that these students are as a result better prepared for college science classes or the workplace. Moreover, no long-term negative consequences have been found; indeed, the research evidence suggests some possible, small additional advantages (Colangelo, Assouline, and Gross 2004). Lubinski (2004), for example, found that many students wished they had been accelerated earlier.

Grouping and the Mathematically Gifted Adolescent

Homogeneous ability grouping, especially of middle school students, has been a point of contention for most of the latter half of the twentieth century—especially between educators of middle school students and educators of the gifted (Loveless 2002; Gallagher, Coleman, and Nelson 1995; Tomlinson 1995; Callahan and Moon 2007). Although the debate continues, it is interesting to note that little research exclusively measures the effects of homogeneous grouping and mathematics at the middle school level devoid of curriculum differentiation. Instead, most studies intertwine some type of homogeneous grouping with accelerated or enriched opportunities, and it is difficult to separate the two. This finding is to be expected, since the only point of homogenously grouping for instruction is to enable the inclusion of such differentiated components. In other words, grouping is an instructional management strategy that provides a mechanism for the teacher to differentiate more effectively. Even with this skill-based and flexible approach to grouping, heated debate continues on the basis of ideology. Organizations represent various points of view on this issue and have published widely about this ongoing dilemma. To gain a sense of how heated the argument is, one can simply search online for position statements from major educational associations and foundations or catalog specific journal issues dedicated to multiple perspectives and research studies on grouping. To complicate matters further, in many instances both sides of the grouping issue cite similar research in support of their arguments for or against ability grouping.

What does the empirical evidence on homogeneous grouping reveal—especially for advanced learners? N. Robinson and colleagues (1997) and A. Robinson, Bradley, and Stanley (1990) conducted two studies involving homogeneous grouping and enrichment that met the criteria for inclusion in the National Math Panel's (2008) report. In the only experimental study to emerge from the panel's literature search of programs for the gifted, N. Robinson and colleagues (1997) randomly assigned equally able gifted students to supplemental enrichment mathematics classes conducted on Saturdays for two years or to no treatment. The enrichment classes, with 28 sessions in all, were constructivist in philosophy, "developmentally appropriate," and aligned with NCTM (1989) guidelines. Teachers created social communities that engaged in open-ended problem solving. At the end of two years, the participants outperformed nonparticipants on a combined mathematics achievement measure. However, there was differential attrition—5 percent in the control group, and 20 percent in the treatment group—and it is possible that the least able students left the program at higher rates than the most able. A statistically significant effect of .401 favored the students who participated in the enrichment program. In this instance, the regular curriculum in the school was not differentiated in any way. Rather, gifted children were challenged through the provision of extracurricular activities—a pullout model, of sorts—and were not explicitly accelerated.

The quasi-experimental study by A. Robinson, Bradley, and Stanley (1990) included in the National Math Panel report is similar to that by Ysseldyke and colleagues (2004) in its use of computer-assisted instruction to adjust pace. However, this after-school mathematics program for gifted elementary students also provided specific enrichment activities that allowed students in the class to add breadth and depth to their learning. Hence, the curriculum was differentiated even further than what was possible in the program investigated by Ysseldyke and colleagues, although A. Robinson, Bradley, and Stanley's study was of one single class and hence involved just one teacher. The performance of the participants was compared with that of nonrandomized control groups composed of students who were selected but did not attend or were selected as alternates. With a statistically significant effect size of .65, the results lend support to the value of differentiating and enhancing the pace of the curriculum for gifted students.

Meta-analyses and reviews of the literature also have tried to make sense of the evidence for homogeneous grouping. These have included studies even if they had methodological limitations or were of varying quality. Still, homogeneous grouping did garner support when the curriculum was differentiated through enrichment (or acceleration as discussed above), but the effects did not appear to be as strong as the results that the meta-analyses showed for acceleration (Benbow 1998; Kulik and Kulik 1982, 1987; Rogers 2007; also see the Fall 2007 *Gifted Child Quarterly*).

Slavin (1990, 1995) also conducted several studies on grouping and found that when groups of similar ability are compared on the basis of grouping alone, the effects of ability grouping are approximately zero, making ability grouping insignificant. In a few instances, however, Slavin (1995) reported effect sizes of .25 with higher-achieving students, but he readily noted that three of his fifteen studies found advantages in favor of heterogeneous grouping for high-ability students. Still, none of the presented data were statistically significant, and acceleration and enrichment were absent in all of the studies.

Using similar methodologies, other studies posit concurrent results, deeming ability grouping as having insignificant effects if the curriculum is not appropriately adjusted to accommodate the various groups of learners (Gamoran and Berends 1987; Mosteller, Light, and Sachs 1996). We would agree that homogeneous grouping without any differentiation would seem pointless even if it produced some small significant effect.

Kulik and Kulik (1992) argue, however, that Slavin (1990) used methodologies for contrived groupings not typically replicated in the real world, including grouping for grouping's sake, grouping decisions based solely on IQ, and grouping with no curricular adjustments. Others argue that Slavin (1990) admittedly omitted the top 5 percent of high-achieving students from his study, making it invalid to generalize for gifted students (Fiedler-Brand, Lange, and Winebrenner 1992). Critics of Kulik and Kulik's (1982, 1987, 1992) research, on the other hand, fault the inclusion of smaller, short-term studies in the meta-analysis and argue that generalizations cannot be made (Ireson and Hallam 1999).

To clarify the debate, Rogers (1998) conducted a more recent meta-analysis of grouping and published her work in a leading middle school journal. She analyzed the benefits and liabilities of ability grouping and made the following generalizations:

1. Advanced groups benefit more academically than low-ability students from grouping with similar students.

2. What is done (e.g., to improve instructional quality, extend instructional time, or reduce class size) when students are grouped is more directly related to achievement than actual placement in a group.

3. Homogeneous groups are more beneficial academically for students of all abilities than heterogeneous grouping.

4. Low-ability students benefit academically when paired with a high-ability partner, but the same may not hold true for the high-ability partner.

5. Both high-ability and low-ability students benefit from more social interactions when grouped within class with like-ability peers.

6. Low-ability students tend to acquire more self-confidence about their abilities when placed in mixed-ability groups. (Rogers 1998, p. 43)

In later work, Rogers (2007) found similar effects and reached similar conclusions.

Thus, homogeneous grouping effects are only as good as the accelerated curriculum and strategies applied. Several studies evaluating such educational arrangements have focused on both mathematics and homogeneous grouping at the middle school level and have coupled grouping in mathematics with accelerated content or individualized instruction. In the majority of those studies, some form of homogeneous grouping (either within-class or between ability-grouped classes) was combined with acceleration, enrichment, or continued practice of basic skills as a function of the needs of the homogeneous groups. Such combinations evinced positive results (Rogers 2007). Success, then, can be enjoyed by students of all ability levels if both flexible groups and appropriately meaningful differentiated mathematics content are used (see Sheffield [1999]). In other words, when gifted and general education students do not achieve at appropriate levels, their lack of success is typically due to a lack of rigorous curriculum options, not the grouping of instruction by itself.

Evidence of effectiveness is just one issue to be grappled with when it comes to policies involving the use of homogeneous grouping. A possibly bigger and certainly more controversial issue is that of discrimination. This issue is especially pronounced when homogeneous ability grouping involves between-class ability groupings. Slavin (1995), for example, writes that "ability grouping by its nature works against democratic and egalitarian norms, often creates racial or ethnic divisions, risks making terrible and long-lasting mistakes, and condemns many children to low-quality instruction and low-quality futures" (p. 125). Oakes (1995), in a study of two urban districts, found that both schools incorporated "racially imbalanced classes" in all grade levels, with African American and Hispanic students relegated to lower-achieving groupings, while Asian American and white students were typically placed in higher-achieving groupings. The achievement gap between students in the upper and lower course tracks was significant over time. Further review of the study suggested that students in both course tracks had varied ability and the student placement was based on race rather than student instructional need. This practice is obviously inappropriate.

Groupings intended for middle school mathematics should be based on students' documented academic needs and be flexible in nature (VanTassel-Baska and Stambaugh 2005; Robinson, Shore, and Enersen 2007; Rogers 1998). This point merits emphasis. When groupings meet these criteria, only negligible, nonstatistical differences in race and class are observed (National Education Longitudinal Study of 2002, reporting 2001 test scores; cited in Loveless [2002]). However, questions surrounding the legitimacy and bias of the placement measures arose when ability was factored in, further indicating the need for multiple identification measures, as previously discussed.

When, then, should homogeneous grouping be considered as part of middle school mathematics curriculum? Homogeneous grouping is an important part of a curriculum that is tailored for all students. Whether homogeneous grouping occurs within a classroom or as a direct placement, the grouping will have a marginal effect on the academic needs of students unless the curriculum and instruction are appropriately tailored. In the case of the gifted child, it is best if the curriculum is also accelerated (e.g., both in depth and complexity)—not just exchanged for a higher grade level's curriculum. Moreover, a curriculum that consistently lacks depth is not appropriate for any student. If using such a curriculum is the common practice, contention between varied groups is understandable. When grouping is flexible and tailored to the needs of individual students, there are positive academic effects for all students (Rogers 1998, 2007).

Policy Implications

Diverse and seemingly controversial research findings, coupled with deep-rooted ideologies about grouping, identification, and acceleration of mathematically gifted individuals, confound the creation of equitable policies within a middle school context. Policies that enable students at the lower end of the ability spectrum may harm advanced students, and vice versa. Policymakers at the national, state, and local levels have a difficult task of creating policies that will meet the needs of all constituents without harming certain ability groups either by rigidity or inaction. The following research-based strategies are worth considering when enacting policy for mathematically gifted middle school students:

1. Flexible, homogeneous grouping, coupled with targeted instruction and curriculum matched to a student's abilities in mathematics, is beneficial academically and socially for all students;

2. Acceleration, as previously defined, is beneficial for advanced students, both academically and socially. Acceleration policies should include multiple opportunities for access to advanced classes that provide more depth and complexity and multiple ways of accelerating different levels of gifted students (e.g., subject acceleration, compacting, telescoping, grade skipping, dual enrollment). Policies on acceleration should also include mechanisms for ensuring that students have encountered the regular curriculum, as a way to reduce gaps in exposure to core principles. Many schools accomplish this through telescoping, or the completion of two years of math in one year.

3. When identifying mathematically gifted students for advanced coursework and instruction, multiple assessments, both subjective and objective, should be used.

4. Extreme acceleration opportunities (e.g., beyond eighth-grade algebra 1) should be provided for the highly gifted as identified by above-grade-level assessments, such as the ACT or SAT, in addition to other evidence, such as motivation, grades, and evidence of mathematical thinking.

5. Teachers need ongoing professional development about the characteristics of gifted students and research-based strategies suitable for identifying and providing appropriate instructional strategies and advanced curriculum options for students who are gifted in mathematics.

6. Middle school math teachers need to show evidence of advanced knowledge of mathematics through a degree or a rigorous certificate program. This credential should be required in addition to a teaching certificate.

As acceptable policies in mathematics are crafted, policymakers must ask themselves two questions:

1. What are the potential intended and unintended consequences of this policy?

2. How will this policy affect the future?

Policies crafted for middle school students have the potential to affect a great number of students over time and can create a domino effect. For example, if a middle school implements a policy on student access to advanced courses, then high school policymakers must also create policies to accommodate these students as they matriculate. As high school policies are implemented, higher education initiatives and undergraduate programs need to adapt their ways of teaching to accommodate this new group of students. The more prepared students are to solve sophisticated mathematical problems and become mathematical thinkers in middle and high school, the more rigorous college coursework and subsequent preparation for the workplace will become. In summary, we must provide mechanisms to aid our advanced students in gaining access to the most rigorous mathematics courses available when these students are ready for the challenge—not when the curriculum or system is conveniently ready for them.

Conclusion

Middle school educators and educators of the gifted may differ from each other with respect to their philosophical beliefs about the education of mathematically gifted adolescents. Adequate and confirmatory research supports acceleration, homogeneous grouping, and multifaceted identification opportunities so that all students, including those gifted in mathematics, have access to appropriately rigorous curriculum and teaching. It is only when we overcome ideologies and examine the research base and effects of policies and services for all populations, including the gifted, that we can adequately prepare the next generation to compete effectively in a global society.

References

Achter, John, David Lubinski, and Camilla P. Benbow. "Multipotentiality among the Intellectually Gifted: 'It Was Never There and Already It's Vanishing.'" *Journal of Counseling Psychology* 43 (1996): 65–76.

Archambault, Francis, Jr., Karen L. Westberg, Scott W. Brown, Bryan W. Hallmark, Christine L. Emmons, and Wanli Zhang. *Regular Classroom Practices with Gifted Students: Results of a National Survey of Classroom Teachers.* Research Monograph 93102. Storrs, Conn.: The National Research Center on the Gifted and Talented, University of Connecticut, 1993.

Benbow, Camilla. "Meeting the Needs of Gifted Students through Use of Acceleration: A Neglected Resource." In *Handbook of Special Education*, vol. 4, edited by Margaret C. Wang, Maynard C. Reynolds, and Herbert J. Wahlberg, pp. 23–36. New York: Pergamon, 1991.

———. "Academic Achievement in Mathematics and Science of Students between Ages 13 and 23: Are There Differences among Students in the Top One Percent of Mathematical Ability?" *Journal of Educational Psychology* 84 (1992): 51–61.

———. "Grouping Intellectually Advanced Students for Instruction." In *Excellence in Educating the Gifted,* edited by Joyce VanTassel-Baska, pp. 261–78. Denver: Love, 1998.

Benbow, Camilla, David Lubinski, and Babette Suchy. "Impact of the SMPY Model and Programs from the Perspective of the Participant." In *Intellectual Talent: Psychometric and Social Issues,* edited by Camilla Benbow and David Lubinski, pp. 266–300. Baltimore: Johns Hopkins University Press, 1996.

Benbow, Camilla, Susan Perkins, and Julian C. Stanley. "Mathematics Taught at a Fast Pace: A Longitudinal Evaluation of SMPY's First Class." In *Academic Precocity: Aspects of Its Development,* edited by Camilla Benbow and Julian C. Stanley, pp. 51–78. Baltimore: Johns Hopkins University Press, 1983.

Benbow, Camilla, and Julian C. Stanley. "Inequity in Equity: How Current Educational Equity Policies Place Able Students at Risk." *Psychology, Public Policy, and Law* 2 (1996): 249–93.

Bloom, B. *Developing Talent in Young People.* New York: Ballantine, 1985.

Bressoud, David. "Is the Sky Still Falling?" *Notices of the AMS* 56 (2009): 20–25.

Brody, Linda, and Camilla P. Benbow. "Effects of High School Course-Work and Time on SAT Scores." *Journal of Educational Psychology* 82 (1990): 866–75.

Burris, Carolyn, Jay P. Heubert, and Henry M. Levin. "Accelerating Mathematics Achievement Using Heterogeneous Grouping." *American Educational Research Journal* 43 (2006): 105–36.

Callahan, Carolyn. "What Can We Learn from Research about Promising Practices in Developing the Gifts and Talents of Low-Income Students." In *Overlooked Gems: A National Perspective on Low-Income Promising Learners,* edited by Joyce VanTassel-Baska and Tamra Stambaugh, pp. 44–46. Washington D.C.: National Association for Gifted Children, 2007.

Callahan, Carolyn, and Tonya R. Moon. "Sorting the Wheat from the Chaff: What Makes for Good Evidence of Effectiveness in the Literature in Gifted Education?" *Gifted Child Quarterly* 51 (2007): 305–19.

Clark, Barbara. *Growing Up Gifted.* Upper Saddle River, N.J.: Prentice Hall, 2006.

Colangelo, Nicholas, Susan G. Assouline, and Miraca U. M. Gross, eds. *A Nation Deceived: How Schools Hold Back America's Brightest Students.* Iowa City, Iowa: The Connie Belin & Jacqueline N. Blank International Center for Gifted Education and Talent Development, 2004.

Csikszentmihalyi, Mihaly, Kevin Rathunde, and Samuel Whalen. *Talented Teenagers: The Roots and Success of Failure.* Cambridge: Cambridge University Press, 1993.

Csikszentmihalyi, Mihaly, and Barbara Schneider. *Becoming Adult: How Teenagers Prepare for the World of Work.* New York: Basic Books, 2001.

Dark, Veronica, and Camilla P. Benbow. "Mathematically Talented Students Show Enhanced Problem Translation and Enhanced Short-Term Memory for Digit and Spatial Information." *Journal of Educational Psychology* 82 (1990): 420–29.

———. "Differential Enhancement of Working Memory with Mathematical and Vertical Precocity." *Journal of Educational Psychology* 83 (1991): 48–60.

———. "Type of Stimulus Mediates the Relationship between Performance and Type of Precocity." *Intelligence* 19, no. 3 (1994): 337–57.

Ernest, Paul. *The Philosophy of Mathematics Education.* London: Falmer Press, 1991.

Fiedler-Brand, Ellen, Richard E. Lange, and Susan Winebrenner. "Tracking, Ability Grouping, and the Gifted." *Pennsylvania Association for Gifted Education Bulletin* 1, no. 3 (1992): 1–7.

Friedman, Thomas. *The World Is Flat: A Brief History of the Twenty-First Century.* New York: Farrar, Straus, and Giroux, 2005.

Fuchs, Lynn, Doug Fuchs, Carol L. Hamlett, and Kathy Karns. "High-Achieving Students' Interaction and Performance on Complex Mathematical Tasks as a Function of Homogeneous and Heterogeneous Pairings." *American Educational Research Journal* 35 (1998): 227–68.

Gagne, Francoys. "Building Gifts into Talents: Detailed Overview of the DMGT 2.0." In *Leading Change in Gifted Education: The Festschrift of Dr. Joyce VanTassel-Baska,* edited by Bronwyn MacFarlane and Tamra Stambaugh, pp. 61–81. Waco, Tex.: Prufrock Press, 2009.

Gallagher, James, Mary Ruth Coleman, and Susanne Nelson. "Perceptions of Educational Reform by Educators Representing Middle Schools, Cooperative Learning, and Gifted Education." *Gifted Child Quarterly* 39, no. 2 (1995): 66–75.

Gamoran, Adam, and Mark Berends. "The Effects of Stratification in Secondary Schools: Synthesis of Survey and Ethnographic Research." *Review of Educational Research* 57 (1987): 415–35.

Horowitz, Frances Degen, Rena F. Subotnik, and Dona J. Matthews. *The Development of Giftedness and Talent across the Life Span.* Washington, D.C.: American Psychological Association, 2009.

Ireson, Judith, and Susan Hallam. "Raising Standards: Is Ability Grouping the Answer?" *Oxford Review of Education* 25 (1999): 343–58.

Janos, Paul, and Nancy M. Robinson. "The Performance of Students in a Program of Radical Acceleration at the University Level." *Gifted Child Quarterly* 29, no. 4 (1985): 175–79.

Kulik, Chen-Lin, and James A. Kulik. "Effects of Ability Grouping on Secondary School Students: A Meta-analysis of Evaluation Findings." *American Educational Research Journal* 19 (1982): 415–28.

Kulik, James. "Meta-analytic Studies of Acceleration." In *A Nation Deceived: How Schools Hold Back America's Brightest Students*, vol. 2, edited by Nicholas Colangelo, Susan G. Assouline, and Miraca U. M. Gross, pp. 13–22. Iowa City, Iowa: The Connie Belin & Jacqueline N. Blank International Center for Gifted Education and Talent Development, 2004.

Kulik, James, and Chen-Lin C. Kulik. "Effects of Accelerated Instruction on Students." *Review of Educational Research* 54 (1984): 409–25.

———. "Effects of Ability Grouping on School Achievement." *Equity and Excellence* 23 (1987): 22–30.

———. "Meta-analysis Findings on Grouping Programs." *Gifted Child Quarterly* 36 (1992): 73–77.

Learned, William, and Ben D. Wood. *The Student and His Knowledge: A Report to the Carnegie Foundation on the Results of the High School and College Examination of 1928, 1930, and 1932.* New York: Carnegie Foundation for the Advancement of Teaching, 1938.

Levin, Henry. *Accelerated Schools for At-Risk Students.* CPRE Research Report Series RR-010. New Brunswick, N.J.: Center for Policy Research in Education, 1988.

Loveless, Tom. *The 2002 Brown Center Report on American Education: How Well Are American Students Learning? With Sections on Arithmetic, High School Culture, and Charter Schools.* Washington, D.C.: Brookings Institution Press, 2002.

Lubinski, David. "Introduction to the Special Section on Cognitive Abilities: 100 Years after Spearman's (1904) 'General Intelligence,' Objectively Determined and Measured." *Journal of Personality and Social Psychology* 86 (January 2004): 96–111.

Lubinski, David, Camilla P. Benbow, Daniel L. Shea, Hossain Eftekhari-Sanjani, and Marcy B. J. Halvorson. "Men and Women at Promise for Scientific Excellence: Similarity Not Dissimilarity." *Psychological Science* 12, no. 4 (2001): 309–17.

Lunny, John F. "Fast-Paced Mathematics Classes for a Rural County." In *Academic Precocity: Aspects of Its Development*, edited by Camilla Benbow and Julian C. Stanley, pp. 79–85. Baltimore: Johns Hopkins University Press, 1983.

Lynch, Sharon. "Fast-Paced High School Science for the Academically Talented: A Six-Year Perspective." *Gifted Child Quarterly* 36 (1992): 147–54.

Ma, Xin. "A Longitudinal Assessment of Early Acceleration of Students in Mathematics on Growth in Mathematics Achievement." *Developmental Review* 25, no. 1 (2005): 104–31.

Mason, DeWayne, Darline D. Schroeter, Ronald K. Combs, and Karen Washington. "Assigning Average-Achieving Eighth Graders to Advanced Mathematics Class in an Urban Junior High." *The Elementary School Journal* 92, no. 5 (1992): 587–99.

Mezynski, Karen, Julian C. Stanley, and Richard F. McCoart. "Helping Youth Score Well on AP Examinations." In *Academic Precocity: Aspects of Its Development*, edited by Camilla Benbow and Julian C. Stanley, pp. 86–112. Baltimore: Johns Hopkins University Press, 1983.

Moon, Carolyn, Carol A. Tomlinson, and Carolyn M. Callahan. *Academic Diversity in the Middle School: Results of a National Survey of Middle School Administrators and Teachers.* Research Monograph 93102. Storrs, Conn.: The National Research Center on the Gifted and Talented, University of Connecticut, 1995.

Mosteller, Frederick, Richard Light, and Jason Sachs. "Sustained Inquiry in Education: Lessons from Skill Grouping and Class Size." *Harvard Educational Review* 66, no. 4 (1996): 797–828.

National Association for Gifted Children (NAGC). Acceleration. NAGC position statement. Washington, D.C.: NAGC, 2009. http://www.nagc.org/uploadedFiles/PDF/Position_Statement_PDFs/pp_acceleration.pdf.

National Council of Teachers of Mathematics (NCTM). *Curriculum and Evaluation Standards for School Mathematics.* Reston, Va.: NCTM, 1989.

———. *Principles and Standards for School Mathematics.* Reston, Va.: NCTM, 2000.

———. *Curriculum Focal Points for Prekindergarten through Grade 8 Mathematics: A Quest for Coherence.* Reston, Va.: NCTM, 2006.

National Mathematics Advisory Panel (National Math Panel). *The Final Report of the National Mathematics Advisory Panel.* Executive Summary. Washington, D.C.: U.S. Department of Education, 2008.

National Research Council. *How People Learn: Brain, Mind, Experience, and School.* Washington, D.C.: National Academies Press, 2000.

———. *Learning and Understanding.* Washington, D.C.: National Academies Press, 2002.

Niehart, Maureen, Sally Ries, Nancy M. Robinson, and Sydney Moon, eds. *The Social and Emotional Development of Gifted Children: What Do We Know?* Waco, Tex.: Prufrock Press, 2002.

Oakes, Jeannie. "Two Cities' Tracking and Within-School Segregation." *Teachers College Record* 96, no. 4 (1995): 681–90.

Olszewski-Kubilius, Paula. "Research Evidence regarding the Validity and Effects of Talent Search Educational Programs." *Journal of Secondary Gifted Education* 9 (1998): 134–38.

Olszewski-Kubilius, Paula, and Marilynn J. Kulieke. "Using Off-Level Testing and Assessment for Gifted and Talented Students." In *Alternative Assessments with Gifted and Talented Students,* edited by Joyce L. VanTassel-Baska, pp. 89–106. Waco, Tex.: Prufrock Press, 2008.

Park, Gregory, David Lubinski, and Camilla P. Benbow. "Contrasting Intellectual Patterns for Creativity in the Arts and Sciences: Tracking Intellectually Precocious Youth over 25 Years." *Psychological Science* 18 (2007): 948–52.

Paterson, Donald. "Conservation of Human Talent." *American Psychologist* 12 (1957): 134–44.

Pressey, Sidney L. *Educational Acceleration: Appraisals and Basic Problems.* Columbus, Ohio: Ohio State University Press, 1949.

Prevost, Fernand J. "Soundoff: Let's Not Teach Algebra to Eighth Graders!" *Mathematics Teacher* 78, no. 8 (1985): 586–87.

Robinson, Ann, Robert H. Bradley, and T. D. Stanley. "Opportunity to Achieve: Identifying Mathematically Gifted Students." *Contemporary Educational Psychology* 15, no. 1 (1990): 1–12.

Robinson, Ann, Bruce M. Shore, and Donna L. Enersen. *Best Practices in Gifted Education.* Waco, Tex.: Prufrock Press, 2007.

Robinson, Nancy M., Robert D. Abbott, Virginia W. Berninger, Julie Busse, and Swapna Mukhopadhyay. "Developmental Changes in Mathematically Precocious Young Children:
Longitudinal and Gender Effects." *Gifted Child Quarterly* 41, no. 4 (1997): 145–58.

Rogers, Karen. "Using Current Research to Make 'Good' Decisions about Grouping." *National
Association of Secondary School Principals Bulletin* 82 (February 1998): 38–46.

———. "Lessons Learned about Educating the Gifted and Talented: A Synthesis of the Research on Educational Practice." *Gifted Child Quarterly* 51, no. 4 (2007): 382–96.

Seashore, Carl E. "The Gifted Student and Research." *Science* 56 (1922): 641–48.

Sheffield, Linda, ed. *Developing Mathematically Promising Students.* Reston, Va.: National Council of Teachers of Mathematics, 1999.

Siegle, Del, and D. Betsy McCoach. "Issues Related to the Underachievement of Gifted Students." *In Leading Change in Gifted Education: The Festschrift of Dr. Joyce VanTassel-Baska,*
edited by Bronwyn MacFarlane and Tamra Stambaugh, pp. 61–81. Waco, Tex.:
Prufrock Press, 2009.

Singham, Mano. "The Achievement Gap: Myths and Reality." *Phi Delta Kappan* 84, no. 8
(2003): 589–91.

Slavin, Richard. "Ability Grouping and Student Achievement in Middle Grades: Achievement
Effects and Alternatives." *Elementary School Journal* 93 (1990): 536–52.

———. *Student Team Learning: A Practical Guide to Cooperative Learning.* Washington, D.C.:
National Education Association, 1991.

———. "Detracking and Its Detractors: Flawed Evidence, Flawed Values." *Phi Delta Kappan* 77,
no. 3 (1995): 220–21.

Sosniak, Lauren. "Learning to Be a Concert Pianist." *In Developing Talent in Young People,*
edited by Benjamin Bloom, pp. 19–89. New York: Ballantine, 1985.

Southern, Thomas W., and Eric D. Jones. "Types of Acceleration: Dimensions and Issues."
In *A Nation Deceived: How Schools Hold Back America's Brightest Students,* edited by
Nicholas Colangelo, Susan G. Assouline, and Miraca U. M. Gross, pp. 5–12. Iowa
City, Iowa: The Connie Belin & Jacqueline N. Blank International Center for Gifted
Education and Talent Development, 2004.

Sriraman, Bharath. "Discovering a Mathematical Principle: The Case of Matt." *Mathematics in
School* 33, no. 2 (2004): 25–31.

Stanley, Julian. "Helping Students Learn Only What They Don't Already Know." *Psychology,
Public Policy, and Law* 6 (2000): 216–22.

Stanley, Julian, Daniel P. Keating, and Lynn H. Fox. *Mathematical Talent: Discovery, Description,
and Development.* Baltimore: Johns Hopkins University Press, 1974.

Stanley, Julian, and Barbara S. K. Stanley. "High School Biology, Chemistry, and Physics
Learned Well in Three Weeks." *Journal of Research in Science Teaching* 23 (1986):
237–50.

Swiatek, Mary Ann, and Camilla P. Benbow. "A 10-Year Longitudinal Follow-Up of Participants in a Fast-Paced Mathematics Course." *Journal for Research in Mathematics Education* 22 (1991a): 138–50.

———. "Ten-Year Longitudinal Follow-Up of Ability-Matched Accelerated and Unaccelerated
Gifted Students." *Journal of Educational Psychology* 83 (1991b): 528–38.

Terman, Lewis. "The Discovery and Encouragement of Exceptional Talent." *American Psychologist* 9 (1954): 221–30.

Tomlinson, Carol. "Deciding to Differentiate Instruction in Middle School: One School's Journey." *Gifted Child Quarterly* 39 (1995): 77–87.

Tyler, Leona. *The Psychology of Individual Differences.* New York: Meredith, 1965.

VanTassel-Baska, Joyce. "Illinois' State-Wide Replication of the Johns Hopkins Study of Mathematically Precocious Youth." In *Academic Precocity: Aspects of Its Development,* edited by Camilla Benbow and Julian C. Stanley, pp. 179–91. Baltimore: Johns Hopkins University Press, 1983.

———. *Excellence in Educating Gifted and Talented Learners.* Denver: Love, 1998.

———. *Alternative Assessment with Gifted and Talented Students.* Waco, Tex.: Prufrock Press, 2008.

VanTassel-Baska, Joyce, and Tamra Stambaugh. *Comprehensive Curriculum for Gifted Learners.* Boston: Allyn & Bacon, 2005.

Webb, Norman L., ed. *Assessment in the Mathematics Classroom.* 1993 Yearbook of the National Council of Teachers of Mathematics (NCTM). Reston, Va.: NCTM, 1993.

Wertheimer, Richard D. "Definition and Identification of Mathematical Promise." In *Developing Mathematically Promising Students,* edited by Linda Sheffield, pp. 9–26. Reston, Va.: National Council of Teachers of Mathematics, 1999.

White, Paula, Adam Gamoran, Andrew Porter, and John Smithson. "Upgrading the High School Math Curriculum: Math Course-Taking Patterns in Seven High Schools in California and New York." *Educational Evaluation and Policy Analysis* 18 (1996): 285–307.

Willerman, Lee. *The Psychology of Individual and Group Differences.* San Francisco: Freedman, 1979.

Wright, Paul, Sandra P. Horn, and William L. Sanders. "Teacher and Classroom Context Effects on Student Achievement: Implications for Teacher Evaluation." *Journal of Personnel Evaluation in Education* 11 (1997): 57–67.

Ysseldyke, Jim, Steve Tardew, Joe Betts, Teri Thill, and Eileen Hannigan. "Use of an Instructional Management System to Enhance Math Instruction of Gifted and Talented Students." *Journal for the Education of the Gifted* 27 (2004): 293–310.

Program Models: Matching the Program to the Abilities, Needs, and Interests of Mathematically Talented Students

Ann Lupkowski-Shoplik

◆ A variety of options should be available for mathematically talented students, both within and outside of school, so that school programs and other services can be matched to the abilities and needs of individual students. Mathematically talented students are not well served by a one-size-fits-all program.

◆ Acceleration needs to be included in the menu of available options, especially for exceptionally mathematically talented students.

◆ Appropriate assessment is vital to determining the type of program needed for an individual student.

◆ The question is not, Is the student going to run out of math? but, How does the student get access to more math?

Well-meaning school personnel sometimes devise programs for mathematically talented students "on the fly," to keep these students busy and out of trouble, without thinking about challenging them appropriately or moving them forward in a systematic progression. An example of such an inappropriate "program" is giving a talented student a book to study on his or her own in the back of the room. Although the offer of the book represents an attempt to recognize the student's needs and somehow provide a differentiated curriculum, school personnel don't do students any favors with this type of program. Few students—no matter how talented—have the maturity, independence, or motivation to work through a challenging curriculum on their own.

Accelerating a student or somehow modifying the curriculum in a way that puts the student out of sequence with his or her age-mates, then suddenly discovering that there is no math class left for the student to take, and ultimately requiring the student to repeat a year of math is also inappropriate. The goal of this chapter is to show how careful planning, proper pacing, and judicious placing of students in appropriate programs result in a program in which mathematically talented students consistently learn new mathematics throughout their school years. This consistent exposure to new learning is the most important goal for the students. New learning fuels students' enjoyment of mathematics, responds to their desire for more challenging mathematics, and, ideally, provides opportunities for students to learn mathematics at a deeper level.

Acceleration and Enrichment

Before explaining the variety of program options for mathematically talented students and reviewing their advantages and disadvantages, it is important to discuss acceleration and enrichment. *Acceleration* means moving students more quickly than is typical through the mathematics curriculum. Acceleration can occur in many different ways, such as by allowing students to skip grades, move up a grade for math, or take a fast-paced math class designed for talented students. *Enrichment* typically means extending or broadening the regular curriculum by elaborating on the topic that is currently being studied or by introducing a new topic that is not offered in the regular curriculum. Rather than putting acceleration and enrichment in two different and opposite camps, it is more productive to think about how the two approaches can complement each other. Good acceleration contains enrichment components, and good enrichment in mathematics is accelerative (Stanley 1979).

The first time that educators encounter a decision about whether to accelerate a student, they are often very concerned about the social ramifications of such a move. Will moving a student up a grade or placing a student in a math class with older students be detrimental? To respond to this question, it is important to look at the many research studies investigating the short-term and long-term effects of acceleration in mathematics. The findings of these studies can be summarized briefly: differences favor the accelerated students, regardless of the type of acceleration used (see Benbow and Stanley [1996]). In summarizing findings of his meta-analysis, Kulik (2004) repeats the point: "The overall message from these studies is therefore unequivocal: Acceleration contributes greatly to the academic achievement of bright students" (p. 15).

In their classic paper, Brody and Benbow (1987) reviewed data from a follow-up study of students from the Study of Mathematically Precocious Youth (SMPY) at Johns Hopkins University and found no harmful effects of acceleration and many positive effects. Students who were more accelerated in school tended to earn more awards, attend more selective colleges, and be more likely to plan to earn doctorates or other advanced degrees than less accelerated students of similar abilities. No differences were found between the two groups in social and emotional adjustment. Kulik and Kulik's (1984) meta-analysis of twenty-six research studies revealed that gifted students' achievement was significantly higher in accelerated classes than in non-accelerated classes.

Other findings about the effects of acceleration include the following:

- Students taking fast-paced summer classes in mathematics found that those classes were challenging and prepared them for the next level of studies (Mills, Ablard, and Lynch 1992).

- No signs of ill effects of acceleration on friendships or work have been found (Brody and Benbow 1987).

- Acceleration benefits social and emotional adjustment (Benbow 1991).

- Acceleration appears to increase educational ambition (Kulik 2004).

- Accelerated students tend to perform in school like their bright, older, non-accelerated classmates. The accelerated students usually score almost a grade level higher on achievement tests than bright, same-aged students who are not accelerated (Kulik 2004).

"Literally hundreds of studies have shown that advancing talented students in their studies so that they are working with curricula designed for older students (i.e., acceleration) is effective in enhancing achievement" (Lubinski and Benbow 2006, p. 334). Longitudinal studies conducted by SMPY complete the story. Ten and twenty years after mathematically talented thirteen-year-olds participated in fast-paced mathematics classes, their achievements were compared to those of equally able students. Students who had participated in the accelerated math classes were twice as likely to be in math or science career tracks. "[B]eing challenged by intellectually rigorous math-science educational opportunities that are responsive to one's learning needs increases the likelihood of being in a STEM career 20 years later" (Lubinski and Benbow 2006, pp. 334–35). Acceleration works.

The reader might suppose that the population studied by SMPY is a tiny, phenomenally talented group made up of the type of students that a teacher might meet only once in a lifetime. That is not the case. Many of the cohorts studied by SMPY include students whose talents have been measured as being in the top 1 in 200 (top 0.5 percent). That fraction means that a number of students with this level of talent are in *every* school.

The literature demonstrating the success of acceleration for mathematically talented students is dominated by the studies of the SMPY researchers. However, other groups have described similar findings. Much of the recent research on acceleration has been summarized in *A Nation Deceived* (Colangelo, Assouline, and Gross 2004).

Matching Program Options to Levels of Mathematical Talent: The "Pyramid of Educational Options"

Figure 2.1 shows the "Pyramid of Educational Options" that Assouline and Lupkowski-Shoplik (2005) developed to describe a variety of educational options for math-talented youth. The arrangement of the pyramid helps to show that students exhibiting different levels of mathematical talent need different types of programs. The figure represents one way of thinking about the options. Enrichment-oriented options complementing the regular curriculum should be widely available to all mathematically talented students. They are shown at the bottom of the pyramid, not because they are less valued, but because they should be available to *all* mathematically talented students.

Higher on the pyramid, the options become more and more accelerative and are ideal for a smaller and smaller number of math-talented students. Close to the top, the options are best suited to the most talented students. In other words, many math-talented students would benefit from enrichment within the regular classroom. A smaller number of students need enrichment plus the challenge provided by a fast-paced, accelerated curriculum. The more talented the student, the less the regular curriculum is an appropriately challenging match, and the greater the need for acceleration. The most talented students need the most accelerative options.

For example, a moderately mathematically talented student may be adequately challenged by enrichment and extensions within the regular classroom, participation in contests or competitions, and participation in occasional weekend enrichment classes provided by a local university. This student may be most appropriately challenged by the "regular" curriculum—as long as it is a curriculum that presents rigorous mathematics in depth and allows the student time to explore topics of interest, wrestle with challenging problems, and talk with teachers and peers about interesting mathematical ideas.

Students exhibiting greater levels of talent require additional challenges. The level and pace of the regular curriculum is not an adequate match for

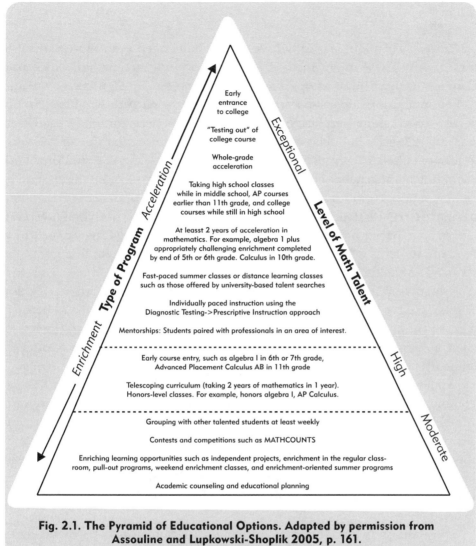

Fig. 2.1. The Pyramid of Educational Options. Adapted by permission from Assouline and Lupkowski-Shoplik 2005, p. 161.

their talents. Challenges may be provided by early entrance to classes such as algebra 1 in seventh grade or honors math classes in middle school and high school. Depending on the curriculum provided by the local school, a student who has demonstrated knowledge of the elementary school and middle school mathematics curricula moves on to higher-level classes, which might be called "algebra 1," "geometry," or "integrated math 1 and 2." (See the discussion of the DT→PI model [p. 41] for more information about appropriate assessment and placement of students.) These students still benefit from studying mathematics in depth, struggling with challenging problems, and talking with teachers and peers about interesting mathematical ideas. However, the *level* of mathematics that they study is more advanced. Thus, it is called *accelerative*.

Exceptionally mathematically talented students need even more radical interventions. These might include participation in a mentorship, which pairs a student with an adult who is a mathematics professor, engineer, or scientist. Other options include fast-paced summer classes, such as those offered by university-based talent searches; two or more years of acceleration in mathematics; taking high school classes while in middle school; and taking Advanced Placement classes at a much younger age than is typical. As stated previously, such students also benefit from participation in contests, competitions, and enrichment opportunities in math. All of these varied experiences give students a chance to refine their talents, struggle with challenging problems, and enjoy the creative process of "doing" mathematics. These stimulating opportunities feed the students' abilities and interests, and encourage them to pursue studies in STEM fields.

Using Assouline and Lupkowski-Shoplik's Pyramid of Educational Options allows us to recognize that math-talented students are not all alike. They need a variety of programs, and those programs need to be matched to the level of their abilities. The more exceptionally talented the student, the greater the student's need for accelerative options.

What is the *best* program for mathematically talented students? This is a common question from both experienced and inexperienced teachers, and it would be simple to answer if only there were one best program to recommend. The response is complex because of two major issues: (a) many programming models or options are available, as shown in the pyramid, and (b) the group known as "mathematically talented students" is composed of students who vary considerably with respect to general ability, specific aptitude, and prior achievement.

Two basic steps are required to devise programs for mathematically talented students. First, the student's ability, aptitude, and achievement are determined through appropriate assessment (Assouline and Lupkowski-Shoplik [2005] provide a useful chapter on educational assessment). Second, the best method of programming is identified to match the results of the assessment. The remainder of this chapter presents examples of many different types of programs shown in the Pyramid of Educational Options, starting at the bottom of the pyramid and working up.

Differentiated instruction within the regular classroom

The most common option for math-talented students is differentiation within the regular classroom. In this situation, the regular classroom teacher recognizes the student's mathematical ability, either through formal assessment or by classroom performance. The teacher devises strategies to challenge the student within the classroom. The teacher may do this quite independently, finding things on his or her own to introduce to the talented student, either in a planned or haphazard manner. As an example of haphazard enrichment, consider the case of the teacher who goes to a conference or in-service program, learns about an activity that "kids really like," and returns on Monday morning to try the activity with the students. Suppose that when Tuesday comes, though, she's back to the regular curriculum, and nothing has really changed.

Enrichment means adding depth and complexity to the curriculum. Good enrichment does not mean providing busy work or assigning more of the same (for example, telling a student, "You're so talented that you can do *all* the problems, not just the even-numbered ones, at the end of the chapter"). Teachers providing good enrichment opportunities give students time to explore topics of interest in depth, offer them resources to use in pursuing these extensions, and support them as they grapple with challenging mathematics problems.

What works best is systematically planned differentiation, in which challenging activities are tied to the regular curriculum and provide extensions to that curriculum. Bonner (2009), a fifth-grade classroom teacher and gifted education specialist, offers one example of planned differentiation in the regular classroom in her description of the fifth-grade math program in Owen J. Roberts School District in Pottstown, Pennsylvania. Fifth graders in Bonner's school district are grouped heterogeneously for mathematics. For instance, one class of sixteen students might include four identified gifted students and three learning support students. The school district has developed a systematic plan for differentiating instruction for these students within the regular classroom. Although a few students in the district have been accelerated in mathematics, the vast majority of the mathematically talented students are served by the regular classroom program described below.

Several years ago, a math task force revised the district's entire K–12 mathematics curriculum to reflect the NCTM Standards and the Pennsylvania Department of Education standards. The task force also relied heavily on *Elementary and Middle School Mathematics: Teaching Developmentally* (Van de Walle 2007). Members of the task force were gifted support teachers, Title I teachers, and regular classroom teachers. According to Bonner, they chose not to use textbooks but rather to use the textbook money to purchase resources. District personnel determined relevant content at each grade level and developed pretests for each unit taught. The goal was to pretest each student, analyze the data, and tailor instruction and enrichment on the basis of that data. The revised curriculum placed an emphasis on content enrichment in the regular classroom and studying topics in detail. One principal in the district says the teachers don't "water ski," skimming the surface; rather, they go "scuba diving," studying mathematics in depth with their students.

In one fifth-grade classroom, Bonner teaches three different levels of mathematics for gifted, learning support, and Title I students. Before starting a new unit (usually on a Friday), she administers the district-developed pretests (also called "inventories") to assess the level of a student's mastery of each topic. Over the weekend, she grades the pretests and designs instruction for the following week, drawing on the resources available. She conducts this pretesting for each unit, and teaches seven or eight units per year.

Although students in the district are assigned to heterogeneous classes, within her fifth-grade classroom Bonner groups the mathematically talented students together. She uses math centers with differentiated activities to manage her classroom. At the beginning of each unit, students sign contracts with her to specify what they will do to satisfy the requirements of the unit. Bonner compresses the curriculum and uses the time saved for enrichment in math. This model gives the talented students an opportunity to work on enrichment problems that don't have quick answers. This is good training for their future study of mathematics, when the mathematical concepts are more abstract and it is hard for the student to "see" the answer immediately.

Although Bonner teaches several sections of fifth-grade mathematics, she is also the gifted education teacher for her building. Mathematics is offered at different times throughout the day so that she can teach mathematics to different classrooms of students. She also spends part of her day teaching in the gifted program. In addition, her schedule includes time to meet with other members of the instructional team. This allows her to interact with other teachers who teach math to gifted students and to share ideas for providing challenging instruction for them. Because the district uses this approach, groups of teachers feel "ownership" of the students, and the teachers do not feel threatened if Bonner makes suggestions to them for differentiating instruction for their mathematically talented students.

Since the beginning of this program, one of the big challenges for teachers is to shift their thinking from placement-oriented assessment to teaching-oriented assessment. By making this shift, teachers focus specifically on what the students know and don't know, and they tailor their instruction to the students' needs. Bonner finds that this new program requires a different type of thinking from what most educators and parents have previously experienced. District personnel have found that their teachers have benefitted from professional development, and they have also instituted a "Family Math Night" program so that they can better inform parents about the program.

Pull-out gifted programs

In pull-out programs for math, students are removed from the regular classroom some of the time so that they can be grouped with similarly talented students for instruction. These pull-out programs often offer only an hour or so of instruction each week. In a pull-out program (which is typically a stand-alone program), students study challenging topics that may or may not be related to the regular math program. For example, a sixth grader might be studying the regular sixth-grade mathematics but be pulled out for an hour each week to work with talented peers on enrichment topics such as geometry or probability and statistics. Such sixth graders are often still responsible for assignments in the regular classroom and must make up any work or tests that they miss. These pull-out programs serve three purposes: (1) recognize students' talents, (2) group students with other talented peers, and (3) give students more challenging mathematics to study. Two of the major drawbacks of this type of program are that students are often responsible for making up work that they miss, and that they are still placed in the regular classroom for mathematics. In other words, their instruction isn't necessarily differentiated in the regular classroom. This can lead to frustration for the mathematically talented student and a feeling of being "punished" with extra work for being "smart" in math.

Outside-of-school enrichment programs: Weekend classes and competitions

Some organizations offer challenging math programs for gifted students to supplement what they study in school. For example, the weekend workshops provided by the Carnegie Mellon Institute for Talented Elementary and Secondary Students (C-MITES) include opportunities for math-talented students to work together with talented teachers on selected enrichment topics. Students may take classes with titles such as "The Math and Art of It" (which shows how mathematics can be applied in artistic ways), "Building a Geodesic Dome" (where students learn about geometry and build a room-sized model of a geodesic dome), and "Mini Math Olympiad" (in which students learn problem-solving strategies and try out their skills on contest problems from various competitions). Students spend three hours or more studying advanced topics. (More information about these workshops can be found at www.cmu.edu/cmites.)

Contests and competitions offer another opportunity to challenge students outside of the regular classroom. Students may meet regularly outside of their assigned math classes to practice math problems and learn problem-solving strategies. They may form a math team that attends contests or participates in an in-school competition. Examples of math competitions for middle school students include the Mathematical Olympiads for Elementary and Middle Schools (MO-EMS; see www.moems.org), MATHCOUNTS (see www.mathcounts.org), and AMC 8 (www.unl.edu/amc). The goal of these competitions is to provide fun and expose students to creative problems that challenge them mathematically.

These outside-of-school enrichment programs offer mathematical challenges to students, give them opportunities to study more advanced mathematics and interact with intellectual peers, provide a chance to work with teachers and other adults who enjoy math and want to inspire students to challenge themselves math-ematically, and give the students recognition for their mathematical achievements. The greatest drawback of these programs is that they have no direct impact on the regular school mathematics program. Students might be achieving great things in mathematics competitions or studying advanced topics in a weekend class, but those experiences do not guarantee that the mathematics that they study in the regular school program is challenging. However, parents and students view the ex-periences as important in helping the students to realize their talents, encounter a challenging environment (perhaps for the first time), experience the joy of study-ing rigorous mathematics, and meet peers and teachers who also love math.

Ability grouping in school: Honors classes and advanced classes

When students are grouped by ability for mathematics, they might be grouped together every day for the math period, or they might be grouped for mathematics with other similarly able students only once or twice a week. This grouping may or may not result in acceleration. One district groups math-talented students by ability only twice a month, for "Math Challenge Day." The students do enrichment activities for fun on those days. In this example, stu-dents are grouped by ability, but their math progression is not systematic, nor is it accelerative.

In contrast, one large suburban district, which we will call "Green Valley School District," provides an ability-grouping program for math-talented stu-dents in middle school that offers one year of acceleration. This acceleration occurs daily. In the spring of fifth grade, students take tests from the Compre-hensive Testing Program 4 (Educational Records Bureau). The fifth graders take an above-level test—level 6—designed for students in sixth grade. Students take the "Quantitative Reasoning," "Mathematics Part I," and "Mathematics Part II" sections of the test. Those earning high scores are invited to skip the sixth-grade math course and take seventh-grade prealgebra. Approximately twelve students in each building qualify for this advanced math program. The talented students are grouped together for math instruction. The teacher com-pletes the standard prealgebra curriculum with the class, and the expectation is that successful students will then move on to algebra 1 in seventh grade.

These students are consequently accelerated by one year in mathematics as compared to the majority of students in Green Valley School District. The benefits of such a model include grouping students with similarly able peers, which gives them both social and intellectual advantages. Participating in a curriculum that matches their intellectual needs challenges the students and helps to prevent them from becoming bored and turned off to mathematics at this critical age.

The mathematically talented students in this sixth-grade math class typically move faster through the prealgebra curriculum than the average seventh-grade students. Their teacher provides enrichment and extensions on a regular basis. Although these students have clearly shown the ability to learn the mathematics quickly, district personnel have made a deliberate decision not to allow the students to accelerate any more than one year in mathematics. So the sixth-grade teacher periodically takes a break from the standard prealgebra curriculum to provide mathematical extensions. For example, one Friday the class spent the day working with the Soma cube, invented by Peit Hein (see http://www.fam-bundgaard.dk/SOMA/SOMA.HTM).

Subject-matter acceleration in mathematics: Moving up a grade

Another option for trying to match the curriculum to a student's abilities is subject-matter acceleration. Because gifted students are, by definition, ready for a more advanced curriculum, it seems to be an easy solution to allow them to move ahead in mathematics. This can be done for one student or a group of students.

Students can be identified for this type of acceleration by testing, teacher nomination, parent input, or a combination of these. Advanced students may be placed in a higher grade only for mathematics. It is not essential to have them skip the entire grade. Having an accelerated student in the classroom does not require any special training on the part of the receiving teacher. The student is simply placed in the regular math classroom with older students and is expected to do all of the assignments and tests that they do. This placement offers more of a challenge for talented students and is an attempt to match the curriculum to the student's abilities and needs.

This approach has a number of positive features:

1. The curriculum is more challenging.

2. The student is likely to be given credit for the work that he or she completes.

3. If the student completes the course satisfactorily, he or she is likely to be permitted to move ahead to the next math course.

4. No special training is required on the part of the teacher.

However, the arrangement also has its drawbacks:

1. The student's schedule may be out of sync with that of his or her age-mates.

2. Transportation to the higher class and scheduling the math class so that the student doesn't miss other important classes may be difficult.

3. The pace of the class may still be too slow for the student.

4. If the receiving teacher has no special training in working with mathematically talented students, the depth or complexity of the mathematics presented may still be inappropriate.

5. The student may have no formal math class to take in his or her last year of school in a particular building, requiring school personnel to find alternative ways to provide the right level of math for the student at that time or—worse—may result in the student sitting out of mathematics for a year.

One district that allows math-talented students to accelerate one year submits all of its students to an elaborate identification process. First, the students' nationally standardized achievement test records are examined. Those who have scored in the top 3 percent of the math composite as compared to local norms are invited to take a mathematics screening test developed by district math specialists. Those students who score in the top 20 percent on the screening test and have high grades, an excellent teacher recommendation, and parent support are invited to accelerate one year in math. Those who accept the invitation are placed in the regular math class that is one year advanced above their grade level. For example, a talented fifth grader can take sixth-grade math with sixth graders. In some cases, several accelerated fifth graders will be in the same sixth-grade classroom together.

The school district initiated this process in an attempt to identify mathematically talented students systematically. The district has succeeded in finding exceptionally talented youth and has been pleased that the vast majority of students who have accelerated have been very successful in their math classes. Unfortunately, even those students who are extraordinarily talented in mathematics have the option of accelerating by only one year. Another drawback of the district's approach is that the accelerated students are placed in regular mathematics, albeit at a higher grade level. No additional differentiation is provided for talented students.

Another, more general criticism of skipping a grade in mathematics is that students might miss critical concepts taught in middle school, such as those described in *Principles and Standards for School Mathematics* (NCTM 2000). Having the student participate in a thorough assessment before making the decision to accelerate helps alleviate these concerns (see the discussion of the DT→PI model below for more details on this concept.)

An accelerative university-based program during the school year

The University of Minnesota Talented Youth Mathematics Program (UM-TYMP) has been provided for sixth- to twelfth-grade students for more than thirty years. Highly accelerated, in-depth mathematics courses are offered for exceptionally talented youth. Students are recommended by their schools as eligible for entering the program at the level of algebra 1. Talented students may take the UMTYMP Algebra Qualifying Examination. Each March and April, nearly 900 students test for this program.

During the 2008–09 school year, nearly 400 students were enrolled in twenty-six different classes, which included nine high school level and nine college level courses. These classes are offered in the Minneapolis-St. Paul area, as well as in Rochester, Minnesota. Students begin by studying algebra 1 and may continue through college calculus, differential equations, and linear algebra. Each UMTYMP high school course is equivalent to one full year of high school credit, and students receive credit from the University of Minnesota for the calculus course. On one or two days a week after school, students attend a two-hour class and are assigned eight to ten hours of homework. In each two-hour class, they cover the equivalent of three weeks of regular high school mathematics content. Students who successfully complete the program take algebra, statistics, trigonometry, and geometry. This program is regarded as an outstanding accelerative program that recognizes exceptionally talented students, allows them to move ahead to an appropriate level of mathematics, and provides a rigorous, challenging curriculum. (For more information about the program, see http://www.itcep.umn.edu/umtymp/index.php; the student handbook is available at http://www.itcep.umn.edu/umtymp/WebHandbook09.pdf.)

The DT→PI model: An individualized, accelerative program

Developed by Julian Stanley (1979, 1991), the "Diagnostic Testing → Prescriptive Instruction" (DT→PI) model has the goal of providing a systematic method for challenging exceptionally mathematically talented students. Explained in detail by Assouline and Lupkowski-Shoplik (2005, pp. 105–39), the model ensures that students are appropriately challenged and are allowed to move ahead in a systematic fashion. The model, shown in figure 2.2, includes five steps.

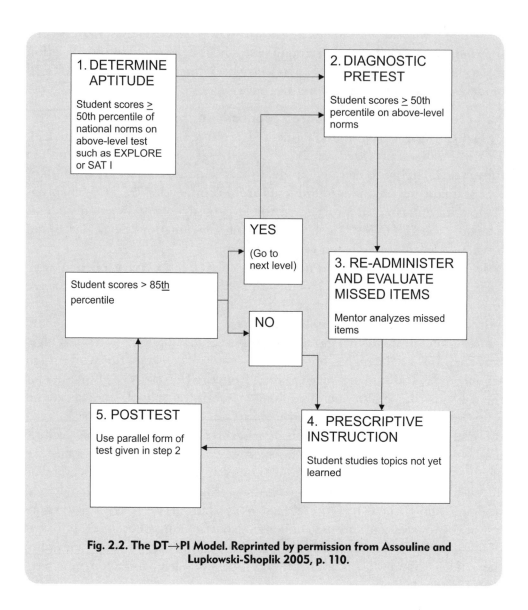

Fig. 2.2. The DT→PI Model. Reprinted by permission from Assouline and Lupkowski-Shoplik 2005, p. 110.

In step 1, students are tested to determine their level of mathematical aptitude. For example, a seventh grader might take the College Board's SAT I test. Students scoring above the 50th percentile when compared to the group for which the test was designed (college-bound seniors) are recommended for the DT→PI model. Other tests that are useful in step 1 with middle school students include the School and College Abilities Test (SCAT), EXPLORE, and the ACT Assessment.

In step 2, the students take a diagnostic pretest to determine what specific topics they have already learned and what they have yet to learn. Tests selected for this step should be above-grade-level achievement tests, since the goal is to determine what the student does and doesn't know. Useful tests for this step include the Stanford Diagnostic Tests of Mathematics, the Comprehensive Testing Program 4, end-of-year tests provided by textbook publishers, the Iowa Algebra Aptitude Test, and the Orleans-Hanna Algebra Prognosis Test. During this step, students take the test under standardized conditions, with one important exception: they are asked to put a question mark next to any item about which they are uncertain.

In step 3, the test proctor scores the test and re-administers items that students missed, skipped, or marked with a question mark. Each student is given the test booklet along with a sheet of paper listing the items that he or she needs to rework and is instructed to complete the items in unlimited time, showing all work. The information gained from this phase of testing is very important, allowing the mentor who is working with the student to determine whether he or she missed an item because of a misunderstanding of the concept or because of a simple mistake.

Step 3 completes the diagnostic phase of the model and leads to step 4, prescriptive instruction—the most important step of the model. The mentor tailors instruction to the student's abilities and achievements, using the very specific information gained from the testing. The goal of the tailored instruction is not to speed through the instructional process but to match the level of curriculum to the intellectual abilities of the student and to provide instruction that helps the student to develop a thorough understanding of the mathematics that he or she is studying.

After studying the mathematics topics for a period of time (a few days or several weeks), the student takes a posttest. The posttest, which constitutes step 5, should be parallel in form to the pretest (the same level of difficulty, but containing different items). Students scoring above the 85th percentile on the posttest are considered to have mastered the material.

This process allows exceptionally talented students to move ahead systematically. It works well for individualized instruction and helps to ensure that students do not have gaps in their mathematical backgrounds. Because it is an individualized program, it avoids some of the pitfalls of simply moving a bright student up to a higher grade. The student studies mathematics with a mentor (and sometimes with a small group of similarly talented students), eliminating some of the social and transportation issues that arise for students who are placed with older students. One of the drawbacks of such an arrangement is the lack of age-mates with whom to discuss mathematical ideas. To overcome this shortcoming, it is useful to have two to four exceptionally talented students grouped together for this type of instruction.

One of the problems with simply moving a student up to a higher grade for math is that talented students often complain that the pace of the class is too slow. Participation in the DT→PI process helps avoid this problem, since the pace of instruction is tailored to the student's abilities and needs.

The DT→PI model has been used in several different ways:

1. Parents have hired a mentor to work with a student on challenging mathematics outside of school. In implementing the DT→PI model in this way, parents need to work with school personnel on issues of placement and credit. Ideally, the student is excused from the regular math class and uses that time to complete mentor-assigned work.

2. Groups of students within a school district have been identified for a DT→PI program provided by the school. These small groups of students usually work together on challenging math. Because this is an in-school program, assigning credit to the student for the work completed presents no problems. The drawback is the expense to the school district of assigning a teacher specifically to the small group of students.

3. The DT→PI model has been used extensively by university-based talent searches in their summer programs (see below for more detail).

The DT→PI model has been researched extensively. Many students have mastered one or more years of instruction in a three-week summer program (Olszewski-Kubilius et al. 1989). Students participating in these fast-paced classes retain what they have learned and perform very well in their next courses in school (Benbow 1992). As described earlier, longitudinal effects are positive, and students participating in these fast-paced math classes were twice as likely to be in STEM careers years later (Lubinski and Benbow 2006).

Talent searches and summer programs: Articulating programs for exceptional students with the school curriculum

Since the early 1970s, university-based talent search programs have provided mathematically talented students with challenging, fast-paced classes as well as opportunities to study and interact with intellectual peers (Lupkowski-Shoplik et al. 2003). To participate in a talent search, middle school students take an above-level aptitude test, such as the SAT I or ACT Assessment (typically for seventh and eighth graders), SCAT (typically for sixth graders or younger students), or EXPLORE (typically for third through sixth graders). Students earning high scores on one of these tests are invited to participate in fast-paced academic summer programs and many other opportunities, such as distance learning classes. These programs provide a unique opportunity for talented students to enjoy the challenge of a rigorous class and be with intellectual peers.

Every year, hundreds of thousands of students participate in these talent searches, which are conducted by the University of Calgary, California State University, Carnegie Mellon University, the University of Denver, Duke University, the University of Iowa, Johns Hopkins University, the University of New South Wales, Northwestern University, the University of Washington, and others. The Talent Searches provide students and their families with test results and assist them in interpreting them and selecting appropriate educational strategies.

Many talent search participants attend summer programs offered at a university. Fast-paced, above-level mathematics classes provided by these summer programs are usually based on the DT→PI model described above. Students are first tested to determine what they already know. Instruction is focused on the concepts that they have not yet mastered. Once they complete a topic, students take a posttest to demonstrate mastery. Bright students are able to move ahead in mathematics at an individualized pace. They can demonstrate mastery of topics that have not formally been taught to them. This helps the students avoid the boredom of sitting through 180 days of mathematics class, when they already know over 80 percent of the material on the first day. Again, the goal is not to speed through the material to break some sort of record; instead, the aim is to match the level and pace of the curriculum to the needs and abilities of the student. In these summer programs provided by talent searches, exceptionally talented students study high-level mathematics at a faster pace than is typical. These summer programs also offer students the opportunity to study mathematics in depth with intellectually able peers and teachers who are excellent mathematical role models.

Once a student successfully completes a course in a talent search summer program, articulation with the regular school program becomes an issue. The immediate question is, How will the school respond to the course just completed? Will the student receive credit for the work and be placed in the next level of the class? Long-term consequences of participation in these classes include the problem of how to accommodate the student several years from now, when he or she may have already completed all the math classes offered in the local school (Olszewski-Kubilius 2003).

School personnel may directly discourage students from participating in such programs because they aren't sure how to articulate completed summer program classes with the mathematics program at their school. Or they may

45

indirectly discourage them by not giving credit for work completed in a summer program. These negative responses are unfortunate, because nearly forty years of research has demonstrated that students who successfully complete talent search summer programs have learned the material well and are well prepared for subsequent courses (Olszewski-Kubilius 2007).

The talent searches strongly recommend that students and their families work with school personnel *before* the student attends the summer program to plan the student's program of mathematics. For example, the Center for Talented Youth (CTY) at Johns Hopkins University makes its summer program syllabi and lists of textbooks available to students before they participate in classes. School personnel can use that information as they plan the student's placement for the coming school year. Together with the students, school personnel are asked to complete a questionnaire before the student attends the summer program. CTY has also put together a parents' guide to assist family members in the process of working with a child's school on credit and placement issues (http://cty.jhu.edu/summer/docs/parentguide_09.pdf).

The goal of these talent search summer programs is to challenge students intellectually. With the DT→PI model, the programs allow students to study mathematics at an appropriate pace. Many students are able to complete an entire course, such as algebra 1 or trigonometry, during a three-week summer program. The goal of the program is clearly acceleration; thus, students should be placed in the next mathematics course when they return to school in the fall. For those students who are unable to complete an entire course in the summer, several alternative arrangements are available. Students might (1) meet with a mentor or tutor for the rest of the summer to complete the course at home, (2) take the course as part of a distance learning program, or (3) continue where they left off in the summer program in an individualized course at school. Much more detail about articulating a talent search course with the school program can be found at the CTY Web site (http://cty.jhu.edu/summer/mathsequence.html).

Distance learning programs

Advances in technology over the last twenty years have allowed an explosion of distance learning opportunities for mathematically talented youth. One of the early leaders in e-learning for mathematically talented students is the Educational Program for Gifted Youth (EPGY) at Stanford University (http://epgy.stanford.edu/overview/index.html). Since EPGY was founded in 1985, more than 50,000 students have taken its courses. Mathematics courses, including algebra, precalculus, and calculus, are available for students in elementary school through graduate school. EPGY courses can be established at a school or on an individualized basis. To qualify for the program, students take mathematics aptitude tests. EPGY courses are designed to replace math courses taught at school, and instructors interact with the students in e-mail exchanges, telephone conversations, or "virtual classroom" sessions. Students are expected to work five to ten hours a week on their classes. Distance learning programs for math-talented youth are also provided by the Center for Talent Development at Northwestern University, the Center for Talented Youth at Johns Hopkins University, the Independent Study High School at the University of Nebraska–Lincoln, and others.

Distance learning classes may be an excellent solution for the accelerated student who has "run out of math" to study in the local school. With these classes, there is no need to transport the student to another location for math class or to hire a special math teacher to teach a class for one student.

Successful students in distance learning classes must be highly motivated and have the ability to work independently, as well as to persevere when things get difficult. The advantages of distance learning classes include the fact that the student can decide when and where to study, and distance learning gives bright students access to advanced classes even if those classes aren't offered in their local school. In addition, schools can provide middle school students with high school classes without needing to deal with the social issues that might arise from placing a younger student in a class with older students (Adams and Olszewski-Kubilius 2007).

Getting students hooked into the technology required for distance learning classes can sometimes be challenging. School personnel and parents might also be concerned that a student will experience feelings of isolation if he or she is always studying mathematics alone. Finally, distance learning courses can be expensive: they can cost as much as $1,000 per semester. Frequently, parents are asked to pay the costs associated with distance learning.

Issues in Planning Programs for Mathematically Talented Students

Assouline and Lupkowski-Shoplik (2005) identified important issues that should be considered when planning a program for math-talented students. These issues include the following:

1. A "one-size-fits-all" program doesn't fit all. Because mathematically talented students have varying abilities, programs designed for them should be varied, too.

2. Students may be gifted in math but not other subjects. Mathematically talented students aren't always identified as "gifted" students

in their schools. They should not be denied opportunities in math because they do not possess high abilities in all subjects.

3. Gifted programs might not address the needs of mathematically talented students. For example, if a gifted program is language-arts based, it might be inadequate for the needs of math-talented students.

4. "Acceleration versus enrichment" is a false dichotomy. Well-thought-out accelerative *and* good enrichment activities should work together to challenge talented students.

5. Acceleration doesn't necessarily produce gaps in a student's mathematical background. Acceleration needs to be implemented in such a way that students progress at an appropriately rapid pace without skipping important concepts. The DT→PI model provides a structure for such an accelerative program.

6. Extremely talented students may make computation mistakes. Talented students perform better on conceptual tasks than on computation tasks. They may make mistakes on routine computation tasks because of carelessness or boredom, or because they have avoided memorizing basic math facts. Talented students shouldn't be denied challenging opportunities because they don't perform perfectly on computation tasks.

7. Appropriately accelerated pacing includes an in-depth study of challenging mathematical ideas. Because gifted students by definition learn faster than typical students, the pace of the material presented to them should be faster than is typical. That faster pace shouldn't result in a quick tour through middle school mathematics for the sake of breaking a record. Instead, it should result in students being consistently challenged by subsequent, well-designed courses in mathematics.

8. Special programs for mathematically talented youth need to be integrated into district-wide objectives so they can survive changes in personnel. Too many times, a successful program falls by the wayside because its chief proponent retired or moved to another position. To help institutionalize the program, it is helpful to take the following actions:

    a. Create ownership by the constituents.

    b. Document how the program works by saving important items such as samples of letters to parents, test results, placement decisions, and annual calendars in a handbook or "how to" manual for running the program.

   c. Develop a written plan, including goals for the program.

   d. Gather data and conduct evaluations of various aspects of the program.

   e. Document success stories by inviting past students to speak to school boards about the impact of the program on their education, or by saving written testimonials and newspaper articles, for example.

   f. Ensure articulation within the curriculum: high school personnel need to be aware of and understand how the middle school program works so that they can be well prepared for students as they move through the grades.

References

Adams, Cheryll M., and Paula Olszewski-Kubilius. "Distance Learning and Gifted Students." In *Serving Gifted Learners beyond the Traditional Classroom*, edited by Joyce L. VanTassel-Baska, pp. 169–88. Waco, Tex.: Prufrock Press, 2007.

Assouline, Susan, and Ann Lupkowski-Shoplik. *Developing Math Talent: A Guide for Educating Gifted and Advanced Learners in Math.* Waco, Tex.: Prufrock Press, 2005.

Benbow, Camilla P. "Meeting the Needs of Gifted Students through Use of Acceleration." In *Handbook of Special Education: Research and Practice,* vol. 4, edited by Margaret C. Wang, Maynard C. Reynolds, and Herbert J. Walberg, pp. 23–36. Oxford, England: Pergamon Press, 1991.

———. "Mathematical Talent: Its Nature and Consequences." In *Talent Development: Proceedings from the 1991 Henry B. and Jocelyn Wallace National Research Symposium on Talent Development,* edited by Nicholas Colangelo, Susan G. Assouline, and DeeAnn L Ambroson, pp. 95–123. New York: Trillium Press, 1992.

Benbow, Camilla P., and Julian C. Stanley. "Inequity in Equity: How 'Equity' Can Lead to Inequity for High-Potential Students." *Psychology, Public Policy, and Law* 2 (1996): 249–92.

Bonner, Mary-Rita. "Meeting the Math Needs of Gifted Students." Paper presented at the annual meeting of the Pennsylvania Association for Gifted Education, King of Prussia, Pennsylvania, April 2009.

Brody, Linda E., and Camilla P. Benbow. "Accelerative Strategies: How Effective Are They for the Gifted?" *Gifted Child Quarterly* 82 (Summer 1987): 105–10.

Colangelo, Nicholas, Susan G. Assouline, and Miraca U. M. Gross, eds. *A Nation Deceived: How Schools Hold Back America's Brightest Students*, vol. 2. Iowa City, Iowa: The Connie Belin & Jacqueline N. Blank International Center for Gifted Education and Talent Development, 2004.

Kulik, James A. "Meta-analytic Studies of Acceleration." In *A Nation Deceived: How Schools Hold Back America's Brightest Students*, vol. 2, edited by Nicholas Colangelo, Susan G. Assouline, and Miraca U. M. Gross. Iowa City: Iowa: The Connie Belin & Jacqueline N. Blank International Center for Gifted Education and Talent Development, 2004.

Kulik, James A., and Chen-Lin Kulik. "Synthesis of Research on Effects of Accelerated Instruction." *Educational Leadership* 42 (October 1984): 84–89.

Lubinski, David, and Benbow, Camilla P. "Study of Mathematically Precocious Youth after 35 Years: Uncovering Antecedents for the Development of Math-Science Expertise." *Perspectives on Psychological Science* 1, no. 4 (2006): 316–45.

Lupkowski-Shoplik, Ann, Camilla P. Benbow, Susan G. Assouline, and Linda E. Brody. "Talent Searches: Meeting the Needs of Academically Talented Youth." In *Handbook of Gifted Education*, edited by Nicholas Colangelo and Gary A. Davis, pp. 204–18. Boston: Allyn & Bacon, 2003.

Mills, Carol J., Karen E. Ablard, and Sharon J. Lynch. "Academically Talented Students' Preparation for Advanced-Level Course Work after Individually-Paced Precalculus Class." *Journal for the Education of the Gifted* 16 (1992): 3–17.

National Council of Teachers of Mathematics (NCTM). *Principles and Standards for School Mathematics.* Reston, Va.: NCTM, 2000.

Olszewski-Kubilius, Paula. "Special Summer and Saturday Programs for Gifted Students." In *Handbook of Gifted Education*, edited by Nicholas Colangelo and Gary A. Davis, pp. 219–228. Boston: Allyn & Bacon, 2003.

———. "The Role of Summer Programs in Developing the Talents of Gifted Students." In *Serving Gifted Learners beyond the Traditional Classroom*, edited by Joyce L. VanTassel-Baska, pp. 13–32. Waco, Tex.: Prufrock Press, 2007.

Olszewski-Kubilius, Paula, Marilyn J. Kulieke, Gordon B. Willis, and Noma Krasney. "An Analysis of the Validity of SAT Entrance Scores for Accelerated Classes." *Journal for the Education of the Gifted* 13 (Fall 1989): 37–54.

Stanley, Julian C. "An Academic Model for Educating the Mathematically Talented." *Gifted Child Quarterly* 35 (1991): 36–42.

———. "Identifying and Nurturing the Intellectually Gifted." In *Educating the Gifted: Acceleration and Enrichment*, edited by William C. George, Sanford J. Cohen, and Julian C. Stanley, pp. 172–80. Baltimore: Johns Hopkins University Press, 1979.

Van de Walle, John. *Elementary and Middle School Mathematics: Teaching Developmentally.* Columbus, Ohio: Allyn & Bacon, 2007.

CHAPTER

3

Using Curriculum to Develop Mathematical Promise in the Middle Grades

M. Katherine Gavin and Linda Jensen Sheffield

◆ Gifted and talented middle-grades mathematics students in the United States have made minimal gains in the last ten years and need a more rigorous, challenging, and articulated curriculum to be able to compete on an international level.

◆ Gifted and talented students need an in-depth understanding of the middle-grades curriculum as outlined in the *Common Core K–12 Mathematics Standards* and NCTM's *Curriculum Focal Points.* The important mathematics outlined for middle school students in these sources is foundational for an understanding of advanced topics and should not be skipped in an attempt to move more quickly to high school topics.

◆ Curriculum for the development of mathematical talent in the middle grades needs to consider both students' mathematical abilities and their attitudes towards mathematics.

◆ Advanced, in-depth curriculum needs four components: creative and complex problem solving, connections within and across mathematical and other contexts, an inquiry-based approach, and appropriate pacing.

◆ Criteria for assessment of student work need to include an appraisal of the students' mathematical understanding and reasoning, communication, problem solving, and creativity.

In *Principles and Standards for School Mathematics* (NCTM 2000, p. 13), the National Council of Teachers of Mathematics asserts that equity in education includes support for exceptionally talented students:

> All students should have access to an excellent and equitable mathematics program that provides solid support for their learning and is responsive to their prior knowledge, intellectual strengths, and personal interests.... Students with special interests or exceptional talent in mathematics ... must be nurtured and supported so that they have the opportunity and guidance to excel.

Exceptionally talented students' needs for support are perhaps especially great in the middle grades, both because of the inherent challenges of adolescence and because of the long history of curricular uncertainty in these grades.

Ever since the beginning of the middle school movement in the early 1980s, what constitutes an appropriate mathematics curriculum for the middle grades has been the subject of debate. International and national test scores have brought into the limelight our problems in developing competence, let alone excellence, in mathematics for our middle school students. This problem is exacerbated for students who are gifted in mathematics.

At the international level, the latest Trends in International Mathematics and Science Study (TIMSS 2008) indicates that although more than 40 percent of eighth graders in Singapore and other Asian countries scored at the most advanced level, only 6 percent of U.S. eighth graders scored at this level. Results from the National Assessment of Educational Progress (NAEP 2008) indicate that even though scores continue to increase, only 7 percent of eighth graders perform at the advanced level. It is at eighth grade that students are expected to use abstract thinking, a cornerstone of high-level mathematics. Moreover, in the period 2000–2007, while the bottom 10 percent of eighth graders showed solid and continued progress (+13 points) on the NAEP, the top 10 percent made minimal gains (only +5 points) (Loveless 2008). Thus, whether we look at international or national measures, our present system of mathematics education, although improving, is not serving the needs of our most capable students.

Why is it that our mathematically promising students are in reality the children who are repeatedly left behind in international and national comparisons? Cossey (1999) suggested that the results of countries other than the United States may reflect the fact that these nations have a more focused mathematics and science curriculum, with concepts covered in greater depth and with more opportunities to apply them. In contrast, the U.S. approach is evident in mathematics texts that cover a wide variety of topics much more superficially, under the assumption that they will be revisited again in future years.

This approach has resulted in a mathematics curriculum that has been labeled "a mile wide and an inch deep" (Schmidt, McKnight, and Raizen 1996). The middle school mathematics curriculum, in particular, has long been criticized for this approach. In fact, Assouline and Lupkowski-Shoplik (2005) share findings from the TIMSS 1998 study that show that the middle school math curriculum (grades 5–8) seems to be a weak link in the U.S. educational system. This curriculum was found to be far less challenging than curricula in other countries where algebra and geometry are included for all students rather than just honors students.

In 2009, the Common Core State Standards Initiative sought to increase the rigor of mathematics standards across the United States by developing a common core of state standards. Also in 2009, NCTM released "Guiding Principles for Mathematics Curriculum and Assessment," noting, "A curriculum is more than a collection of activities: It must be coherent, focused on important mathematics, and well articulated across the grades…. Any national mathematics curriculum must emphasize depth over breadth and must focus on the essential ideas and processes of mathematics" (NCTM 2009, p. 1). In addition to underscoring the necessity of depth in the mathematics curriculum, the draft College- and Career-Readiness Standards from the Common Core State Standards Initiative emphasize the need to develop proficient mathematics students who are experimenters and inventors, who think strategically, and who pursue mathematics beyond the classroom walls. As the draft states, "Encouraging these practices should be as much a goal of the mathematics curriculum as is teaching specific content topics and procedures" (Common Core State Standards Initiative 2009, p. 5).

Overview

In this chapter, we give an overview of the current state of the middle school mathematics curriculum as well as research-based information on how middle school students learn mathematics. This overview serves as a backdrop for issues surrounding developing mathematical talent in middle school students. To develop mathematical talent, we must first recognize the potential in students, and this potential is manifest in different degrees at different levels. In this chapter, we present a model of talent development that is two dimensional, focusing on abilities in and attitudes toward mathematics. Next, we discuss a model for advanced, in-depth curriculum for mathematically talented students. This model has four components: creative and complex problem solving, connections within and across mathematical and other content areas and contexts, an inquiry-based approach, and appropriate pacing. Consideration of all four components is necessary to provide the kind of rigorous curriculum that challenges students to think and act like practicing mathematicians. We then outline each of these components in more detail to give the reader an understanding of how it fits into creating an appropriate curriculum. Examples of sample problems, activities, and classroom vignettes are provided to show the curriculum components in operation. Finally, we discuss how to assess student work and thinking that includes high-level problem solving and creativity.

Development of Mathematical Talent

In determining appropriate curriculum for students, consideration of the level of mathematical talent that they display is important. As identified in the "Report of the NCTM Task Force on the Mathematically Promising" (Sheffield et al. 1995), mathematical promise is a function of four variables: ability, motivation, belief, and experience or opportunity. The report states, "These variables are not fixed and need to be developed so that success for these promising students can be maximized" (p. 310). The reality is that mathematically promising students exhibit a continuum of both attitudes and abilities that should be cultivated and extended (see the model in fig. 3.1). Thus, it is impossible to say that there is a specific mathematics curriculum that meets the needs of all talented students. However, regardless of where students with talent lie on this continuum, we want to provide curriculum and experiences that help them make continuous progress in developing their talent.

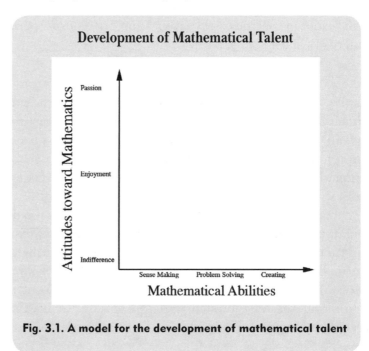

Fig. 3.1. A model for the development of mathematical talent

Mathematical ability in promising and talented students may begin with having a strong number sense, sometimes coupled with strong visual capabilities. Note that this trait, or combination of traits, is different from being fast or accurate at computation but can give students a strong basis for developing computational fluency. Using this number sense, possibly combined with spatial sense, mathematically talented and promising students make sense of the mathematics at hand, sometimes in an intuitive way, and at other times by integrating the new knowledge into their larger understanding of mathematics. To develop their talent, it is important that students build on their previous understanding, making sense of mathematics to help them solve both routine and non-routine problems. The process of problem solving itself has a hierarchy akin to Bloom's taxonomy. Students with talent should be given increasing levels of challenge, with problems calling for application, analysis or synthesis, and evaluation. Problems that require them to use mathematical understanding in real-life situations, compare and contrast mathematical concepts and ideas, and justify their thinking are examples of these hierarchical levels of Bloom's taxonomy. Students move back and forth between sense making and problem solving as they move up in this hierarchy. Moving beyond problem solving, talented students should be encouraged to pose new tasks, questions, and problems, and create new, unique solutions. In fact, these are the activities in which practicing mathematicians engage. Creativity provides both challenge and enjoyment for students with mathematical talent, and they should have opportunities to *play* with mathematics by creating new problems and unique, interesting solutions. This, in effect, is the way in which new mathematics is created, and providing these opportunities can offer an apprenticeship to a budding mathematician.

Some students are quite good at mathematics but apathetic about actually doing math for the sheer joy of learning. Regrettably, for many talented students the goal is simply getting through the required coursework. The phenomenon of a student who is highly successful at algebra or geometry in middle school but does not see this success as something to build on is not uncommon. Rather, such students often see their skill as a means to complete high school graduation requirements in mathematics as quickly as possible, so that they may stop taking mathematics. Some will even get university credit through Advanced Placement Calculus or an International Baccalaureate mathematics course. But then they are happy not to have to take a mathematics course at the university, because they have all the mathematics credits that they need to get a bachelor's degree. We cannot afford to let our best mathematics students think of mathematics as something to get out of the way as quickly as possible. Middle school is a critical time for students to develop an enjoyment in tackling interesting mathematical puzzles and problems as part of a comprehensive, well-articulated curriculum. The ultimate goal is to help as many students as possible become passionate about delving deeply into mathematical concepts and relationships.

Beliefs about Cognitive and Social Development of the Preadolescent

The middle school movement was in part generated by the emergence of the belief that learning plateaus in the early adolescent years and that middle schools need to pay more attention to the affective development of students while limiting their exposure to new content knowledge. The impact of earlier theories of brain functioning and Piagetian studies led some middle school educators to conclude that middle school students are still at the concrete level of thinking and are not capable of higher, more abstract levels of thinking. Thus, they believed that students at this age should practice existing skills and procedures rather than learn new ones (Alexander and George 1981; Toepfer 1990, 1992). This was, and to some extent still is, evident in the middle school mathematics curriculum. *Principles and Standards* (NCTM 2000) notes that some middle school curricula have a "preoccupation with number" (p. 211), even though number concepts and skills are studied in depth in elementary school. In contrast, the development of algebraic and geometric concepts, so important for the study of future mathematics, is limited and often not emphasized in some middle school programs. This certainly does not benefit most middle school students and is definitely harmful to mathematically promising students, who are eager and ready to delve into new and challenging mathematics.

Compounding a repetitive curriculum is the current national emphasis on standardized test scores and the accompanying instructional focus on students who are not meeting grade-level goals. Perhaps even more detrimental is a goal of a single level of proficiency for all students as mandated by the No Child Left Behind Act of 2001. This, in fact, totally ignores the continuous progress of students who have already achieved proficiency.

Today, brain plasticity, the capacity of the brain to change with any type of learning, is well documented. "We now know that the human brain actually maintains an amazing plasticity throughout life. We can literally grow new neural connections with stimulation, even as we age. This fact means nearly any learner can increase their intelligence, without limits, using proper enrichment" (Jensen 2000, p. 149). We know that the brain never stops changing and adjusting—developing and pruning connections, organizing and reorganizing in response to experiences—even growing new neurons.

According to Carol Dweck (2006), a social psychologist and professor at Stanford University, the difference between achieving and not achieving depends on whether a person believes that talent is something inherent that needs to be demonstrated or something that needs to be developed. Seventh-grade students who were struggling with mathematics and were taught a "growth mindset" about intelligence—the belief that intelligence is a potential that can be developed—significantly improved their mathematical performance after they learned about the plasticity of the brain. It is critical that all students realize that they can become far more adept at mathematical reasoning and that the commonly offered excuse, "I don't have a mathematical brain," is not valid.

In *Principles and Standards for School Mathematics* (2000), and more recently, in *Curriculum Focal Points for Prekindergarten through Grade 8 Mathematics: A Quest for Coherence* (2006), NCTM outlines a curriculum that moves beyond a repetition of skills and procedures and introduces important new concepts in number, algebra, geometry, measurement, and data analysis and probability for all students. *Principles and Standards* emphasizes the importance of learning significant new mathematics in the middle grades: "Students are expected to learn serious, substantive mathematics in classrooms in which the emphasis is on thoughtful engagement and meaningful learning" (NCTM 2000, p. 213). The new reform curricula have used NCTM's Standards as guidelines in developing material to be studied by all students. Unfortunately, "all students" does not always include gifted and talented middle school students. Differentiation for our gifted students in terms of increased rigor, depth, and complexity is often given short shrift. "Enrichment," as outlined in many textbooks, consists of worksheets that students are expected to do on their own. But are students who can complete these assignments entirely on their own being challenged appropriately? Do these worksheets give students the type of experiences that develop future mathematicians?

In fact, mathematically gifted students are at special risk when a challenging and rigorous curriculum is not offered to them. In his studies of talent development, Bloom (1985) found that highly productive and talented adults in a variety of fields actually began to seek out challenge in content areas and to develop their own high expectations and even intense passion and focus for their work during the middle school years. If mathematically talented students are presented with a curriculum in which they already understand the concepts, do not need to practice the skills, and are bored by the pace, how can we expect them to develop a love of mathematics, let alone learn new and exciting mathematics? It is imperative that we raise the bar and offer these students an intellectually rigorous and stimulating curriculum that will excite them and encourage them to continue their studies in mathematics and eventually enter careers in the field or in another field that is closely related.

Criteria for a Curriculum for Mathematically Talented Students

To create an advanced, in-depth curriculum appropriate for talented students, we propose a model with four components:

1. Creative and complex problem solving

2. Connections within and across mathematical and other content areas and across a wide range of contexts

3. An inquiry-based approach that focuses on processes used by mathematicians

4. Appropriate pacing

The model appears in figure 3.2.

All four components of the model are equally important, serving as the foundational "legs" that support a curriculum that is advanced and in depth. This type of curriculum is necessary to provide appropriate challenge, rigor, and enjoyment for mathematically talented students. The curriculum should be integrated and coherent, encompassing all the content strands identified in *Principles and Standards* and focusing on all the areas of emphasis targeted in *Curriculum Focal Points*. With a focused, coherent curriculum, students have "opportunities to explore topics in depth, in the context of related content and connected applications, thus developing more robust mathematical understandings" (NCTM 2006, p. 4).

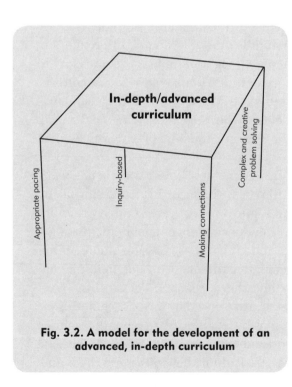

Fig. 3.2. A model for the development of an advanced, in-depth curriculum

In addition to aiding in developing a rigorous curriculum, this model can help in ensuring that students are afforded opportunities to use thought processes akin to those of practicing mathematicians—an instructional strategy recommended by leading experts in gifted education (Renzulli et al. 2000; Tomlinson et al. 2002). Each of these components can be outlined in more detail to provide an understanding of the importance of its contribution to a quality curriculum for talented students.

Creative and complex problem solving

We often teach students that there are four neat steps of problem solving:

1. Understand the problem

2. Determine a strategy to solve the problem

3. Solve the problem by carrying out the strategy

4. Check

However, mathematicians will tell you that when they are struggling with deeper mathematical problems, they do not generally find the solutions by using those four steps. Because a mathematical problem is often defined as something for which we do not have an immediate method of solution, telling students that they should determine and carry out a single solution strategy is a method that might work on exercises or "word problems" but may not be helpful for deeper problems, where creative or complex solutions are required. For these mathematical problems, a much richer heuristic that emphasizes the integration of processes is required. Consider the model in figure 3.3 (Sheffield 2003), for example.

Students who use this model in solving and posing problems may start at any point on the diagram and proceed in any order that makes sense to them. They might do the following:

- Relate the problem to other problems that they have solved, making connections to prior mathematical concepts and perhaps to applications in different contexts.

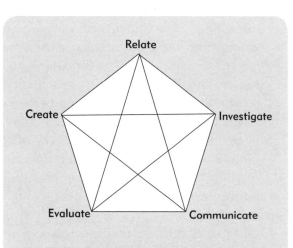

Fig. 3.3. A heuristic for complex and creative problem solving (Sheffield 2003)

- Investigate the problem, perhaps using a variety of strategies and representations.

- Evaluate their findings. What worked, and what did not? Refine and build on aspects that did not seem to work well. Extend and dig more deeply into successful solutions.

- Communicate with peers and others. Discuss strategies as well as results. Can unsuccessful strategies be cultivated or tweaked? Can successful strategies be improved? Is there a more efficient or elegant way to solve the problem? Are there other ways to think about and develop the problem?

- Create new questions and pose new problems to explore as well as create unique and original solutions.

As they begin to think like mathematicians, students might change the order of the steps and the questions that they ask in starting to explore a problem. Throughout the problem-solving process, students should be evaluating their work, making connections, asking questions, communicating results, and creating new problems to investigate.

Connections within and across mathematical and other content areas and contexts

When considering possibilities for students who are mathematically promising, we have customarily asked, "Should we enrich their learning with greater breadth, adding new topics for them to explore beyond the regular curriculum, or should we accelerate them to the next grade level or math course?" This question leads back to the model for the development of mathematical talent (fig. 3.1). Students who are above average in making sense of mathematics and are good problem solvers need to move on to posing new problems and creating mathematics that is unfamiliar to them. This does not mean that we should enrich their mathematics by adding new, disconnected topics or accelerate their mathematics by moving them quickly through a shallow curriculum that emphasizes memorization and basic skills. Genuine enrichment and acceleration do something different. As Schiever and Maker (2003) point out, "without both acceleration and enrichment, more is simply more" (p. 168). They state that the curriculum offered to talented students needs both acceleration and enrichment to such an extent that "more" becomes "different" and the curriculum becomes "qualitatively differentiated" (p. 167). Our model indicates that students who progress along the continuum of talent should have this qualitatively differentiated curriculum. Such a curriculum will be characterized by an increase in the degree of rigorous content and the opportunity to create new questions, new strategies, and new mathematics, along with appropriate pacing commensurate with the students' level of giftedness. And herein lies a key for truly developing mathematical talent and promise. The Common Core State Mathematics Standards (2009) include exemplary performance tasks that are grouped into four categories: exercises, structured tasks, substantial tasks, and target tasks. Target tasks include exemplary problems for challenging mathematically promising students. These tasks "require students to integrate strategic, tactical, and technical skills through connections within mathematics and to the problem context. Some target tasks allow good responses in only 10–20 minutes, though many can stimulate hours of valuable investigation" (p. 2).

An accelerated program that moves middle school students into the next grade-level textbook or high school course designed for all math students is not appropriate for helping students develop their mathematical talents to full potential. In addition, moving rapidly through these courses so that students can take calculus in high school denies students the opportunity to delve deeply into mathematical concepts and does our gifted students a disservice. In fact, it is apparent that this approach has begun to backfire. Rather than instill a love for mathematics and a desire to continue studying mathematics in college, it seems to turn students off from mathematics. We have seen the percentage of students who are enrolled in mathematics classes at four-year institutions steadily decrease relative to the total number of students enrolled in these institutions. In 2005, only a meager 1.02 percent of U.S. college students were enrolled in advanced-level mathematics courses (Bressoud 2009). Clearly, the current way in which we serve our gifted students is not leading them to pursue mathematics as a field of interest or inquiry.

Instead of merely moving rapidly through a shallow curriculum or adding unrelated topics to a curriculum that is "a mile wide and an inch deep," students who are given the opportunity for creative and complex problem solving according to the heuristic discussed earlier (see fig. 3.3) will explore a variety of topics that are often considered "enrichment" or "advanced." Yet, they will also have a solid foundation for connecting this mathematical understanding seamlessly and at a deeper level as they develop into mature mathematicians. They will find that new mathematical concepts are tied to existing mathematical understanding, sometimes with real-world applications or connections to other subject areas. Often, they will discover links among concepts by using a variety of models and representations from a range of mathematical strands— from number theory and computation to algebra, geometry, measurement, and data analysis and probability. This development of mathematical understanding aligns with the recommendations that NCTM has consistently made over time. In *Principles and Standards,* NCTM asserts, "Students' understanding of foundational algebraic and geometric ideas should be developed through extended experience over all three years in the middle grades and across a broad range of mathematics content, including statistics, number, and measurement" (NCTM 2000, p. 213). In *Curriculum Focal Points,* NCTM continues to emphasize the importance of a coherent, fully articulated curriculum for advanced middle school students:

> Those whose programs offer an algebra course in grade 8 (or earlier) should consider including the curriculum focal points that this framework calls for in grade 8 in grade 6 or grade 7. Alternatively, these topics could be incorporated into the high school program. Either way, curricula would not omit the important content that the grade 7 and grade 8 focal points offer students in preparation for algebra and for their long-term mathematical knowledge. (NCTM 2006, p. 10)

An example from algebra

In a typical algebra 1 program, *slope* is introduced with a definition and the formula, and students are asked to practice finding the slope of a line by working with several computational examples that give two points. The idea of a slope is typically presented in one or two lessons. In contrast, Project M^3: Mentoring Mathematical Minds (Gavin et al. 2008), a new research-based curriculum for talent development, guides mathematically promising students in grades 5 and 6 in exploring algebra concepts related to analyzing change over a six-week period. Set in the motivational context of exploring seemingly wacky world records from the Guinness Book of World Records, the curriculum encourages students to focus on analyzing change in situations from a qualitative perspective. This enables them to look more globally at what is happening throughout the situation. They analyze change, including the rate of change, in various situations and learn how to represent it graphically and describe it as the slope of a line. They study slope, *y*-intercept, and points of intersection in the context of change. Rather than learning the meaning of slope as the formula

$$\text{Slope} = \frac{\text{change in } y}{\text{change in } x} = \frac{y_2 - y_1}{x_2 - x_1},$$

students gain an intuitive and conceptual understanding of slope by comparing graphs, tables, and situations, making predictions and then testing those predictions, and creating new situations. After exploring, they are asked to reflect, thinking deeply about the mathematics that they have used or discovered.

These experiences enable the students to make connections to the bigger idea of change in the study of continuous mathematics and to develop mathematical understanding by using processes akin to those of practicing mathematicians. In a study measuring student achievement with the Project M[3] curriculum, Gavin and colleagues (2009) found that mathematically promising students studying this curriculum made highly significant gains in achievement as compared to a group of students of like ability in the same schools.

An inquiry-based approach

The National Council of Teachers of Mathematics (1989, 2000, 2006) promotes inquiry-based curriculum for all students. Indeed, this is the foundation on which the NCTM Content and Process Standards rest and the Curriculum Focal Points were developed. The thought processes that are especially nurtured by experts in the field of gifted and talented education are consistent with those that NCTM promotes in the Process Standards and include critical thinking, creative thinking, and problem solving. However, Tomlinson (1994) cautions that although these processes are laudable goals to develop in all students, it is the *level* at which and *degree* to which students use them that are critical to developing talent. Gifted students need to be encouraged to engage in these processes more frequently and at much higher levels than other students. Challenging and provocative questions and mathematical investigations can provide the encouragement that students need. VanTassel-Baska and Brown (2007) emphasize that inquiry-based strategies that allow students to engage in making choices and that involve complex, creative problem solving and decision making were central to each of nine research-based gifted education curriculum models that they analyzed. They state that emphasis on motivation and student engagement provides an important connection between teacher and learner, and they suggest that this connection may account for greater gains as motivation on the part of both the teacher and the student grow.

In addition, both Usiskin (1987) and Sheffield (1999) state that inquiry-based learning in mathematics, using problem-based strategies rather than simply automatic recall focused on drill and practice, leads to a much deeper understanding among gifted mathematicians. Indeed, research suggests that any review or practice of skills and procedures be spaced rather than concentrated for greater retention of understanding (Dempster 1988; Lupkowski-Shoplik and Assouline 1994). The fact is that talented students need much less practice than other students, and it needs to be spread out, with increasing depth and complexity each time that a topic is revisited, rather than concentrated in one block of time without any real depth. Content must be rigorous and include complex problems to be explored in depth over a longer period than textbooks generally devote to topics.

Appropriate pacing

The fourth component of an advanced, in-depth curriculum is appropriate pacing of instruction. As Sheffield (1999) points out, a program that helps students develop their mathematical talent to its fullest allows them to move faster in class to avoid "deadly repetition of material they have already mastered" (p. 46). Start (1995) actually measured the rates of learning novel concepts of children at different standard deviations on IQ tests. He found that a child with an IQ of 130 (2 standard deviations above the mean) learned eight times faster than a child with an IQ of 70 (2 standard deviations below the mean). These findings certainly offer a rationale for increasing the pace of instruction for mathematically gifted students. In addition, an increased pace for certain content allows students less "down time" in which to become bored or distracted, lose focus, act out, or not do well on assessments because of a lack of attention to detail (Rogers 2007).

However, we must add an important caveat when we talk about appropriate pacing. The pace of instruction depends on the nature of the content being studied. The pace can generally be rapid when mathematically talented students are learning basic skills and procedures, since they are able to master these more quickly than other students. However, when talented students are working on complex problems, we recommend that the pace actually slow down to allow them time to think deeply, discuss their ideas, and explain their reasoning to one another. In fact, mathematicians take a very long time to solve complex problems and prove theorems. Indeed, it is this very perseverance in problem solving that allows time for ideas to percolate and yields the rewarding "aha moment" of discovery. Students need this time to think, let their ideas germinate, and make discoveries for themselves. Having appropriate time to think deeply about problems, communicate with peers of like ability, and go beyond answering the questions to questioning the answers can instill in all students a passion and love for mathematics and a desire to pursue mathematics in high school, college, and beyond.

Learning Environment to Develop Mathematical Talent

In addition to studying rigorous content in depth, gifted students need to be in a classroom with equally talented students or in a mentoring situation with those who can discuss challenging mathematics at high levels. VanTassel-Baska and Brown (2007), in their analysis of research-based curriculum models, recommend that gifted students be grouped instructionally by subject area for work in an advanced curriculum that is flexibly organized and implemented on the basis of students' documented levels of learning within the subject area. These students need stimulating conversations in which they can agree or disagree with one another, add to one other's thoughts, and come up with new generalizations and justifications. It is this kind of rich mathematical discussion that motivates, excites, and challenges students. One such discussion is illustrated in the classroom vignette that follows. This discussion took place when students were studying the Project M^3 unit described in the algebra example. They were thinking and talking about the solution of simultaneous equations in the context of a familiar concrete situation.

Classroom vignette

After studying rates of change and graphing linear relationships, talented fifth graders were given the following scenario about a read-a-thon taking place at the middle school:

> On October 4, Jeremy had not started reading at all and Jamie had read 150 pages. For the next several days, Jeremy read an average of 35 pages a day, and Jamie read an average of 20 pages a day. Who had read the most pages on October 10? On October 12?

After answering the questions, students were asked to think more deeply about the problem. Their teacher asked them to consider the following question: "How might you determine if there was a day when both students had read the same number of pages?" The following conversation took place:

Serina: I made a table to record the data to find out the answer to the questions in the problem. So I look at the table to see if there was a day when the columns matched. [*See fig. 3.4.*]

Rajeev: I don't get what you mean about the columns matching.

Serina: Well, I have one column for the number of days, one for the number of pages that Jeremy read, and one for the number of pages that Jamie read. I'll show you.

Day	Pages Read by Jeremy	Pages Read by Jamie
October 4	0	150
October 5	35	170
October 6	70	190
October 7	105	210
October 8	140	230
October 9	175	250
October 10	210	270
October 11	245	290
October 12	280	310
October 13	315	330
October 14	350	350
October 15	385	370
October 16	420	390

Fig. 3.4. Serina's table showing cumulative numbers of pages read by Jeremy and Jamie, October 4–16

Dorsey: I see. On October 14, the last two columns match. They had both read 350 pages.

Teacher: Is that what you mean, Serina?

Serina: Yeah, that's it.

Teacher: Did anyone else find that they had read the same number of pages on October 14?

Dan: I thought, Jeremy is reading 15 pages a day more than Jamie, so I just thought how long would it take to catch up.

Teacher: What do the rest of you think? Would Dan get the same answer as Serina?

Regina: I don't know what Dan did, but I made a graph.

Teacher: We will come back to the graph in a minute. First, could you explain what you think Dan meant, Regina?

Regina: I am not sure. He said something about Jeremy catching up. Dan, could you please repeat that?

Dan: Every day, Jeremy reads 15 pages more than Jamie. Jamie started out 150 pages ahead.

Regina: Now I get it. If Jeremy reads 15 more pages a day, he could divide 150 pages by 15 to see that it would take 10 days to catch up. You can see on my graph how every day, Jeremy gets closer to Jamie.

[*Regina then shows her graph and explains how she created it. She also describes how she might use Dan's idea to understand that Jeremy is getting 15 pages closer to Jamie each day, with the two graphs intersecting on October 14 and Jeremy reading more total pages than Jamie after that.*]

Teacher: I would like each of you to talk with your partner for two minutes and then write an expression for the number of pages that Jeremy would have read at the end of n days and another expression for the number of pages that Jamie would have read at the end of n days. How could you tell that there will be a day that Jamie and Jeremy had read the same number of pages by using the expressions without making a table or graphing? Be ready to explain your reasoning.

After students discussed this task with their partner, they shared their ideas with the rest of the class. They noted that at the end of n days, Jamie had read $150 + 20n$ pages, and Jeremy had read $35n$ pages. Several students observed that they could use a "guess, test, and refine" strategy and substitute different numbers for n in these expressions until they found an n where the two expressions had the same value. Other students wrote an equation to show when the number of pages Jamie read would be equal to the number of pages Jeremy read ($150 + 20n = 35n$). These students readily determined that on the tenth day (October 14) the two expressions would be equal.

Note that the scenario itself is a type of problem generally studied in ninth grade, with sufficient complexity to allow these fifth-grade students to solve it in a variety of ways. Initially, students used three different ways to find a day when Jamie and Jeremy had read the same number of pages:

1. They created a table of values and looked for a common ordered pair.

2. They created a graph and looked for a point of intersection.

3. They thought analytically about the number of days that it might take Jeremy to catch up with Jamie by reading 15 pages more each day, and then they determined the number of pages that each student had read after ten days.

The teacher extended the mathematical thinking further when she asked the students to write algebraic expressions and use those to determine the day when Jeremy and Jamie would have read the same number of pages. The students needed to think deeply about the meaning of solving simultaneous equations, even though that term and abstract rules for that process (generally studied as part of an algebra curriculum) were not introduced. This is the kind of deep thinking that needs to take place to develop mathematical talent in middle school students.

Assessment

If we wish students to think deeply and make sense of mathematics, we must have assessment that encourages the type of mathematical reasoning and creativity described above. Appropriate assessment tools should provide opportunities for students to pose new problems, generalize patterns, solve problems in a variety of ways, and connect various aspects of mathematics. Simply marking answers to questions as correct or incorrect does not promote rich, innovative solutions or problem-solving techniques.

To assist pupils in developing their fullest mathematical potential, teachers might use some of the following assessment criteria:

- *Depth of understanding*—the extent to which core mathematical concepts are explored and developed

- *Ability to communicate mathematically*—the extent to which ideas are developed and reasoning is supported by clear details, appropriate mathematical vocabulary, and a variety of representations, including charts, graphs, drawings, models, and words

- *Fluency*—the number of different correct answers, methods of solution, or new questions that are formulated

- *Flexibility*—the number of different categories of answers, methods, or questions that are offered

- *Originality*—the extent to which solutions, methods, or questions are unique and show insight

- *Generalizations*—the number of patterns that are noted, hypothesized, and verified for larger categories

- *Extensions*—the number of related questions that are posed and explored, especially those involving "why" and "what if" (Sheffield 2000, p. 419)

Not every problem that students tackle lends itself to all these criteria for assessment of their work, but having students make a portfolio where they can gather examples of their best in-depth investigations is a good way to encourage this type of thinking. Keeping a portfolio gives students an opportunity to spend an extended period of time on a problem, not only solving the original problem and justifying and proving their solutions, but also posing and answering related questions, discovering in the process that the "real mathematics" often begins after the original problem is solved. Students previously identified as gifted should not be the only ones who are encouraged to develop a portfolio of their best work exhibiting these criteria. Evaluating portfolios is a good way to identify gifted, creative, talented, and promising students who may not perform well on standardized tests or other measures.

For example, a portfolio might include work on the following problem, accompanied by the drawings in figure 3.5 (Gavin, Chapin, and Sheffield, in press):

> Nikesha and Rebecca were having fun making towers out of one-inch cubes. They created an interesting design that looked like a pyramid with steps up to the top from four different directions. They built a pyramid that was one layer high (just one block), then two layers, and then three layers. They wanted to build a pyramid that was 25 layers high. What is the total number of blocks they will need? Find the explicit rule for the total number of blocks in n layers.

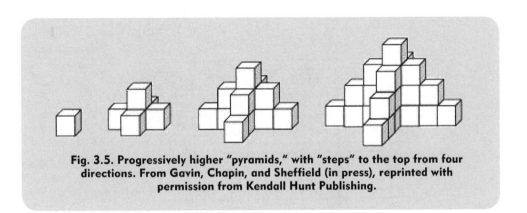

Fig. 3.5. Progressively higher "pyramids," with "steps" to the top from four directions. From Gavin, Chapin, and Sheffield (in press), reprinted with permission from Kendall Hunt Publishing.

Students might begin work on this problem individually and then share their thinking with a partner or small group. The work in figure 3.6 is from a group of students who started by finding the number of blocks needed to build a pyramid six blocks or twelve blocks high in the center. They made a table, graphed the number of blocks needed for different heights, and described an explicit rule for finding the number of blocks needed to make a pyramid x blocks high in the center. A student in another group explained the group's formula as shown in figure 3.7.

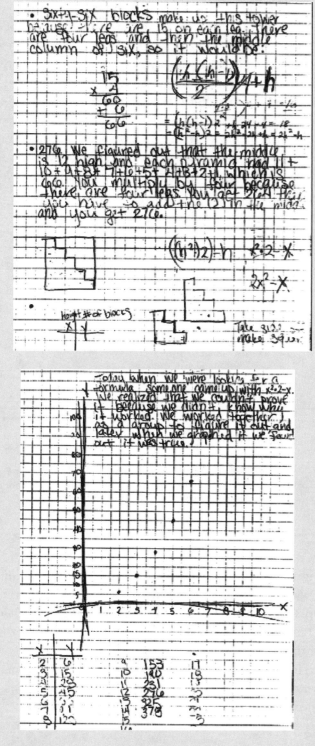

Fig. 3.6. Samples of work from students on the problem of the block "pyramids"

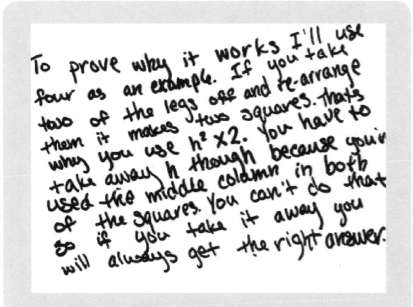

Fig. 3.7. A student's explanation of why the group's formula for the block "pyramids" works

To encourage students to think deeply and make connections between seemingly diverse problems, teachers might invite students to relate their work on the block pyramids problem to earlier work on problems such as the "handshake problem," or to work with triangular or other figurate numbers, or to the task of finding the sum of all the counting numbers from 1 through n. Another problem that might initially seem unrelated is the following:

	1	
3	5	
7	9	11

Look for a pattern and complete the next three lines on the chart according to your pattern. Where will the number 289 appear? List other patterns that you find on the chart. Make and justify generalizations.

A ninth-grade algebra 2 student initially gave the answer shown in figure 3.8.

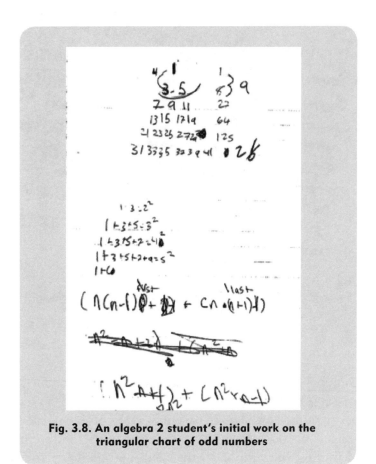

Fig. 3.8. An algebra 2 student's initial work on the triangular chart of odd numbers

Many teachers note that some of their most gifted students are quite satisfied with solving problems in a rough form like this. Once students have solved the problem to their own satisfaction, they often do not wish to go any further. It is important that students learn to express themselves in a manner that others can understand, however. After arriving at the initial solution, this student developed the explanation shown in figure 3.9.

A.

$$
\begin{array}{ccccccc}
 & & & 1 & & & \\
 & & 3 & & 5 & & \\
 & 7 & & 9 & & 11 & \\
 13 & & 15 & & 17 & & 19 \\
21 & & 23 & & 25 & & 27 & & 29 \\
31 & & 33 & & 35 & & 37 & & 39 & & 41
\end{array}
$$

B. The number 289 can be found in the center of row 17. 289 is equal to 17^2. By looking at the chart, one notices that the mean and median (middle number) are equal to the row number squared. For example, the median of the third row is nine (3^2. Therefore, it can be inferred that the median of the seventeenth row is 289 (17^2). The proof behind this is as follows:

Since each row has the number of numbers equal to the row number, one can add the row numbers to determine the number of numbers in total. Therefore, by the end of row n, $1+2+3....+n =$. Then, the fact that the sum of a series is equal to $n(n+1)/2$ combined with the fact that each term equals it's number doubled minus one, one finds that the last term is equal to $(n(n+1)-1)$. Therefore, to find the first term, one merely needs to find the last for the previous row and add two, making $(n(n-1)-1+2)$

Representing the first number in the row by $(n(n-1)-1+2)$ and the last by $(n(n+1)-1)$, the mean is therefore: $((n(n-1)-1+2) + (n(n+1)-1))/2 = ((n^2 + -n +1) + (n^2 + n + -1))/2 = 2n^2/2=n^2$.

C. The sums of the consecutive rows are consecutive perfect cubes-1, 8, 27, 64, 125, etc.
The sums of the of all the numbers from one to n gives us the mean of row n. For example, 1+3=4, mean of row 2. 1+3+5=9, mean of row 3. 1+3+5+7=16, mean of row 4. The diagonal columns increase by 2 more each time as one goes along. 2,4,6,8... from one left diagonal. 4,6,8,10... from one right diagonal. etc. This pattern also holds true for the even numbered triangle of:

$$
\begin{array}{cccc}
 & & 2 & \\
 & 4 & & 6 \\
8 & & 10 & & 12 \\
14 & & 16 & & 18 & & 20
\end{array}
$$

The pattern in part B. doesn't hold true in this even numbered triangle. In this case, the squared row number is one less than the mean of the row whether it is even or odd.

Fig. 3.9. A student's refinement and full statement of a rough initial solution

Note that each of these problems can be solved in a variety of ways, using different models and representations. Students who have minimal experience or expertise in solving problems such as these can still be successful at some level. At all levels, students should be encouraged to look for patterns, make generalizations, and describe both recursive and explicit rules as appropriate. Promising students should be expected to justify their reasoning and give proofs as appropriate. In addition, they should pose and investigate new, related questions. In many cases, working with a partner or small group after initial individual work can help students think more deeply and in different ways about a problem. Sharing and discussing solutions with the whole class can give students even greater insight into diverse and more complex solutions and connections, thus building a deeper, stronger base for future problem solving and problem posing. Students who have the opportunity to read and critique each other's written work also begin to set much higher standards for their own work. Thus, it is important that the curriculum offer interesting, open-ended problems, but it is also essential that the assessment promote higher-level thinking and encourage increasingly complex and creative responses from students at all levels, including those whose work is already at a higher level than that of their classmates.

We cannot design a curriculum that includes all that mathematics students will need in the future, but we can aim for a curriculum that creates an appropriate environment and uses instructional and assessment strategies to enrich it, with the goal of instilling in students the passion, power, and perseverance to define, investigate, solve, and extend the problems that they encounter. This is critical, not only for the well-being of the mathematically promising students themselves, but also for the future of our society, which depends on their leadership in our increasingly technological world.

References

Alexander, William, and Paul George. *The Exemplary Middle School.* New York: CBS College Publishing, 1981.

———. *Developing Math Talent: A Guide for Educating Gifted and Advanced Learners in Math.* Waco, Tex.: Prufrock Press, 2005.

Bloom, Benjamin. *Developing Talent in Young People.* New York: Ballentine Books, 1985.

Bressoud, David. "Is the Sky Still Falling?" *Notices of the AMS* 56, no. 1 (2009): 20–25.

Common Core State Standards Initiative. College- and Career-Readiness Standards for Mathematics: Draft for Review and Comment (July 16, 2009). http://www.edweek.org/media/draftmathstandards-july162009-07.pdf.

———. Common Core State Mathematics Standards for College and Work Readiness: Examples (June 11, 2009). http://www.corestandards.net/mathexemplars.html.

Cossey, Ruth. "Are California's Math Standards Up to the Challenge?" *Phi Delta Kappan* 80, no. 6 (1999): 441–43.

Dempster, Frank. "The Spacing Effect: A Case Study in the Failure to Apply the Results of Psychological Research." *American Psychologist* 43, no. 8 (1988): 627–34.

Dweck, Carol. *Mindset: The New Psychology of Success.* New York: Random House, 2006.

Gavin, M. Katherine, Tutita Casa, Jill Adelson, Susan Carroll, and Linda Sheffield. "The Impact of Advanced Curriculum on the Achievement of Mathematically Promising Elementary Students." *Gifted Child Quarterly* 53, no. 3 (2009): 188–202.

Gavin, M. Katherine, Suzanne Chapin, Judy Dailey, and Linda Sheffield. *Project M³: Mentoring Mathematical Minds.* 12 vols. Dubuque, Iowa: Kendall Hunt, 2008.

Gavin, M. Katherine, Suzanne Chapin, and Linda Sheffield. *Prove It: Focusing on Mathematical Reasoning and the Pythagorean Theorem.* Dubuque, Iowa: Kendall Hunt, in press.

Jensen, Eric. *Brain-Based Learning.* San Diego: The Brain Store, 2000.

Loveless, Thomas. *Part 1: An Analysis of NAEP Data.* Washington, D.C.: The Thomas B. Fordham Institute, 2008.

Lupkowski-Shoplik, Ann, and Susan Assouline. "Evidence of Extreme Mathematical Precocity: Case Studies of Talented Youths." *Roeper Review* 16, no. 3 (1994): 144–51.

National Assessment of Educational Progress. "The Nation's Report Card: Mathematics 2007." Washington, D.C.: National Center for Education Statistics, U.S. Department of Education, 2008. http://nces.ed.gov/nationsreportcard/pdf/main2007/2007494.pdf.

National Council of Teachers of Mathematics (NCTM). *Curriculum and Evaluation Standards for School Mathematics.* Reston, Va.: NCTM, 1989.

———. *Principles and Standards for School Mathematics.* Reston, Va.: NCTM, 2000.

———. *Curriculum Focal Points for Prekindergarten through Grade 8 Mathematics: A Quest for Coherence.* Reston, Va.: NCTM, 2006.

———. "Guiding Principles for Mathematics Curriculum and Assessment." 2009. http://www.nctm.org/standards/content.aspx?id=23273.

Renzulli, Joseph, Jann Leppien, Thomas Hays, and Carol Tomlinson. *The Multiple Menu Model: A Practical Guide for Developing Differentiated Curriculum.* Mansfield Center, Conn.: Creative Learning Press, Inc., 2000.

Rogers, Karen. "Lessons Learned about Educating the Gifted and Talented: A Synthesis of the Research on Educational Practice." *Gifted Child Quarterly* 51, no. 4 (2007): 382–96.

Schiever, Shirley, and C. June Maker. "New Directions in Enrichment and Acceleration." In *The Handbook of Gifted Education*, 3rd ed., edited by Nicholas Colangelo and Gary Davis, pp. 163–73. Boston: Allyn & Bacon, 2003.

Schmidt, William H., Curtis C. McKnight, and Senta A. Raizen. "Splintered Vision: An Investigation of U.S. Mathematics and Science Education." Washington, D.C.: U.S. National Research Center, 1996.

Sheffield, Linda. "Creating and Developing Promising Young Mathematicians." *Teaching Children Mathematics* 6 (February 2000): 416–19, 426.

———. *Extending the Challenge in Mathematics: Developing Mathematical Promise in K–8 Pupils.* Thousand Oaks, Calif.: Corwin Press, 2003.

Sheffield, Linda, ed. *Developing Mathematically Promising Students.* Reston, Va.: National Council of Teachers of Mathematics, 1999.

Sheffield, Linda, Jennie Bennett, Manuel Berriozábal, Margaret DeArmond, and Richard Wertheimer. "Report of the Task Force on the Mathematically Promising." *NCTM News Bulletin* 32 (December 1995): 3–6.

Start, Kenneth. "The Learning Rate of Intellectually Gifted Learners in Australia." Paper presented at the Supporting the Emotional Needs of the Gifted conference, San Diego, July 1995.

Trends in International Mathematics and Science Study (TIMSS). "TIMSS 2007 Results." Washington, D.C.: National Center for Education Statistics, U.S. Department of Education, 2008. http://nces.ed.gov/pubs2009/2009001.pdf.

Toepfer, Conrad. "Implementing Turning Points: Major Issues to Be Faced." *Middle School Journal* 21, no. 5 (1990): 18–21.

———. "Middle Level Curriculum: Defining the Elusive." In *Transforming Middle Level Education,* edited by Judith Irvin, pp. 203–243. Boston: Allyn & Bacon, 1992.

Tomlinson, Carol. "Gifted Learners: The Boomerang Kids of Middle School?" *Roeper Review* 16 (February 1994): 177–82.

Tomlinson, Carol, Sandra Kaplan, Joseph Renzulli, Jeanne Purcell, Jann Leppien, Deborah Burns, Cindy Strickland, and Marcia Imbeau. *The Parallel Curriculum: A Design to Develop High Potential and Challenge High-Ability Learners.* Thousand Oaks, Calif.: Corwin Press, 2002.

Usiskin, Zalman. "Why Elementary Algebra Can, Should, and Must Be an Eighth-Grade Course for Average Students." *Mathematics Teacher* 80 (September 1987): 428–38.

VanTassel-Baska, Joyce, and Elissa Brown. "Toward Best Practice: An Analysis of the Efficacy of Curriculum Models in Gifted Education." *Gifted Child Quarterly* 51, no. 4 (2007): 342–58.

Preparing Teachers for Mathematically Talented Middle School Students

Carole Greenes, Dawn Teuscher, and Troy P. Regis

◆ Teachers of gifted middle school students need special expertise in mathematics, reasoning, and problem solving.

◆ Teachers of gifted middle school students must be able to identify the mathematical talents of gifted students and differentiate instruction to enhance their enthusiasm for and understanding of mathematics and its many applications.

◆ Teachers of gifted middle school students need to understand the cognitive, emotional, and behavioral development of middle school–aged students.

Identifying the characteristics and competencies of mathematics teachers who can effectively capitalize on, and develop the talents of, gifted students is a major challenge for school districts. Mathematics education programs in colleges and universities face similar concerns in the preparation and evaluation of teachers to work with exceptionally talented students. This challenge is further complicated by the fact that gifted students differ from other learners with respect to interests, talents, developmental trajectories, and idiosyncratic ways of learning (Maker 1982; VanTassel-Baska and Johnson 2007). In this chapter, we summarize what is known about effective teachers of gifted and talented students in general, consider specific qualities of teachers of mathematically talented students, and describe a program of study to prepare teachers to work with mathematically gifted and talented middle school students. We conclude with recommendations of ways in which middle school mathematics teachers of the gifted can remain connected with one another and can regularly update their knowledge of new content, technologies, instructional approaches, and assessment strategies.

Since the 1980s, several studies have examined and described characteristics of teachers who have been able to nurture and develop the talents of gifted students (Berliner 2004; Hanninen 1988; Laczko-Kerr and Berliner 2003). In 2007, the National Association for Gifted Children (NAGC) and the Council for Exceptional Children (CEC), together with CEC's special interest division, The Association for the Talented and Gifted (TAG), collaborated to produce the NAGC-CEC Teacher Knowledge and Skill Standards for Gifted and Talented Education. This document was created to assist state departments of education in developing standards for teachers of gifted students in kindergarten through grade 12 and to help colleges and universities focus their teacher education programs on preparing teachers to work with gifted and talented students. Although most of the studies, as well as the NAGC-CEC standards, do not specifically address teachers of mathematically gifted and talented youth, many of the qualities that they identify are applicable to teachers in this role.

In summary, the research findings and Teacher Knowledge and Skill Standards indicate that teachers of gifted and talented students must be—

1. flexible thinkers who can quickly analyze and respond to students and ideas;

2. appreciative of creative approaches to solutions of given problems and the creation of new problems;

3. curious about how things work;

4. persistent in finding solutions to hard problems and in the search for more elegant solutions to those problems; and

5. confident in their own abilities to solve problems, including those that may be generated on the spot by students.

As well as satisfying these general requirements, teachers of mathematically talented students should—

1. understand a wide range of mathematical concepts and skills;

2. possess a "toolbox" of problem-solving heuristics;

3. be armed with mathematical problems and challenges that will continue to stimulate students' interest in, curiosity about, and engagement with mathematics; and

4. love doing mathematics (Greenes and Mode 1999; Assouline and Lukowski-Shoplik 2005).

As we consider the preparation of middle school teachers to work with mathematically gifted students, we must address the following question: Do our current teacher education programs adequately prepare teachers to work with mathematically talented middle school students?

The mathematical requirements for middle school mathematics certification vary by state. In some states—for example, Arizona—elementary teachers are certified to teach kindergarten through grade 8, and secondary teachers are certified for grades 7 through 12. As a consequence, some middle school teachers may have minimal preparation in mathematics—often, only one or two courses in mathematics education. Other states—for example, Massachusetts—have separate certification for elementary, middle, and high school mathematics teaching, with extensive training in mathematics at all levels. Table 4.1 shows numbers of states that require either mathematics middle school certification or endorsement to teach in grades 4–9, and numbers of states that require endorsement to teach gifted students. "Gifted" courses are usually generic, not grade-range or content specific.

Table 4.1. Numbers of states with middle school certification or endorsement

Type of Certification or Endorsement	Number of States
Mathematics middle level license/certification or endorsement	44 + DC
Mathematics middle level licenses	30 + DC
Mathematics middle level endorsements	14
Gifted students endorsement	10

Source: NAGC Web site

Teacher Preparation: What Should Teachers of Gifted Students Know and Be Able to Do?

Historically, the answer to this question is based on the U.S. reaction to the launching of Sputnik in 1957. This watershed event prompted political, business, and social groups to urge critical examination of American mathematical, scientific, and technical education (Fey and Graeber 2003), resulting in major recommendations for teacher education programs. "More knowledge of mathematics leads to better teaching of mathematics," was the theme of the redesign (Ferrini-Mundy and Graham 2003). In response, colleges and universities nationwide increased the number of liberal arts mathematics courses required for preservice secondary school teachers, including those specializing at the middle school level, and diminished the importance of "education" courses.

However, teachers' greater knowledge of mathematics does not appear to motivate students sufficiently (Csikszentmihalyi, Rathunde, and Whalen 1993). Talented students need teachers who can move beyond the traditional "teacher role" of a dispenser of information to that of a role model who is passionate about learning, able to translate that passion into action, aggressively curious, and comfortable with this change of role.

More recently, "pedagogical content knowledge," or knowledge of the mathematics and appropriate instructional methods, has gained favor as an alternative to the "more advanced math courses" approach to teacher preparation (Ball and Bass 2000). This alternative approach promotes a deep understanding of mathematical concepts and skills, including methods for developing them, and an appreciation for how those concepts and skills become more robust.

We favor this approach but also believe that teachers should engage their talented students in applying mathematics to problems in the multiple domains of mathematics (e.g., number theory, algebra, geometry), as well as in other disciplines (e.g., economics, geography, physics). To accomplish this goal, teachers themselves need to gain greater insight into the related domains and disciplines; they need to gain "applications content knowledge"—that is, knowledge of the settings of the applications.

In summary, prospective and current teachers of gifted middle school mathematics students must—

1. know the "big mathematical ideas" to be developed;

2. learn and feel competent with problems and projects;

3. gain experience with multiple problem-solving methods and become expert problem solvers themselves;

4. have an arsenal of challenging extensions to problems as well as new explorations; and

5. be mentored by successful teachers of gifted and talented students as they observe, assess, and work with these students.

Before considering a preparation program, it is important to address the question of why we need such a program. Almost every college and university program of study offers an academic major, and within the major are specializations with unique sets of courses. In biology, for example, specializations may include biotechnology, ecology, urban horticulture, microbiology, cellular and molecular biology, marine biology, bioinformatics, and so on. Special education has specializations in learning disabilities, speech and language disabilities, emotional disturbance, mental retardation, and so forth.

By contrast, in gifted education, the few programs that do exist provide generic K–12 preparation. A search of states' DOE certification programs reveals no specialized programs by content area. We strongly recommend that a program of study be implemented and required for middle school teachers who wish to be certified or endorsed to teach mathematically talented middle school students.

The program that we propose consists of a sequence of five workshops or courses beyond certification for secondary school teachers of mathematics:

- Workshop/Course 1: Problem-Solving Lab

- Workshop/Course 2: Assessing Talent and Differentiating Instruction

- Workshop/Course 3: Instructional Strategies

- Workshop/Course 4: Exploring Situational Math

- Workshop/Course 5: Concept Study

Our program is intended to provide teachers with opportunities to gain greater insight into talented students' thinking and learn ways to identify and engage students who are mentally agile, reason quickly, transfer ideas easily to new settings, demonstrate originality in their interpretations of displays, and have differences in their depths of understanding, the interests that they hold, or the pace at which they acquire ideas.

This program can be implemented as a professional development opportunity that a school district or several collaborating districts offer for middle or high school teachers of mathematics. Alternatively, the program can be integrated into current undergraduate or graduate teacher education programs, possibly supplanting some of the generic courses. The experiences are designed to enable mathematics teachers to become model investigators who can bring the study of mathematics to life and foster students' desires to do more—and increasingly more challenging—mathematics.

Workshop/Course 1: Problem-Solving Lab

With the publication of George Pólya's (1945) book *How to Solve It*, the art of problem solving gained momentum as a key process in the teaching and learning of mathematics. Professional organizations of mathematics educators identified problem solving as one of the five major process skills that should be promoted across grade levels (NCSM 1977; NCTM 1989, 2000). These process skills form the framework for workshop or course 1.

The term *lab* conveys the nature of this workshop or course: it is hands-on and involves investigation, group collaboration, and the use of various technologies to enhance problem solution, while at the same time encouraging creativity. Unlike methods courses that focus on instructional strategies to be used with students to advance their learning, the lab is designed to enable current and future teachers to know what it feels like to wrestle with ideas, identify ambiguous statements, make conjectures, locate and gather critical data, analyze different approaches, and search for more elegant solutions. The mathematics required to solve the problems comes from the middle and high school curricula, concurrently providing participants with a review of key concepts and skills and their growth across the grades.

Since the publication of Pólya's book, several problem-solving models have been described. We favor the following six-step approach for solo or group work on problems or projects, recognizing that problem solvers may be stalled at any one of the steps and need to start over or reconsider a prior step:

1. Take the problem statement apart. Identify any ambiguities or assumptions to be clarified. Restate the problem by paraphrasing, symbolizing, or stating the problem in reverse.

2. Brainstorm with others. List all information about the problem, including what is given and what is missing. Record conjectures about the nature of the solutions or solution methods. Identify any mathematical ideas that are familiar and any ideas that burst forth during the discussion.

3. Determine whether any of the following strategies can be applied:

    • Simplify the problem?

    • Display information?

    • Find patterns?

    • Try special cases?

4. Formulate hypotheses about the solution.

5. Try your best idea: Which strategies (from step 3) will you apply? In what order? Which strategies are more closely aligned to your hypotheses?

6. Check out the result: Does it make sense? Is your solution the most elegant or efficient?

If at any time you reach a roadblock, be willing to scrap what you have done so far, change direction, and try different routes.

An additional step may be to pose new problems that are suggested by the solutions or solution methods to the original problem (Greenes, Gregory, and Seymour 1977).

Designing mathematical walking tours

Designing and conducting mathematical walking tours for gifted middle school students is an example of an activity that will increase teachers' awareness of mathematics in the environment. The tour will not only show teachers how mathematics can be used to model phenomena but also develop their skills as problem posers. The tour locale can be any place (e.g., historic site, museum, ball park, zoo, mall) that is a reasonable distance from school. Such a tour, typically three to four hours in duration, provides compass directions to various locations where students obtain measurements or gather data to solve problems posed in a tour guide. Problems focus on the application of key mathematical ideas and reasoning methods. Initially, tours can be used as mathematical field trips for students. Subsequently, they can be used to stimulate students to create their own mathematical walking tours. "The Memorial Mine," a problem designed for a mathematical walking tour of parts of historic downtown Boston (Greenes 1995, p. 18), offers an example of an integrated problem.

In the Boston Common is a very large ball-shaped mine, retrieved from the North Sea during World War I and used as a memorial to those who served in the armed forces. Using a coin—specifically, a quarter—to "eclipse" the mine, and a yardstick to make distance measurements, "tourists" estimate the circumference of the mine, and then, for a challenge, consider ways to determine if the mine is spherical.

Although any circular coin can be used, a quarter offers the advantage of having a diameter of 25 millimeters, or about 1 inch, which simplifies computation. Holding the coin at arm's length, tourists measure the distance from eye to coin, obtain an estimate of their distance from the mine by measuring the length of one walking step and counting walking steps from the eclipse point to the mine, and set up a proportion:

$$\frac{\text{Distance from eye to quarter}}{\text{1 inch (diameter of quarter)}} = \frac{\text{Distance from eclipse position to mine}}{D \text{ (diameter of mine)}}$$

From the estimate of the diameter of the mine, tourists can estimate the circumference. To solve this problem, they bring to bear concepts of measurement (formulas, conversions), geometry (spheres), and number (proportions), and they gain insight into the science of eclipses.

Workshop/Course 2: Assessing Talent and Differentiating Instruction

A substantial amount of literature focuses on differentiated instruction to address the needs of gifted and talented students in heterogeneous classes.

Some believe that the needs of gifted and talented students can be met if teachers have comprehensive training in curriculum differentiation and spend the time and effort required to meet individual needs (Croft 2003). Others believe that gifted students cannot be well served or challenged in regular classroom settings and should be taught in their own classrooms (Croft 2003). As Assouline and Lupkowski-Shoplik (2005) note, "The typical elementary and middle school curriculum is not challenging enough for mathematically talented students" (p. 226). Gifted and talented students should be grouped with other students of talent for exploration of challenging mathematics that requires them to think differently.

To differentiate instruction, even in a class of mathematically gifted students, teachers need to identify each student's specific talents and interests. To accomplish this, we recommend that prospective and current teachers construct a Mathematics Individualized Learning Plan (MILP) for each student. Unlike the Individualized Education Plan (IEP), the MILP is talent-based and identifies not only a student's level of achievement in mathematics, but also the student's special talents in reasoning and creativity, degree of perseverance, oral and written communication abilities, and collaboration skills. Once these special talents are identified (a task that often takes several weeks of observation and work with the students), a plan for instruction can be prepared. Plans should be updated every four or five months.

In workshop or course 2, teachers learn strategies for assessing the achievement, perseverance, problem-solving talent, and communication and collaboration skills of mathematically talented students. Participants consider standardized tests for identifying mathematical talent, like the SAT (www.collegeboard.com), ACT (www.act.org), and Ravens Advanced Progressive Matrices tests of abstract reasoning (http://www.personality-and-aptitude-career-tests.com/ravens-test.html). They explore the use of portfolios and performances for revealing talent. They also design and conduct individual think-aloud problem-solving sessions to identify heuristics, individual clinical interviews to probe a student's depth of understanding, and group problem-solving observation surveys to assess curiosity, communication, and collaboration talents. All assessment and observation activities are carried out with middle school students, and participants analyze and use data from these assessments to construct MILPs.

Workshop/Course 3: Instructional Strategies

Workshop or course 3 focuses on three aspects of instruction that present special challenges in the teaching of gifted students: (1) problem and project selection, (2) mentoring, and (3) creating an appropriate learning environment.

Problem and project selection

Effective teachers select and use problems and projects that promote solving problems and justifying solution paths, stretch mathematical know-how, allow for divergent approaches, promote curiosity about related mathematical ideas and their contexts, and require application of knowledge from other fields. As examples, consider the following projects selected from the Math Explorations and Group Activities (MEGA) program (Greenes et al. 1996). The first involves making a number "bracelet" like that shown in figure 4.1 (MEGA Projects, Grade 6, Card 37).

Bracelets: A Mathematical Curiosity

Start with any two single-digit numbers. Record them in the two "start" links (see fig. 4.1). Add the numbers. Record the ones digit of the sum in the adjacent link to the right. Continue to add the last two digits, each time recording only the ones digit of the sum in the next link. Eventually, the sequence repeats. Just before the repeat starts, STOP. Attach the last digit in the sequence to the first digit, making a bracelet of digits. The sequence starting with 1, 3 makes the bracelet shown in figure 4.1.

1. How many pairs of numbers will generate this same bracelet?

2. Beginning with any two single-digit numbers, how many different bracelets are possible?

3. How many links are in each bracelet? Which bracelet has the greatest number of links? The least number of links?

4. How do you know that you found all possible bracelets?

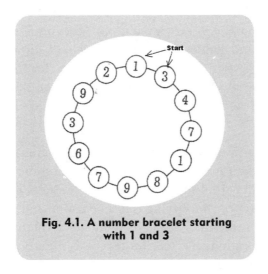

Fig. 4.1. A number bracelet starting with 1 and 3

The second project involves thinking about the map of the United States in a new way (MEGA Projects, Grade 6, Card 18).

State Boundaries: A Demographics Connections Exploration

You probably know that Rhode Island is the smallest state (land area). But did you know that its population is greater than that of Montana, the fourth largest state? Imagine a map where the size of each state is based on its population. Rhode Island would be larger than Montana. Draw a *fictional map* of the Continental United States (48 states) where the area of each state represents its population but maintains its current configuration.

The MEGA Projects program provides sets of such projects, five per theme, with ten themes for each level, grades 4–8, with accompanying teachers' guides.

An excellent source of challenging problems is MATHCOUNTS, a national enrichment, coaching, and competition program for students in grades 6–8. MATHCOUNTS provides sets of non-routine mathematics problems for practice by students in preparation for the various competitions at the school, state, and national levels. Problems from previous years are available at the MATHCOUNTS Web site (https://mathcounts.org/).

Like MATHCOUNTS, Math Olympiads for Elementary and Middle Schools (MOEMS) holds club meetings designed to prepare students for contests using sets of non-routine problems designed by MOEMS board members. Competition problems from previous years are released for each division—upper elementary and middle school. Information about MOEMS can be obtained at http://www.moems.org/program.htm.

For projects that integrate mathematics with other content areas, a good source is *Mathematics and Economics, Connecting for Life, Grades 6–8*, produced by the National Council of Economics Education in 2002. Another useful source is ScienceProject.com (http://www.scienceproject.com), a Web site that provides project ideas and guides for secondary school students in the areas of biology, chemistry, physics, earth and space science, health, energy, engineering, and computer science. Project Lead the Way (http://beta.pltw.org), offers integrated curricula with an engineering or biomedical sciences focus.

Mentoring learning

As opposed to traditional instruction, which introduces new concepts and skills that students then practice and apply, instruction for gifted students often follows a different path. Initially, the teacher presents a challenge for either solo or group exploration, specifying the time frame and the means by which the solution is to be presented. Students then tackle the problem.

During the exploration, the teacher serves as mentor, anticipating where students might reach an impasse and aiding them in identifying and gaining access to needed materials and other sources of information, including outside experts.

Workshop or course 3 focuses on developing teachers' mentoring talents by helping them identify at what points students might get stuck in solving particular problems or projects, and when and how to assist at those points without giving away the solution.

An appropriate learning environment

A learning environment that cultivates the talents of mathematically gifted students must include satisfactory amounts of time for (1) thinking "big thoughts," (2) going "off task" when an exciting opportunity for investigation arises, (3) sharing and evaluating potential solution paths, and (4) presenting and assessing solutions. These types of activities cannot take place in a class period of forty-five or fifty minutes. They require extended lab periods during school time or can take place in after-school programs, including Saturday classes and summer enrichment or acceleration programs.

Workshop/Course 4: Exploring Situational Math

The first part of workshop or course 4 has two components. In the first, teachers study previously constructed long-term integrated projects appropriate for exploration by teams of mathematically advanced middle school youngsters. In the second, they design new projects and use them as the centerpiece of their work with talented middle school students, either during school or in after-school sessions, while being mentored by university faculty in mathematics or science education, or by faculty from related fields.

In the design of long-term integrated projects appropriate for exploration by teams of talented middle school students, teachers have two goals. Not only do they want to engage students in the application of mathematics to the solution of problems in various domains of mathematics and in other contexts, but they also want to develop students' collaboration and communication skills. After creating integrated projects and using them with middle school students, teachers evaluate the students' learning and present the results of their evaluations. With its project design and evaluation elements, this course or workshop might satisfy the applied projects requirement that many university programs have for their degree programs.

Workshop/Course 5: Concept Study

In contrast to the popular "lesson study" model for pedagogical development (Wang-Iverson and Yoshida 2005), "concept study," focuses on a key mathematical concept (Greenes et al. 2007). Teams of mathematics teachers study how the concept is manifested in the secondary school curriculum, how students' understanding of it becomes more robust within and across grades, how it is developed in instruction in related content areas, and how it can be introduced, maintained, enriched, and assessed.

Workshop or course 5 recognizes that concept study is particularly important for teachers of gifted students. Often gifted and talented students develop concepts very early, and in unexpected ways. When working with mathematically talented students, teachers need to consider alternative ways to approach concepts and to capitalize on what the students already know, while leading them into deeper study of the concepts than the same teachers might do with other students. (Note that the same can be said about groups of students who struggle with mathematics.) The work of learning to recognize students' levels of understanding and achievement can be difficult for teachers of gifted students. Concept study can help to sort out these difficulties.

As an example, consider the case of a key mathematical concept and reasoning method—proportional reasoning. This concept is central not only in algebra but also in other content strands identified by NCTM (2000), including number and operations with numbers (e.g., construction of equivalent fractions, computation of percents), geometry (e.g., identification of similar triangles), measurement (e.g., conversion among measurement units, interpretation of scale drawings and time lines), and probability and statistics (e.g., computation of simple probabilities, chi square analysis). In the sciences, problem solvers reason proportionally when they solve problems dealing with simple machines in physics, calculate dosages in medicine, and determine concentrations in chemistry. Sorting out appropriate examples of proportional reasoning for gifted students, recognizing what the students already know, and deciding how their knowledge can be expanded are all good topics for concept study.

Proportional reasoning is just one example of such a topic. Others might include equality, variables as unknowns in equations and systems of equations, variables as varying quantities in functions (including formulas), and inductive reasoning.

Beyond the Program of Study Provided by the Five Workshops or Courses

Not only should teachers promote lifelong learning of mathematics for their students, but they should also adopt that perspective for themselves (Csikszentmihalyi, Rathunde, and Whalen 1993). There are a variety of ways in which teachers can grow in their abilities to solve problems, gain greater insight into alternative solution approaches, and communicate with other teachers. One way is to participate in workshops and courses offered online, such as those provided by the Math Forum at Drexel University (http://mathforum.org).

Math Forum programs engage teachers from across the country and internationally in discussions of their own approaches to solving problems, as well as considerations of the work of students.

Another way for teachers to continue to develop expertise in mathematics and problem solving is to participate in courses, programs, or workshops that are offered at colleges and universities, particularly those that integrate mathematics with other content areas. One such program is the Mars Education Program at Arizona State University (http://marsed.asu.edu). In partnership with NASA, this program matches teachers and talented middle and high school students with scientists for Mars explorations activities, with the goal of "firing up" students' imaginations and stimulating their unique skills while introducing teachers to new ways of teaching.

The United States has several centers for gifted education (e.g., Center for Gifted Education, College of William and Mary; National Research Center on the Gifted and Talented, University of Connecticut; The Belin-Blank Center for Gifted Education and Talent Development, University of Iowa) that offer professional development opportunities for preservice and in-service teachers. There are also multiple national and state gifted associations that offer workshops, conferences, and other types of programs for teachers. A listing is available on the Web site of the Center for Talent Development at Northwestern University (http://www.ctd.northwestern.edu/resources/gifted).

Conclusion

We need middle school teachers who are passionate about mathematics, charismatic, and well prepared to identify and develop the talents of mathematically gifted middle school students. Unfortunately, there are too few programs—if any—designed specifically to address the needs of mathematics teachers for these students. Such teachers need to be able to wrestle with ambiguities. They need a rich mathematical background from which to select problems that will elicit students' talents. They need to be able to support students who go off course intellectually—and sometimes they must go off course themselves. They need to learn about ways to mentor and counsel students to take the right series of courses and programs. Perhaps most importantly, teachers of mathematically gifted students must be committed to lifelong learning, intellectual flexibility, and the joy of thinking in new ways. With this type of preparation, no mathematically talented student will go unrecognized, underestimated, or unchallenged.

References

Assouline, Susan, and Ann Lupkowski-Shoplik. *Developing Math Talent: A Guide for Challenging and Educating Gifted Students.* Waco, Tex.: Prufrock Press, 2005.

Ball, Deborah L., and Hyman Bass. "Interweaving Content and Pedagogy in Teaching and Learning to Teach: Knowing and Using Mathematics." In *Multiple Perspectives on Teaching and Learning,* edited by Jo Boaler, pp. 83–104. Westport, Conn.: Ablex Publishing, 2000.

Berliner, David C. "Describing the Behavior and Documenting the Accomplishments of Expert Teachers." *Bulletin of Science, Technology & Society* 24, no. 3 (2004): 200–212.

Croft, Laurie J. "Teachers of the Gifted: Gifted Teachers." In *Handbook of Gifted Education,* 3rd ed., edited by Nicholas Colangelo and Gary Davis, pp. 558–71. Boston: Allyn & Bacon, 2003.

Csikszentmihalyi, Mihaly, Kevin Rathunde, and Samuel Whalen. *Talented Teenagers: The Roots of Success and Failure.* Cambridge: Cambridge University Press, 1993.

Ferrini-Mundy, Joan, and Karen Graham. "The Education of Mathematics Teachers in the United States after World War II: Goals, Programs, and Practices." In *A History of School Mathematics,* vol. 2, edited by George M. A. Stanic and Jeremy Kilpatrick, pp. 1193–308. Reston, Va.: National Council of Teachers of Mathematics, 2003.

Fey, James T., and Anna O. Graeber. "From the New Math to the Agenda for Action." In *A History of School Mathematics,* vol. 1, edited by George M. A. Stanic and Jeremy Kilpatrick, pp. 521–58. Reston, Va.: National Council of Teachers of Mathematics, 2003.

Greenes, Carole. *A Mathematical Historical Tour of Boston.* (Printed for the 75th NCTM Annual Meeting.) Palo Alto, Calif.: Dale Seymour Publications, 1995.

Greenes, Carole, John Gregory, and Dale Seymour. *Successful Problem Solving Techniques.* Palo Alto, Calif.: Creative Publications, 1977.

Greenes, Carole, and Maggie Mode. "Empowering Teachers to Discover, Challenge, and Support Students with Mathematical Promise." In *Developing Mathematically Promising Students,* edited by Linda Jensen Sheffield, pp. 121–32. Reston, Va.: National Council of Teachers of Mathematics, 1999.

Greenes, Carole, Steve Rosenberg, Kathleen Bodie, Donna Chevaire, Charles Garabedian, Daniel Wulf, Ann Halteman, Kevin Wynn, and Eileen Herlihy. "The Professional Development of Leaders and Teachers of Mathematics." *NCSM Journal* (Spring 2007): 16–24.

Greenes, Carole, Linda Schulman, Rika Spungin, Suzanne Chapin, Carol Findell, and Arthur Johnson. *Math Exploration and Group Activity (MEGA) Projects.* Palo Alto, Calif.: Dale Seymour Publications, 1996.

Hannimen, Gail E. "A Study of Teacher Training in Gifted Education." *Roeper Review* 10, no. 3 (1988): 139–43.

Laczko-Kerr, Ildiko, and David C. Berliner. "In Harm's Way: How Uncertified Teachers Hurt Their Students." *Educational Leadership* 60, no. 8 (2003): 34–39.

Maker, C. June. *Curriculum Development for the Gifted.* Rockville, Md.: Aspen, 1982.

National Association of Gifted Children and the Council for Exceptional Children. Teacher Knowledge and Skill Standards for Gifted and Talented Education. 2007. http://www.nagc.org/index.aspx?id=1863.

National Council of Supervisors of Mathematics. Basic Mathematical Skills. NCSM position paper. 1977. http://www.mathedleadership.org/resources/index.html.

National Council of Teachers of Mathematics (NCTM). *Curriculum and Evaluation Standards for School Mathematics.* Reston, Va.: NCTM, 1989.

——. *Principles and Standards for School Mathematics.* Reston, Va.: NCTM, 2000.

Pólya, George. *How to Solve It: A New Aspect of Mathematical Method.* Princeton, N.J.: Princeton University Press, 1945.

Wang-Iverson, Patsy, and Makoto Yoshida, eds. *Building Our Understanding of Lesson Study.* Philadelphia : Research for Better Schools, 2005.

VanTassel-Baska, Joyce, and Susan K. Johnsen. "Teacher Education Standards for the Field of Gifted Education: A Vision of Coherence for Personnel Preparation in the 21st Century." *Gifted Child Quarterly* 51 (Spring 2007): 182–205.

Extracurricular Opportunities for Mathematically Gifted Middle School Students

Richard Rusczyk

♦ Extracurricular opportunities in mathematics are an important aspect of talent development for middle school students.

♦ Extracurricular options include math clubs, specialized texts, summer and after-school programs, distance learning, and math circles.

♦ The role of teachers as facilitators of these opportunities for mathematically gifted students is as important as their role as classroom mathematics instructors.

♦ Appropriate levels and complexity of challenge in out-of-school options can minimize boredom and repetition, which can ultimately lead to underachievement in talented students.

I recently received an e-mail from a fellow alumnus of my Ivy League alma mater. He was lamenting that he hadn't had access to appropriate resources when he was a student. He thought that the lack of such resources had left him unprepared for mathematical study in college. But he couldn't point to poor performance in middle and high school as a cause of his difficulties. In fact, he wrote, "I went through junior high and high school without ever missing a question on a math test, and then took [college math] 103 and 104, which was one of the most unpleasant and bewildering experiences of my life, and poisoned me on math for years."

Students who ace every math test in middle and high school are not necessarily success stories for their schools. Such students present their teachers with an important challenge: to give them the best preparation for the greater challenges that they will face in college and beyond. This chapter focuses on strategies for creating or developing outside-the-classroom experiences that may help. Because teachers of the gifted are the main source of mathematical information for many of their students, it is particularly important for them to know about these opportunities.

Gifted students often report that their work outside the classroom on problems of greater depth yields benefits that go far beyond their mathematical knowledge. I saw this firsthand in college. I attended an average high school; we had a graduation rate of 60–70 percent, and very few students went to college out of state. I took only two AP tests and did not attend any college classes while in high school. I was concerned that I wouldn't be as prepared as my Princeton classmates who went to magnet high schools or elite private schools. I quickly found that my training in challenging problem-solving mathematics through math contests had prepared me very well for Princeton—and not just for my math classes.

Examinations and homework problems in college science, computer science, engineering, and economics classes offer challenges like those found in high school math contests. These college courses, which are designed to challenge even the strongest students, require problem-solving skills rather than memorization and mechanical repetition. Students often develop these essential problem-solving skills in math clubs and on math teams in middle and high school.

Although acceleration through the usual school curriculum can offer opportunities for many gifted students, those who are highly gifted sometimes do not find the challenges that they need in courses designed for the general student. This is often the case even when highly gifted students are accelerated by a year or two. However, extracurricular work with these students is not subject to the requirements of accountability or accessibility that can bind school curricula. Some schools have a sufficiently high concentration of very high-performing students that they are able to offer a curriculum specifically designed for them, but many schools do not have enough of these students to fill a classroom. The strategies presented in this chapter can be pursued as alternatives or supplements to acceleration and include the following:

- School-sponsored math clubs and teams
- Summer programs
- Independent study
- Distance learning
- Privately run math circles and after-school programs

Math Clubs and Teams

School-sponsored math clubs and teams provide important exposure to challenging mathematics. Although these activities are ostensibly "extracurricular," they are major sources of math education for many highly gifted students. Members of clubs or teams that enter competitions derive additional benefits.

Advantages of math clubs and teams

Math clubs and teams provide numerous benefits to talented students whether or not their in-school mathematics is accelerated:

- *More challenging mathematics.* It is important that students learn early how to wrestle with difficult problems. If they wait until college, they may come to believe that anything that is not easy is impossible. Worse, they may have formed the idea that mathematics is a dull and routine subject. Math clubs and teams—and particularly math contests—offer many students their first true mathematical challenges. Because math clubs and teams can be tailored specifically to the most interested and able students, they can offer deeper challenges to middle school students than most accelerated curricula can.

- *Mathematics outside the curriculum.* Math clubs and teams can expose students to rich areas and applications of mathematics that are missing from the standard curriculum. Examples of such topics include discrete math, cryptography, graph theory, and group theory.

- *Indications of the importance of mathematics.* Many middle school students are very attuned to what is "cool." Signals that sports and music are more cool than math come not just from their peers or popular culture. Nearly all schools provide specialized teams and training for their best athletes (school sports teams), musicians (the band or glee club), and writers (the school paper). Thus, when schools do not also offer specialized avenues for their best math students, they send a clear signal to students that their peers and television are correct: math isn't cool. Middle school students don't generally see the job satisfaction surveys or career compensation lists that clearly indicate that out in the professional world math is very cool indeed. The establishment of a math club or team can send a clear signal that the school values its best math students as much as it does its best athletes and musicians.

- *Social groups in which mathematics is highly valued.* Although the adage "Show me your friends, and I'll show you *you*" may not be entirely true, the positive effects of supportive peer groups on students' academic development are a significant part of the value of math clubs and teams. Higher salaries, greater professional opportunities, and higher social status for mathematical and scientific careers provide clear, immediate signals to adults of the value of mastery of mathematics. These signals are not of immediate import to most middle school students, who are inundated with the social cues provided by their middle school peers, most of whom aren't concerned yet about salary or social status based on intellectual contributions to society. A math club or team creates a social group in the school with values that more constructively reinforce the interests of those students who value learning mathematics.

Additional benefits provided by math competitions

Competitions extend the benefits of math clubs in numerous ways. Entry into competitions can provide the following:

- *A focus for the club.* Imagine a basketball team without games against other schools, a band without performances, or a drama club without the school play. Math contests can provide a similar organizing focus for a math club.

- *A yardstick for the top students.* The best students in any school will be measured in their future careers against those who were the best students in schools all over the world. The sooner these students start measuring themselves against these other outstanding thinkers, the more prepared they will be psychologically for nationally and internationally competitive careers.

- *Exposure to a wide array of mathematical topics.* Math contests usually include problems from important areas of mathematics, such as discrete mathematics, which are underrepresented in most curricula. Moreover, since most contests cover many areas of math, they allow students to revisit areas of mathematics regularly, reviewing as they apply fundamentals in solving challenging problems.

- *Mental recreation.* Competitions are for playing—not just for winning. Some students are not attracted to—and others are turned off by—competition. The point of the competition is not to win but to play. On the one hand, students who are intimidated or embarrassed by competition should never be forced to participate. On the other hand, students who initially believe that competitions are not for them may find that simple exposure unveils the mystique of competition. For them, such opportunities may open up a whole new world of friends. The adviser of a math club must find the right balance for his or her group of students between competitive mathematics and individual or cooperative work.

Steps in building a school-sponsored math club

The first step in building a math club is to attract the students. Three tips are very useful for getting a math club off the ground:

- *Offer food.* A little candy and an occasional pizza go a long way.

- *Provide games.* Jeff Boyd, three-time National MATHCOUNTS champion coach, explains that he started his first math club by hosting weekly game days featuring "thinking" card and board games. Good games for math clubs include Blokus, Boggle, Carcassonne, chess, Connect 4, Diplomacy, Dots and Boxes, go, Othello, Puerto Rico, Qubic, Risk, Scrabble, SET, Settlers of Catan, Stratego, and Ticket to Ride. Students who enjoy such games often will also enjoy greater mathematical challenge.

- *Start young.* When building a new club at a school, it helps to start with the youngest students. The club can hope to have them for more than one year, and they will help establish the necessary culture to make the club thrive. Although the range of activities for younger students is narrower, and the literature is scarce, involving them first is well worth the effort. The oldest students in the school will be gone at the end of the first year, and recruitment will have to start over the following year. Moreover, older students are harder to attract because they're much more likely to be involved in other activities.

Activities for math clubs

Once a math club has recruited students, it must have activities to engage and "hook" them. Clubs can offer a variety of activities, including contests, explorations of new subjects, and projects.

Math contests

Options for math contests include the following:

- *MATHCOUNTS (www.mathcounts.org).* MATHCOUNTS is the premier middle school contest in the United States. The competition consists of four rounds with participants from progressively wider fields:

school, chapter (local), state, and national. A school's team consists of four students, and the contest has both team and individual components. The school round is administered by teachers in the school; the other rounds are invitational events outside the school, administered by volunteers. The chapter, state, and national levels of the contest give students opportunities to meet other outstanding students from many other schools, thereby expanding their peer group of students with common interests.

- *MOEMS (www.moems.org).* The Math Olympiads for Elementary and Middle Schools (MOEMS) program is an excellent starting point for younger students in mathematical problem solving. MOEMS consists of five rounds during the school year, and the contest is administered by teachers in their classrooms. The problems do not require algebra, and the program has a heavy emphasis on non-routine problems that have multiple solution methods. MOEMS is a starting place for students who find MATHCOUNTS too difficult.

- *AMC (www.unl.edu/amc).* The American Mathematics Competitions of the Mathematical Association of America administers the series of tests that determine the United States team for the International Mathematical Olympiad, a competition that pits top high school students from the United States against those from other countries. AMC test scores are requested by many of America's top colleges, such as MIT and Caltech. Most of the top students in the AMC started participating in these tests while in middle school. In addition to the high school competitions, the AMC also offers a middle school contest, AMC 8, as early preparation for the high school contests.

- *Mail-in and Internet contests.* Middle school students are eligible to participate in many mail-in and Internet contests. Some of the larger ones are Continental Math League, NatAssessment, National Math League, Rocket City Math League, and Purple Comet. Very advanced middle school students also participate in some mail-in and Internet contests for high school students, including ARML Power Round, Mandelbrot, and USAMTS. (Currently, participation in Purple Comet and USAMTS is free of charge.) All of these mail-in and Internet contests have readily accessible Web pages. Some of the contests are for teams, and others are for individuals.

- *Local events.* There are many local, on-site contests throughout the United States. In these contests, a high school or college usually hosts teams from surrounding communities. Local contests are a great way for students to meet top math students from other schools, and they also provide very good practice for the more established national events. They teach students how to handle time pressure on difficult tests while giving them regular opportunities to revisit various math concepts, with something staked on the outcome. Even more important, they're just plain fun.

- *Self-run contests.* A club can start its own contest and invite schools from the community to participate. This can be an excellent service activity for the club and can strengthen the local academic culture.

Most math contests require many skills that are not developed in most curricula. Therefore, students typically need specialized training for success in these programs. Fortunately, over the last few decades, many useful training materials have been developed. Some effective and commonly used materials are identified below:

- *Past contests.* Many programs publish past contests as preparation materials for future contests. Some of these are available as books, and others are available online. Students who are serious about competition can work the problems from the past contests under test conditions. These past contests also make excellent homework, group activities, or class discussion tools, and they are excellent sources for problems to integrate into honors classes.

- *Textbooks for contests.* Several textbooks are designed to help students prepare for contests. These texts typically include many problems from a variety of contests and highlight the types of advanced problem-solving strategies required to tackle challenging problems. Texts for middle school students include *Art of Problem Solving, Volume 1: The Basics* (Lehoczky and Rusczyk 2006), *Creative Problem Solving in School Mathematics* (Lenchner 2007), and *First Steps for Math Olympians* (Faires 2005).

- *MATHCOUNTS School Handbook and Club Program.* Each school year, MATHCOUNTS produces two publications, the MATHCOUNTS School Handbook and the MATHCOUNTS Club Program, both of which are provided without charge to any requesting middle school. The handbook includes three hundred problems with solutions, grouped roughly by difficulty. The Club Program includes a resource guide for club meetings and activities for math clubs throughout the year, such as monthly math challenges. The Club Program also offers rewards and recognition for club performance throughout the program. For a fee, MATHCOUNTS also offers an online resource called OPLET, which makes available more than 10,000 past MATH-COUNTS problems, sorted by subject and difficulty, for teachers to use in producing worksheets, problems of the day, or flash cards for classroom use.

Explorations of new subjects

Math clubs offer opportunities to study areas of mathematics that are not included in the standard curriculum. For example, clubs might provide semester-long courses in areas like discrete mathematics, short introductions to areas of higher mathematics, or a series of single-day activities centered on a single problem or mathematical concept. Abundant resources are available for these long- and short-term explorations of nontraditional topics:

- *Texts and Web sites.* Possibilities include the following:

  » *Introduction to Counting and Probability* (Patrick 2005) and *Introduction to Number Theory* (Crawford 2006). Each of these texts supports a one-semester course in its respective subject area.

  » *Mathematical Circles* (Fomin, Genkin, and Itenberg 1996). This book offers more than a dozen chapters, each of which can serve as a three- to ten-day course in a subject area that is not covered, or only lightly covered, in the standard curriculum.

  » www.cut-the-knot.org. This Web site includes hundreds of articles that can serve as the inspiration for one- to three-day explorations for a math club. Many topics are far too advanced for middle school students, but examination of the site will turn up appropriate materials. Lovers of mathematics will find the site very addictive.

  » *Solve This: Math Activities for Students and Clubs* (Tanton 2001). This book, published by the Mathematical Association of America, contains a compilation of engaging activities for math clubs.

- *Association meetings and conventions.* State, regional, or national meetings of national associations for mathematics or gifted education (e.g., NCTM, NAGC) typically include sessions that offer methods for introducing interesting areas of mathematics that are outside the standard curriculum.

- *The work of Martin Gardner.* I once met a parent from India who explained that as a child he would walk many miles each month to the local village simply to read Martin Gardner's columns in the *Scientific*

American in the village library. Although most of Gardner's readers don't have to walk miles to enjoy his work, a great many of them can point to it as the starting point of a lifelong love of mathematics. Many of his articles can easily be converted into one- or two-day activities for a math club. Gardner was extremely prolific, and many of his articles have been collected in books or on CDs.

Projects

Individual projects in mathematics loom large in both curricular and extracurricular activities on the high school level. These activities can build to significant, and sometimes even publishable, mathematical results. Although most middle school students cannot hope for this level of achievement, there are meaningful mathematical projects that they can complete, often with encouragement or direction offered in a math club. They can also often enter these projects in local science fairs, since a math fair on the middle school level is unusual. Many of the resources listed above for explorations are also excellent sources of ideas for projects.

A note to math club advisers: Sometimes, so-called "math projects" actually turn out to be "history projects" or "art projects"—the project is really an investigation of math history or an artistic application of math in which the vast majority of the work and exploration is art, not math. Although these activities may be fun for some students, they are historical or artistic activities first and foremost—not mathematical ones. Some useful sources for reading about the history of mathematics include *Fermat's Enigma* (Singh 1998), *Journey through Genius* (Dunham 1991), and *Music of the Primes* (du Sautoy 2004).

Ensuring a math club's growth

After a math club has been launched, it may encounter several challenges to its survival or growth. Keys to a club's vitality include the following:

- *Good meeting times.* Most clubs typically start by meeting after school or at lunch. Of course, these options place extra demands on the teachers, the students, and, if the club meets after school, even the parents, who must adjust carpooling schedules. After-school meetings also run the risk of time conflicts with other activities—particularly as the students get older. For these reasons, many successful math teams and math clubs have integrated their meetings into the regular school day, through either a math enrichment class or a math seminar. Some groups meet once a day, whereas others meet two or three times a week. Similar allowances of time are made in most schools for participation of the top athletes in sports teams and the top musicians in band or orchestra, so it is reasonable to ask that schools make such an allowance for its top math students. Providing a regular class period for a math club can mitigate the difficulties that students and teachers often have in finding time for more challenging mathematical study. Students in many schools are overwhelmed with homework and extracurricular activities. By replacing a regular class with a math club class period, schools can avoid burdening students with "extra" work. The students simply replace less useful work that they would have in another class by work that is more valuable and meaningful to them. In addition, having a class period during the day for the math club makes the club a part of a teacher's regular school-day schedule—not extra work that he or she must do on a voluntary basis.

- *Supportive parents.* Many successful math teams have two primary features in common: a very dedicated teacher and a small army of parents supporting that teacher. It's very hard (but not impossible) for a teacher to go it alone and build a strong program with no support. Occasionally, a team can thrive even without a teacher at the center, but only if parents are heavily involved. Parents can help a math team by providing snacks or transportation or by hosting practices or club social events at their homes. They can also lend a hand with funding. Math teams can have booster clubs, just like bands and sports teams. Some employers match donations or provide donations in amounts that are based on parents' volunteer work. Sometimes parents can also help in training students in the club.

- *Publicity.* Whenever a club has a notable success, it is important to publicize it, both inside the school, through the daily announcements, for example, and outside the school, in the local press. Local publicity reflects well on the school's administrators, and this positive attention makes them more likely to support future events. It also makes local fund-raising easier and induces parents and others to volunteer to support the club. Promoting the club's success within the school adds to the prestige associated with involvement in the math club. This helps draw more students and keeps students connected to the club as they get older. Typically, the regard that students most value is that which they earn from their immediate peers. By giving students the opportunity to excel and earn peer admiration through success at a locally recognized endeavor, a club encourages their continued interest and growth at an age when peer pressure can be a powerful influence. Securing publicity for the club's achievements can go a long way towards constructively influencing these local values.

- *An informed and involved administration.* It is important to keep the school administration informed of the progress of the math club, and especially of any successes. Spreading the credit liberally for those successes secures goodwill for the program and can help to protect it from the periodic cuts that all school systems endure.

- *Ties with the local high school.* If a local high school has a math club, it can help support a middle school math club. Many high school math clubs or honor societies have a community service requirement that members can fulfill by helping out in the local middle school. This avenue for assistance becomes particularly fruitful after a middle school club has existed for a few years, because many alumni of the program are then at the local high school.

- *Links with feeder elementary schools.* It is useful to encourage the elementary schools that feed into the middle school to form math clubs of their own. At the very least, they can participate in the Math Olympiads for the Elementary and Middle Schools (MOEMS) problem-solving program.

Summer Programs

Several summer programs are designed for outstanding math students. This section focuses on the national residential summer programs. Some communities have day camps hosted by universities or after-school programs. National summer programs give students a variety of advantages:

- *An outstanding peer group.* Because these programs have a national reach and very challenging entrance requirements, their students provide gifted students with the type of peer group that top universities like MIT offer college students. Many students find some of their closest lifelong friends at these programs, and the intellectual culture of these summer experiences can inspire students throughout the remainder of the year.

- *Interaction with professional mathematicians.* Most summer programs provide a great deal of interaction with professional mathematicians (usually college professors). This allows participating students to receive tutelage from mathematically sophisticated instructors who serve as role models who use mathematics professionally.

- *An immersive experience in mathematics.* At summer programs, mathematics doesn't compete with four or five other subjects for students' attention, so students can indulge their passions and make great intellectual strides.

That said, two other major factors also determine whether or not a student enjoys a mathematics summer program:

- *Genuine interest.* Does the student want to go? Parents should make sure that their child really wants to attend a summer program before enrolling him or her. Many students who do not enjoy a summer program experience were forced to attend by their parents.

- *Age appropriateness.* Is the camp age appropriate for the student? Aside from the usual social concerns that accompany accelerating students into classes with much older students, particular academic concerns make it desirable to aim for an age-appropriate camp. A summer program that describes its target student body as "high school students" does not aim to attract middle school students who are studying high school mathematics. Such a program is usually intended for high school students who are ready for college-level mathematics (or beyond). Middle school students who attend a camp that is designed for much older students may find themselves mathematically in way over their heads, socially isolated, and deprived of the consolation of academic success. Major summer programs have outstanding staff with a great deal of experience in challenging the best students in the country. So even if a student is the very best at an age-appropriate camp, he or she won't be held back by peers of lesser ability.

Other factors should also be taken into consideration when choosing a camp. These factors include the following:

- *Duration.* Younger students and first-timers may prefer shorter camps.

- *Cost.* Most residential camps are fairly expensive, though some offer financial aid.

- *Geography.* Some programs are at different universities each year, whereas others are always in the same place. Some parents may prefer to have their children in programs near home or relatives.

- *Mathematical emphasis.* Some programs are specifically designed to help students with contests. Others are designed to introduce advanced areas of mathematics that most students won't encounter until college. Some focus on a single area of mathematics, and others take a more eclectic approach. Still others focus mainly on applications of mathematics, such as cryptography.

- *Structure.* Some programs are very highly structured, specifying which classes students must take and what homework they must do. Others are much less rigid, leaving the student to decide which classes to attend and what work they would like to do. Which environment is best depends on the student's personality and preferred approach to learning.

Parents and students should consider all these factors when choosing a program, and they should research many programs to find the one that is the best fit.

Some major national programs that offer instruction specifically for high-performing students of middle school age include the following:

- *AwesomeMath (www.awesomemath.org).* The primary focus of Awesome-Math is on preparing students for problem-solving competitions.

- *Center for Talented Youth (CTY) (www.cty.jhu.edu), Center for Talent Development (CTD) (www.ctd.northwestern.edu), and Duke Talent Identification Program (TIP) (www.tip.duke.edu).* CTY, CTD, and TIP are well-established and highly regarded gifted education organizations at Johns Hopkins, Northwestern, and Duke universities, respectively. They all offer a wide variety of courses for gifted students in many academic fields at many different locations. Other more localized opportunities are found at many universities around the country, including the University of Iowa, University of Minnesota, University of Buffalo, and Carnegie Mellon University.

- *MathPath (www.mathpath.org).* MathPath offers both contest preparation and exposure to intriguing areas of mathematics that are not part of either the typical middle and high school curriculum or major national contests (such as graph theory or game theory).

- *MathZoom (www.mathzoom.com).* The primary focus of MathZoom is to prepare students for problem-solving competitions.

Graduating eighth graders might consider a variety of high school programs. Possibilities include Canada/USA MathCamp, Hampshire College Summer Studies in Mathematics, PROMYS, and the Ross Mathematics Program. More details about all of these programs can be found with a quick Internet search.

Independent Study

My most important high school math teacher taught me very little mathematics directly, but indirectly she was the source of nearly all of my math education in high school. She realized that the best role for her to play in relation to me was as someone who could provide me with appropriate challenges and make me realize that there was more to mathematics than simply getting an A+ on the next test. She took our math team to competitions all over the southeastern United States, and she accompanied us to national Mu Alpha Theta competitions each summer. She provided me with numerous problem sets from past competitions that I could study to learn more mathematics. Later, I would realize that they were the backbone of all my education. They taught me how to approach problems that I had never seen before and how to learn independently. I developed these skills in no small part because a teacher realized that the best way for her to help me was to set appropriate goals for me, provide adequate resources, and allow me the freedom to learn how to use those resources to attain those goals.

Independent study is an important part of the development of advanced students in any discipline. These students require adequate resources and inspiration from their teachers more than they need direct instruction. Advanced students also require time and freedom to explore their academic passions and reach their potential. Students can be so overwhelmed with homework and extracurricular activities that they have little time to explore, find academic passions, and then develop their talents in these areas to the fullest. Giving students the freedom to do so in middle and high school may be the most important educational experience that we can offer.

Independent study also teaches students how to develop their own plans for attaining their goals. The most productive individuals don't get a to-do list or daily homework from others. They prioritize tasks to meet vaguely defined long-term goals. Even as early as middle school, students can learn to do this through independent study for an examination or in completing a mathematics project.

Moreover, independent study teaches students how to learn new skills on their own. This "meta-skill"—the skill of learning new skills—is particularly critical for students today. I graduated from college in 1993, and most of the jobs I've had since then did not exist when I graduated from high school. How could my middle school or high school teachers have provided me with specific skills to perform tasks that didn't yet exist? Tectonic shifts in necessary career skills occur even more frequently today. Rather than aspiring to teach students specific employable skills, part of our focus should be on providing students with more general skills that they can use later to teach themselves the specific skills that they will need to confront unforeseen future challenges.

Forms of independent study

Independent study can take various forms. Two common ways to structure a more challenging independent study are as a supplement to or a replacement for a regular class.

Supplements to regular classes

To supplement a regular class for a mathematically promising student, a teacher might do the following:

- *Include more difficult problems on homework and tests.* Challenging problems can be added to weekly homework and tests and offered for extra credit or in place of more routine problems for regular credit. Finding the right advanced problems and deciding how to award credit for them can be difficult—and evaluating this sort of student work can be still more difficult. But the benefits to high-ability students, especially those not easily identified as such, will repay this effort. Math contests or books on recreational mathematics are good sources of more challenging problems. The opportunity to try these problems can be offered to the entire class, giving all students equal access, and opening up the possibility of identifying students whose previous poor performances were the result of boredom with easy material.

- *Provide concurrent work in a supplementary text.* Students can be offered texts that are designed to be more challenging and address shortcomings in the standard curriculum. Good options are texts on discrete mathematics and advanced problem solving. Homework loads for advanced students should be reduced accordingly, to give them time to explore the supplementary text.

Replacements for regular class

Some students are so far ahead of their classmates that keeping them in any regular class significantly constrains their mathematical development. If such students are mature enough to progress on their own, then removing them from their regular math classes should be considered. Various options for these students include a self-paced, ability-appropriate curriculum; distance learning; and self-paced acceleration within the standard curriculum. The last option has its difficulties. Often, it does not address the insufficiency of the standard curriculum to develop the advanced students' mathematical skills. And equally often, it devolves into a situation where an advanced student is left alone with a book, while the teacher's time is occupied in working with the other students.

Texts for independent study

Many sources are appropriate for independent study. Texts recommended for mathematically gifted middle school students include the following:

- *Introduction to Algebra* (Rusczyk 2008)

- *Introduction to Counting and Probability* (Patrick 2005)

- *Introduction to Geometry* (Rusczyk 2009)

- *Introduction to Number Theory* (Crawford 2006)

- *Intermediate Algebra* (Rusczyk and Crawford 2007)

- *Intermediate Counting and Probability* (Patrick 2007)

- *Algebra* (Gelfand and Shen 2003)

- *Art of Problem Solving, Volume 1: The Basics* (Lehoczky and Rusczyk 2006)

- *Geometry* (Jacobs 1987)

- *Kiselev's Geometry* (Kiselev [adapted from Russian by Givental] 2006)

- *The Heart of Mathematics* (Burger and Starbird 2009)

- *Mathematical Circles* (Fomin, Genkin, and Itenberg 1996)

- *A Survey of Mathematics with Applications* (Angel, Abbott, and Runde 2008)

- *Lessons in Elementary Geometry* (Hadamard 2009)

Challenges of independent study

Independent study for mathematically promising middle school students has a number of inherent challenges involving a variety of issues. A few of these are discussed briefly below.

Maturity

Some students are not sufficiently emotionally mature to be entirely responsible for their own progress. It is important to provide guidance and clear expectations in the first few months of an independent study program and to offer support and praise throughout.

Equity

Different students have different educational needs. To the degree that it is feasible in a school, it is beneficial for students' education to be tailored to their interests and abilities. For a successful independent study program, it is important to establish clear standards in advance regarding who may be permitted to omit a regularly scheduled class or discontinue work in it and instead pursue independent study.

Two good standards are desire and performance. Qualified students themselves need to want to study independently—not just because their parents are pushing them. If a student is asking to do independent study—and not just because a friend is doing it—then independent study is quite likely to be a good option. If a teacher is unsure of a student's readiness for independent study, or if the student is a first-time independent learner, then it is particularly important to have a way to measure his or her progress. A simple way is to have the student take the regular class tests along with the class. If students who are pursuing independent study perform well on these tests, then there is no need to worry about their doing the regular homework or about their falling behind their peers. If they perform poorly, then scaling back or ending the independent study should be considered.

Time

Once mathematically gifted students have access to appropriate educational resources, the main limitation on their development is usually time. If gifted students must complete all the regular class work in addition to self-paced, self-determined work in the independent study that they have earned the privilege of pursuing through outstanding performances on earlier class work, then they lose critical time to an activity that they have already shown is insufficient to their needs. As students take on more independent work, it is useful to reduce the regular class work accordingly to give them sufficient time to study material that is more appropriate for them.

Grades

Performance on exams probably provides sufficient evidence for assigning grades for students who are pursuing independent study. Alternatively, an independent study might be structured with specific goals, such as completing a particular textbook or completing an online course of study. Students who pursue independent study often earn A's easily in regular classes and shouldn't be penalized for taking on a greater challenge. The bar for an A in an independent study course should not be set higher than in the regular classroom. Whatever method is used to determine grades for students in independent study, it is often best to deemphasize the role of grades. This can be done more easily in middle school than in high school, where grades have an impact on class ranking and college admissions. In middle school, removing the relevance of grades from those students whose performance has already exceeded the grading scale eliminates the stress of grades, enabling the students to flourish in and enjoy their independent study.

Distance Learning and Online Resources

Although some traditional correspondence courses are still available to students, "distance learning" now mainly means "online learning." Considerations about the appropriateness of distance learning for mathematically gifted students overlap with considerations about the appropriateness of independent study in general. However, students' ability to maintain the pace of the particular course in question deserves special attention.

Classes

Distance-learning classes are available for different purposes. For example, they provide rapid acceleration, contest preparation, a broader and deeper curriculum, and exposure to areas of mathematics outside the traditional curriculum. Students should thoroughly research a class before enrolling to make sure that it suits their goals. Distance learning works best for emotionally mature students who work very well independently. Less mature students who require daily assignments and very specific direction are not good candidates for most of these courses. Such students may fall behind in classes that are more aggressively paced, or they may develop significant gaps in their knowledge of math if they are using these courses for rapid acceleration. Students who are not ready for significant independent study can still benefit from such classes as enrichment, but not as the backbone of their math education.

Many organizations offer online classes specifically designed for high-performing students. The following list offers a sampling:

- Art of Problem Solving (www.artofproblemsolving.com)
- Center for Talent Development (www.ctd.northwestern.edu)
- Center for Talented Youth (www.cty.jhu.edu)
- Duke Talent Identification Program (www.tip.duke.edu)
- Educational Program for Gifted Youth (www.epgy.stanford.edu)
- Institute for Mathematics and Computer Science (IMACS) (www.eimacs.com)

If a school offers credit for work done through distance learning, the rigor of both the courses and evaluation methods of the classes should be investigated. Alternatively, the student might be required to pass regular class exams to receive credit.

Online learning systems

Online learning is a relatively new option for mathematically talented students looking for education outside the classroom. Most online learning systems consist of a database of problems and some degree of structure to guide the student through the problems. Some of the systems include text lessons, and others include video lessons. Some adapt interactively to some degree, adjusting the problems that they offer to students on the basis of their success on previous problems.

Although most online learning systems describe themselves as ideal for gifted students, this usually means that they offer gifted students a way to go through the same material as remedial students, except at a much faster pace. When choosing an online learning system, it is important to investigate the degree to which the system is designed to challenge gifted students by offering difficult problems, and the degree to which it accelerates the student by offering simple problems that require more advanced tools.

Online learning systems are a very new educational resource, and more options are likely to appear every year. Four such systems are listed below as examples only:

- Alcumus (www.artofproblemsolving.com/Alcumus/Introduction.php)

- Educational Program for Gifted Youth (www.epgy.stanford.edu)

- ALEKS (www.aleks.com)

- Indian Math Online (www.indianmathonline.com)

The first two of these are specifically designed for gifted students. The latter two are primarily structured around the standard curriculum and when used by gifted students are primarily tools for rapid acceleration. As with online classes, schools should have some internal method for determining whether or not a student who has completed an online learning system has really mastered the subject.

The Web offers many other resources that can be useful in distance learning. A few good starting points for math explorations for gifted students include the following:

- *Art of Problem Solving (www.artofproblemsolving.com)*. This site includes many free resources, including a real-time interactive game, "For the Win," which allows students to compete online at any time against other students from around the world.

- *Cut the Knot (www.cut-the-knot.org)*. This site features hundreds of mathematical investigations, many with interactive Java applets. Numerous articles at the site can serve as excellent starting points for projects, research, or enjoyment of beautiful ideas.

- *Hoagies' Gifted (www.hoagiesgifted.org).* This site includes many links to sites of interest to gifted students, their parents, and their teachers, including sites related to math.

- *MathForum (www.mathforum.org).* This site is intended for a wide math audience and includes numerous resources that might be starting points for class discussions, including problems from a problem-of-the-week program and lesson plans contributed by teachers.

Math Circles and After-School Programs Not Run by Schools

Many cities have thriving "math circles" or after-school programs run by private individuals, universities, or foundations rather than the school itself. The recent math circle movement in the United States has been inspired to a large degree by the math groups for middle and high school students hosted at universities in Russia and Eastern European countries, where university professors play a much larger role in developing mathematical talent than they do in the United States. Many private after-school programs have been developed by parents and educators from Asian countries, where attendance at such programs is very common.

Math circles and after-school programs can take many different forms. Some are free, supported by grants or large volunteer efforts. Others are funded primarily by private donations. Some are essentially private schools, where students must pay tuition to attend classes. Some programs are designed mainly for preparation for math contests, others focus on introducing students to new areas of mathematics and encouraging greater interest in pure mathematics, and still others mainly supplement students' schoolwork by extending and enriching the standard curriculum.

These programs offer largely the same social and intellectual benefits as math clubs and summer programs. Students are exposed to more challenging mathematics, work with mathematically sophisticated instructors, and are in a social environment in which their intellectual abilities are encouraged and rewarded.

Conclusion

This chapter has covered many educational options for gifted students outside the classroom. The role of the teacher in the context of many these options is quite different from the role of the teacher in the classroom. The teacher provides a portal to opportunities and serves as a facilitator and advocate for the student, removing obstacles and inspiring the student to reach for more than is in the classroom.

Now more than ever, it is critical that we develop the skills of our strongest students. To a greater extent than ever before was possible, technology allows us to leverage the efforts of a few for the benefit of many. By helping our best students, we help ourselves, because they hold in their hands not only their own futures but our shared future, as well.

Print Resources Cited

Angel, Allen R., Christine D. Abbott, and Dennis C. Runde. *A Survey of Mathematics with Applications*. New York: Addison-Wesley, 2008.

Burger, Edward, and Michael Starbird. *The Heart of Mathematics*. New York: Wiley, 2009.

Crawford, Mathew. *Introduction to Number Theory*. Alpine, Calif.: AoPS, 2006.

Dunham, William. *Journey through Genius: The Great Theorems of Mathematics*. New York: Penguin, 1991.

Faires, J. Douglas. *First Steps for Math Olympians: Using the American Mathematics Competitions*. Washington, D.C.: Mathematical Association of America, 2006.

Fomin, Dmitri, Sergey Genkin, and Ilia Itenberg. *Mathematical Circles (Russian Experience)*. Translated by Mark Saul. Providence, R.I.: American Mathematical Society, 1996.

Gelfand, I. M., and Alexander Shen. *Algebra*. Boston: Birkhäuser, 2003.

Hadamard, Jacques. *Lessons in Elementary Geometry*. Providence, R.I.: American Mathematical Society, 2009.

Jacobs, Harold R. *Geometry*. New York: W.H. Freeman & Company, 1987.

Kiselev, A. P. *Kiselev's Geometry, Book 1: Planimetry*. Adapted from Russian by Alexander Givental. El Cerrito, Calif.: Sumizdat, 2006.

Lehoczky, Sandor, and Richard Rusczyk. *Art of Problem Solving, Volume 1: The Basics*. 7th ed. Art of Problem Solving Introduction Series. Alpine, Calif.: AoPS, 2006.

Lenchner, George. *Creative Problem Solving in School Mathematics*. 2nd ed. New York: Mathematical Olympiads, 2007.

Patrick, David. *Introduction to Counting and Probability*. Alpine, Calif.: AoPS, 2005.

———. *Intermediate Counting and Probability*. Alpine, Calif.: AoPS, 2007.

Rusczyk, Richard. *Introduction to Algebra*. Alpine, Calif.: AoPS, 2008.

———. *Introduction to Geometry*. Alpine, Calif.: AoPS, 2009.

Rusczyk, Richard, and Mathew Crawford. *Intermediate Algebra*. Alpine, Calif.: AoPS, 2007.

Sautoy, Marcus du. *Music of the Primes: Why an Unsolved Problem in Mathematics Matters*. New York: Harper Perennial, 2004.

Singh, Simon. *Fermat's Enigma: The Epic Quest to Solve the World's Greatest Mathematical Problem*. New York: Anchor, 1998.

Tanton, James. *Solve This: Math Activities for Students and Clubs*. Washington, D.C.: Mathematical Association of America, 2001.

CHAPTER

6

Articulation

Janet Lynne Tassell, Rebecca Ruth Stobaugh,
Beth Duvall Fleming, and Chloe R. Harper

◆ Purposeful interconnection among levels of instruction is essential to the successful educational experience of mathematically promising students.

◆ Close coordination is required among elementary, middle, and high schools to guard against gaps or overlaps in the mathematics curriculum.

◆ Curricular articulation extends beyond local curriculum alignment and involves district, state, and national standards.

◆ Academic advisers must understand the unique cognitive and social needs of gifted students.

In education, *articulation* refers to the connectedness of curriculum from one section to another. An articulated mathematics curriculum is one that has been consistently and systematically examined for gaps and redundancies in the mathematical knowledge, skills, and relationships that it communicates to students, to ensure that all students make continuous progress and smooth transitions from first grade through graduation.

Articulation is closely linked to the selection of standards for education, an activity to which a number of groups have recently turned their attention. Standards can guide articulation, but simply writing down a list of standards, for whatever level, does not accomplish articulation. Reciprocally, the need for articulation can serve as a guide for writing standards. Common standards give teachers "focus, direction, and priority—making sharing natural and productive" (Schmoker 2001, p. 88). Schmoker found that these common standards act as an "instructional insurance" to promote high expectations and collaboration among teachers to reach those levels. Others have also noted this effect: "A common, coherent, and challenging curriculum can transform mathematics education in the United States" (Schmidt 2004, p. 6).

This chapter provides a review of the literature and discusses issues related to articulation of the middle school mathematics curriculum at the classroom, building, district, and national levels. Within these broad areas, the chapter addresses issues of curriculum, pedagogy, and policy.

Classroom-Level Articulation

Consider the comments of a middle school mathematics teacher:

> Allie and Dan both entered middle school at the sixth-grade level, having already mastered sixth-, seventh-, and eighth- grade concepts. One option was to accelerate both students to seventh-grade prealgebra. Both students possessed the academic ability and had already acquired the needed mathematical skills to be successful in the seventh-grade class. Allie's parents chose not to accelerate her, as Allie expressed a desire to remain in mathematics classes with her current peers. Allie progressed through the middle school mathematics curriculum with numerous opportunities for enrichment activities. Dan was accelerated to prealgebra in the seventh grade, took algebra 1 as an eighth grader, and studied geometry through independent study in a virtual schools program. Both students had comparable scores on various standardized tests at the end of middle school.

Middle school students enter the mathematics classroom with a wide array of talents, as well as a wide range of growth rates in cognitive, physical, emotional, and social areas. In constructing a mathematics program that will meet the needs of students in middle school, a frequent misunderstanding, as Assouline and Lupkowski-Shoplik (2005) observe, is that "gifted students respond equally well to the same curriculum" (p. 5). As the example above demonstrates, the best mathematics program for one gifted student may be totally different from the best program for another.

Meeting the needs of diverse learners is a task that teachers face daily with all students—not just gifted students. In examining this process, educators have pointed out a number of issues that have particular importance in working with gifted students. Assouline and Lupkowski-Shoplik (2005) indicate the necessity of making good choices in the selection of educational settings, which include enrichment in the regular classroom, ability grouping, individualized instruction, and single-subject acceleration. These researchers also highlight the importance of the selection of curricula and materials, of getting away from a "random assortment of enrichment topics" (p. xxi) and moving toward studying a core curriculum in a systematic manner.

Part of the challenge of articulation is the debate about acceleration versus enrichment. Both have merits, and both have drawbacks. Stanley (1979) describes four forms of enrichment: busywork, irrelevant academic enrichment, cultural enrichment, and relevant academic enrichment. The last, of course, is the most appropriate for gifted students. Any program of enrichment should include a constant review of both the depth of cognitive complexity and the relevance of the work presented to students. The enrichment approach, as Sheffield (1999) points out, should include a close look at mathematics, giving students the opportunity to develop an understanding of the beauty of mathematics through a deep exploration of the content.

Acceleration must also be implemented correctly and can take many forms. *A Nation Deceived* (Colangelo, Assouline, and Gross 2004) describes eighteen types of acceleration. Badly articulated, acceleration may skip over vital topics or treat them superficially. Thoughtful articulation is a key to appropriate implementation of acceleration. For example, students may enter kindergarten early, skip grades, or receive credit by examination (Assouline and Lupkowski-Shoplik 2005). All these forms of acceleration, and others, have produced remarkable, well-documented gains.

Middle schools often attempt to meet the needs of gifted math students by simply placing them in an existing advanced course. But often, more is needed: courses designed for average students have to be adjusted to the needs of the gifted students placed in them. Typically, mathematically gifted students can learn mathematics faster and at a deeper level than others. This faster pace is not detrimental to their learning. Thus, *Foundations for Success* (National Mathematics Advisory Panel 2008) recommended that mathematically gifted students be allowed to proceed through the curriculum at a much faster rate.

Both acceleration and enrichment introduce problems in articulation. For example, students often move from school to school, even on the same grade level. In such situations, the risk for gifted students whose learning has been enriched or accelerated is that they may be placed in classes where they learn nothing new. An accelerated or enriched environment in one school may not be parallel to the environment in another. Schools need to develop reliable mechanisms for assessing a student's level of achievement, interest, and potential for future growth. Similar problems occur as students move into middle school from elementary school and into high school from middle school.

Students must possess an in-depth knowledge rather than a shallow understanding of fundamental concepts to master high school honors mathematics classes. Selections of classroom materials for advanced middle school mathematics classes should take into account critical thinking, enrichment activities, and technological extensions that provide deeper learning opportunities than fast-paced, textbook-driven units of study (Rothery 2008).

Several researchers have pointed out that acceleration "versus" enrichment is in fact a false dichotomy. Like Stanley (1979), Shriever and Maker (1997) found that each is more effective when used in combination with the other than when implemented on its own. As Assouline and Lupkowski-Shoplik (2005) state, "By definition, relevant enrichment in mathematics must have some acceleration and appropriate acceleration will have an enrichment component" (p. 185).

School-Level Articulation

A college student who is a preservice middle school mathematics teacher describes the following experience in learning mathematics:

> My mathematics education has been a roller coaster of experiences over the years. It began somewhat smoothly in elementary school. I excelled at mathematics and was always looking to be challenged in the subject. When the time came for students to be tested for the "Gifted and Talented Program," my inadequate reading abilities at the time kept me out. I was placed in the average math classes, learning material which seemed basic and simple. So, I was not nearly as prepared for the advanced math courses in middle school as I should have been. With a little hard work I caught up with the other students who had entered the Gifted and Talented Program. Not until my eighth-grade year would I really be challenged again.

Assouline and Lupkowski-Shoplik (2005) explain that some erroneously believe that "mathematically talented students cannot be identified until high school" (p. 10). In fact, some students show talent as early as the beginning of kindergarten. Screening can identify students early so that they quickly become part of the mathematically gifted pool. If learning is denied them, students can lose their hunger to learn. Worse, problems in articulation, such as those described in the vignette above, can postpone the identification of gifted students. Indeed, since students develop at different rates and times, it is appropriate to consider identification as an ongoing process: schools must be ready to identify gifted students at many different times during their academic careers.

But the vignette also points out another issue: mathematically gifted students may be overlooked because of a mismatch of their talents and the measures used. Poor performance on a test dependent on "reading skills" may mask a gift for mathematics. Similarly, students gifted in mathematics may not always have strong and speedy computation skills, and a test dependent on such skills may not reveal a student's gifts.

Another myth about gifted students is "early ripe, early rot" (Assouline and Lupkowski-Shoplik 2005, p. 3)—that is, the notion that students who are identified and supported early will "burn out." In fact, a number of studies (Benbow and Lubinski 1996; Benbow and Stanley 1983) reveal that students who are discovered to be talented at an early age can and do continue to achieve in adulthood if provided with appropriate educational opportunities.

A middle school principal indicates some of the complex issues that schools consider in accelerating students in mathematics:

> One area of contention is whether too many students are taking algebra and whether to use testing to tighten the limits on how many could take the course. If those numbers were reduced, how would that affect our team structure? If algebra weren't offered by both teams, it would make one team have most of the higher-ability students. For accelerated students ready for geometry, an easier accommodation was to have advanced students go to the high school for this class.

Many educators now advocate algebra in the middle school. Some argue that this move should be made for all students, although others think it should be limited to those of high ability. School structures affect this decision. High schools that have schedules with five or more periods a day (rather than block schedules) sometimes offer fewer opportunities to take above-level mathematics classes. This can create an articulation problem for students entering with advanced work. Also, if gifted students have not been accelerated into algebra in middle school, the only way to accelerate them in high school may be to teach them algebra and geometry in the same year. Offering these students algebra in middle school can avoid this awkward situation.

Principles and Standards for School Mathematics (NCTM 2000) advocates a focus on algebra and geometry in the middle grades, with the goal of providing a strong foundation in algebraic and geometric concepts by the end of eighth grade. Middle-grades students should experience a rich curriculum that integrates geometry and algebra instead of presenting them as separate entities to be learned in single courses.

NCTM outlines a comprehensive, well-articulated mathematics program for middle school in *Curriculum Focal Points for Prekindergarten through Grade 8 Mathematics: A Quest for Coherence* (NCTM 2006, p. 10):

> Those who are involved in curriculum planning for grades 6–8 should note that this set of curriculum focal points has been designed with the intention of providing a three-year middle school program that includes a full year of general mathematics in each of grades 6, 7, and 8. Those whose programs offer an algebra course in grade 8 (or earlier) should consider including the curriculum focal points that this framework calls for in grade 8 in grade 6 or grade 7. Alternatively, these topics could be incorporated into the high school program. Either way, curricula would not omit the important content that the grade 7 and grade 8 focal points offer students in preparation for algebra and for their long-term mathematical knowledge.

Foundations for Success (National Mathematics Advisory Panel 2008) gives a stronger recommendation, advocating that algebra be studied in grade 8 at the latest (p. 16, table 1). Useful lists in this report include "Critical Foundations of Algebra" (p. 17) and "Benchmarks for the Critical Foundations" (p. 20, table 2).

The middle school landscape is varied: some schools include algebra for all students, although others offer it only to those who are gifted. These differences in program create problems in articulation when students enter high school.

Still more variation occurs in this landscape: "There is a debate about how to fit algebra into the overall middle-grades curriculum. It is important to be thoughtful about what we mean by 'algebra' and what algebra instruction should look like in the middle grades," (Goldsmith and Kantrov 2001, p. 44). *Foundations for Success,* among other sources, recommends the integrated approach, in which instruction in algebra is spread among the three years of middle school mathematics. According to the Trends in International Mathematics and Science Study (TIMSS 2008), most high-achieving countries use an integrated approach, in high school as well as middle school. *Principles and Standards for School Mathematics* gives the following advice:

> Students' understanding of foundational algebraic and geometric ideas should be developed through extended experience over all three years in the middle grades and across a broad range of mathematics content, including statistics, number, and measurement. How these ideas are packaged into courses and what names are given to the resulting arrangement are far less important than ensuring that students have opportunities to see and understand the connections among related ideas. This approach is a challenging alternative to the practice of offering a select group of middle-grades students a one-year course that focuses narrowly on algebra or geometry. All middle-grades students will benefit from a rich and integrated treatment of mathematics content. Instruction that segregates the content of algebra or geometry from that of other areas is educationally unwise and mathematically counterproductive. (NCTM 2000, p. 213)

However algebraic instruction is delivered, its inclusion in middle school mathematics raises yet another issue in articulation: should middle school teachers use high school curricula and assessments? Or is another approach more developmentally appropriate for middle school students? And are approaches that are appropriate for gifted middle school students different from those that are suited to the general population? If other approaches are used besides those that the high school uses or expects, how are the curricula articulated?

Counseling Issues Related to Articulation: Meeting the Individual Needs of Exceptional Learners

A middle school counselor offers the following perspective on the counselor's role in ensuring articulation:

> Many middle schools offer advanced math classes. Prealgebra may be offered to mathematically superior sixth- and seventh-grade students. Algebra 1 is often offered for high school credit to eighth-grade students. Some middle school students have a distinct plan for their future, while most have yet to determine a realistic career path. Gifted and talented students often crave career guidance and enjoy counseling sessions related to college and career planning. Students flourish academically when they see a connection between the work they are doing and their future plans.
>
> Middle school counselors play a key role in assisting students in the high school registration process. A freshman student's class selections may determine the path for their entire high school program. Parents sometimes push students to take all honors classes and speed through the math program at a rapid pace, when that student may actually learn more if courses are not taken so quickly. As a ninth-grade counselor, [I see that] many of my students' parents want their children to remain in honors classes, even if they are not performing well.
>
> As a school counselor, I monitor the grades and progress of gifted students, as well as struggling students. Parents of middle school students often have less communication with teachers and are unaware when their gifted students are not reaching their full potential. Parents sometimes advocate for a mathematics program to allow their child to accelerate, with no concern about depth of understanding. Counselors should be more concerned about finding that class for the student that propels him or her toward mathematical success, rather than towards course completion.

Counseling is a key mechanism for articulation. Assouline and Lupkowski-Shoplik (2005, p. 175) suggest steps for finding the "optimal match":

Step 1: Assess academic abilities and achievements.

Step 2: Choose the general grade level of curriculum for further assessment of specific knowledge.

Step 3: Offer curriculum-based assessment using chapter tests and pretests.

Step 4: Place the student in the appropriate level of the curriculum for instruction.

Step 5: Reassess—is the student being challenged but not overly frustrated?

These steps allow parents and students to be involved in the decision-making process.

A middle school counselor remarks on the social and emotional issues facing gifted middle school students:

> Middle school teachers must address the emotional needs of gifted students. Middle school students face numerous insecurities, and a supportive classroom environment celebrating success and discovery motivates students to learn. Most middle school students fear being singled out in class, and some gifted students do not want to appear different. Differentiation of instruction must be done in a manner that respects both the students' social and academic needs.
>
> Meeting the needs of middle school gifted and talented students is challenging both for teachers and counselors. Gifted students often begin middle school eager and motivated, looking for opportunities to showcase their abilities. As the social scene emerges, middle school students often develop a strong desire to fit in and blend with the crowd.

Blackwell, Trzesniewski, and Dweck (2007) have shown how counseling can help students who are experiencing high levels of difficulty understand the developmental period through which they are passing. Lowenthal, Thurnher, and Chiriboga (1975) found that 40 percent of their respondents rated adolescence as the "worst time of life."

Middle school is a critical point in a child's development, when problems emerge that are rarely experienced earlier. Younger children may be well behaved, have good self-esteem, and generally do well in school. Yet, when they go through adolescence, a decline in their self-esteem can affect behavior, grades, and general engagement in school life (Eccles 2004; Harter 1998; Simmons and Blyth 1987; Watt 2004; Wigfield et al. 1991; Wigfield, Eccles, and Pintrich 1996). Elder (1968) thinks of entering seventh or eighth grade as a formal rite of passage in American society. Some students never recover from this difficult time (Eccles, Lord, and Midgley 1991; Gutman and Midgley 2000; Midgley, Feldlaufer, and Eccles 1989; Wigfield, Eccles, and Pintrich 1996). Students making this transition often need emotional as well as intellectual support.

There is a special pitfall in work with gifted students. Sometimes these students perform at a high level academically, even in an enriched or accelerated environment. Yet, their performance sometimes comes at an emotional cost that teachers, counselors, and administrators may not detect. The social and emotional needs of gifted students can be masked by their academic success. As articulated by Assouline and Colangelo (2006), "Academic gifts tend to be unrecognized as an important characteristic in the typical teenage environment in America. The challenge to the individual adolescent, therefore, is integrating intellectual integrity within the teenage environment so that 'membership' to this dubious group can be realized. This is a monumental task" (p. 66).

A middle school counselor makes the following points about the struggle of adolescents to find themselves academically:

> Gifted middle school students can be polar opposites: Some students are excessively concerned and emotional about grades and learning, while others lack the focus and motivation to perform well on a daily basis. As a counselor, I help students overcome anxiety and face fears of not achieving perfection. Some students identified as gifted in elementary school falter in middle school for various reasons, and counselors must provide support to help these students regain academic success. Disadvantaged students and underachieving students may need additional interventions. Other students shine in middle school and are identified as gifted for the first time. Counselors must carefully analyze student test scores and compare those scores to students' actual classroom performance.

In other words, counselors can play a major role in identifying, as well as nurturing, gifted students.

The need to weigh a student's social adjustment against an accelerated placement for the student is the focus of the following middle school counselor's comments:

> Careful consideration must be taken when accelerating students to higher grade level mathematics classes, and teachers must be aware of social adjustment issues. Occasionally parents wish for the child to be accelerated, while the student wishes to remain with grade-level peers. Parents, teachers, and students must all be involved for acceleration to be successful. At the same time, teachers should respect students' desires to fit in socially and refrain from drawing excessive attention to giftedness.

Elementary school is typically a supportive and student-centered environment. Therefore, some students' problems may not be apparent at this level. When these same children proceed to middle school, however, they are often not given the same amount of support. Furthermore, in many middle schools, students find an increase in academic challenge along with a decrease in support (Blackwell, Trzesniewski, and Dweck 2007). In other schools, the imbalance is reversed: the school focuses on the social and emotional development of the student and neglects the academic challenge. In any level of schooling, these two goals should reinforce, rather than compete with, each other. The National Middle School Association and the National Association for Gifted Children (2005) have developed a joint position paper on this topic.

Approaches to Achieving Articulation within a Middle School

Consider the comments of a middle school principal about collaborative instructional planning at the school:

> Collaborative teamwork among our teachers seems to result in improved school test scores. Teachers collaboratively designed curriculum maps, assessments, and lesson plans. Unit tests included several curriculum items from previous tests focusing on particular areas of difficulty to reinforce these concepts. They tracked data and celebrated the success of students meeting the established goals. I enjoyed wearing a "Pi" shirt for Pi Day and receiving a pie in my face.

For any educational program to succeed, teachers must "buy into" it. For some teachers, this may mean exercising their "academic freedom" to try out their own ideas. For others, it may mean participating in a group that chooses and differentiates the curriculum. School principals must be aware of the benefits and drawbacks of each approach—and all approaches between these extremes. Again, the challenges are greater in dealing with gifted students, since the variety of instructional activities may be greater than in regular classes.

District-Level Articulation

A middle school principal describes improvement in articulation from the school's feeder elementary schools:

> As a middle school principal, I felt that mathematics must be a priority at our school. Initially the five feeder schools lacked common agreement on what was to be taught at each grade level. However, as the years progressed, the state department began to delineate math standards for each grade level, and the district made efforts to create a common curriculum map and adopt common resources.

Vertical and horizontal articulation of standards has been a challenge across the nation. With the decentralization of education decision making in many states, decisions about curriculum are often made in local schools. Schools that are separated by only a few miles often have different expectations or provide different learning opportunities. Kher and colleagues (2007) revealed clear differences among classes with the same title.

Some districts make formal efforts to communicate expectations at each level. Scope and sequence charts outlining content taught in each grade level help ensure the building of concepts over time. Some districts articulate standards through common curriculum maps, common formative and summative assessments, or banks of suggested lesson plans. When these items are benchmarked to standards, schools can develop coherence, ensure accountability, and improve the program.

This situation has particular meaning for gifted students. Whether curriculum for these students is enriched or accelerated—or both—it is likely to be more varied than that for general students. Teachers are likely to choose more unusual activities. Two gifted classrooms are less likely to resemble each other than two classrooms serving average students. Instruments of articulation must be carefully tailored to the nature of the classroom, allowing teachers the freedom to match the talents of the students in the class to the chosen learning activities.

The challenge of shaping gifted instruction to ensure articulation is the focus of the following comments from a middle school principal:

> When considering the educational programming for mathematically talented students, I found it challenging to design a program that all stakeholders could consistently believe in from elementary to middle school. Teachers at the elementary level tend to be overly concerned about the computational fluency, more so than creating students that can problem solve and reason. With the understanding that we are, right now, teaching students for jobs that do not yet exist, I believe that we want students who can think!

In *Foundations for Success* (National Mathematics Advisory Panel 2008), some emerging themes provide guidance on the importance of articulation. First and foremost is the finding that all levels, pre-K–grade 8, need to have a streamlined mathematics curriculum, and the early elementary grades should emphasize clearly defined topics. Of the important themes in the report, the following need to be recognized:

1. Students need a strong start.

2. Conceptual understanding, procedural fluency, and automaticity of facts need to be part of the balanced mathematics curriculum.

3. Effort along with talent "counts" in achievement.

Articulation from Middle School to High School

Consider the perspective of a middle school principal:

> I often have to help teachers grapple with the question of whether they should move on to the next topic despite clear assessment data stating that students did not understand the previous concept. The teacher typically feels pressure to cover a list of topics. Some other schools would cover certain areas of math at each grade level and go into depth with these areas and skip other content in the standards, leaving it for other grade levels to address. I was not brave enough as a principal to skip these standards and risk a drop in test scores. Perhaps that is what I should have advised. But what if the topic omitted is critical to success in high school?

Schmidt, Wang, and McKnight (2005) confirm the observation that mathematics courses cover more topics at each grade level in the United States than in many other high-performing countries. On the basis of the TIMSS report, Schmidt and colleagues (1999) comment that U.S. standards are dispersed over many topics and lack rigor when judged by international standards. In an articulated program, content standards are learned at a basic level, and deeper understanding evolves. For gifted students, it is critical that topics continue to be treated in greater depth, without monotonous repetition.

The "mile wide and an inch deep" phenomenon raises another problem in articulation involving gifted students. If accelerated—even at a completely appropriate rate—some students collect four years of high school credit very early—even by the time when they enter high school. What mathematics will these students take? Sometimes, a careful probing of the problem reveals a flaw in the acceleration: students have been pushed through the curriculum, passing standardized tests, but lack a deep understanding of the content. When such students face more rigorous high school mathematics classes, they may lose their motivation to persevere with confidence in their own abilities (Rothery 2008).

At other times, however, students have been appropriately accelerated, and they seemingly "run out" of mathematics to take. Worse, they opt out of taking mathematics once they have finished the required sequence of courses. Although this is a high school problem, it can be anticipated in middle school. Counselors or administrators can then confer with their high school colleagues to decide how such a student will be served.

It is perhaps important to point out that this last situation may arise for a tiny number of students in any single year. It is easy for administrators to overlook such students. But these students are perhaps the most likely members of the cohort to make momentous contributions in the future. Administrators must be aware of this fact, which can put into perspective the inconvenience that such students cause for the school.

Articulation of Teacher Education and Preparation

A professor whose area of study is gifted mathematics education offers the following remarks on teacher preparation:

> Often, the top middle-grades math students are taught by teachers who do not have middle-grades or secondary math certification. They may be certified in the area of gifted education, or in general elementary education. This situation has many implications for articulation. In many states, it prevents schools from offering high school credit for these math courses. Since these are our very best students, this course should be at a much deeper, richer level than the corresponding high school course.

Students who take algebra in the middle school must not be forced to take it again in the high school because of a discrepancy in teacher credentials. This problem can be avoided with foresight.

But there is a larger issue here. We need knowledgeable teachers in all our classrooms, and this presents a challenge in all areas and at all levels. Gifted students in the middle school need teachers who know the deeper implications of beginning algebra or intuitive geometry. Mathematicians can play a role in meeting this need. More cooperation is called for between schools of education, which prepare teachers, and college and university departments of mathematics. Mathematicians on the college level can distinguish core themes, even in elementary mathematics, that lead to profound insights later on. The tradition of examining "elementary mathematics from an advanced standpoint" (see Klein [1932]) needs continued development.

Beyond the Pre-K–12 Scope: National Articulation Concerns

A college student who is a preservice middle school mathematics teacher shares a personal experience with learning gaps resulting from a move from one school to another:

> A little over a month into the school year, my family and I relocated out of state. This new area not only had different curriculum, but also a different academic calendar. It was the end of the first semester at this school, and I was very behind in the algebra 1 course that I was enrolled in. The class had just covered the topic of trigonometry and was moving on to a new chapter. Although this hindered me at the time, I would later grasp this concept with help from peers and teachers.

Without a national curriculum, states vary widely in performance, their learning expectations are moving targets, and gaps readily occur. This is no longer acceptable as leaders in the United States recognize the need for education to be more unified.

Currently, as a result of the kinds of problems that the vignette above illustrates, the Common Core Standards Initiative (Council of Chief State School Officers 2009) is formulating a common set of standards for participating states. Recommendations to ensure quality and rigor are offered by the ACT College Readiness Benchmarks (ACT 2007). One concern is that too many students taking the "core" curriculum are still unprepared for the first-year demands of college-level coursework. Of those students surveyed who took mathematics courses beyond the recommended core curriculum, 59 percent did better in mathematics than those who did not. Of students who did not take a substantial number of additional courses, no more than 75 percent were ready for the first year of college. Even though higher percentages of students are meeting the College Readiness Benchmarks and taking the recommended core curriculum, no more than 75 percent are ready for the mathematical rigor of first-year college courses.

A coordinator of gifted and talented programs describes the challenges of simultaneously accelerating students, articulating their math programs, and keeping them interested:

> A concern that some of our district's teachers had is that the school would run out of courses if the students advanced too quickly. This was a valid concern in that we needed to be mindful that the courses contained depth and that we were aware of the students' futures. The goal is not to "get the mathematics out of the way" but rather to get these mathematically talented students in courses for learning more mathematics *and* keep them in the pipeline.

The coordinator's comments relate to middle and high school, but they also apply to other levels of education. Bressoud (2009) found that most students studying calculus in high school do not receive college credit for the course. Although the number of students taking calculus in high school is increasing, there is no similar increase in the number taking calculus for college credit. Furthermore, the number of students enrolled in calculus in college has been the same for the past 25 years. Growth is occurring in calculus enrollment at research universities, which often include schools of engineering. At other universities, enrollment is declining.

Worse, students are opting out of advanced mathematics courses in college, having fulfilled their mathematics requirements with a credit in calculus. Preparation for calculus is often cited as one reason to accelerate students in middle school. But does this strategy help students progress toward a career in scientific or mathematical fields? To answer this question, we must go beneath the surface of middle school education and raise deeper questions about its relationship to preparation for STEM careers. Mathematics education is at a turning point. Society is no longer going to accept poor mathematics achievement. According to the RAND Mathematics Study Panel (2003), "every student now needs competency in mathematics" (p. 2). This goal is essential, since education, career, and financial opportunities are directly correlated to mathematics achievement (Checkley 2006, pp. 5, 10–11).

If high school graduates complete higher-level mathematics courses, they are more likely to earn a bachelor's degree:

- Of students who complete algebra 1, 8 percent will earn a bachelor's degree by age 30. Of those who complete calculus in high school, 80 percent will earn a bachelor's degree by age 30. (Adelman 1999)

- Of students who earn two or more credits of algebra 2 or higher mathematics, more than half will earn more than $40,000 a year. (Carnevale and Desrochers 2002)

- High school graduates who have taken one extra course in algebra or geometry will enjoy 6.3 percent higher earnings in their lives. (Rose and Betts 2001)

Thus, mathematics opens up career paths. However, Silver and Strong (2003) note a problem: the longer students are in school, the less they trust their own mathematical ability. These researchers found that 75 percent of all students graduating from high school do not believe that they have the gifts to handle higher-level mathematics. This finding presents us with a challenge: we must stop turning out "math-haters" but instead nurture a culture of "math-lovers."

Conclusion

As the name indicates, "middle school" serves students at a crossroads in their lives. At every level of a student's learning, educators must look back at what the student has accomplished as well as forward to what the student can achieve. By middle school, most (but not all) gifted students have been identified, and the question is how to engage them in mathematics, optimize their learning opportunities, and serve them best.

The problem should not be seen as a matter of fitting the student to the school, but rather of using the school's resources to the advantage of the student. Every student should learn something new in school every day. Ensuring that this happens is a challenge that teachers, administrators, and parents must face together. The solution must include articulation of the middle school experience with elementary, high school, and college-level education, and even with teacher professional development.

Our country is on the brink of making some important decisions about mathematics education programs. We will need to invest the same effort that we currently invest in crafting programs for individual students on behalf of the nation as a whole. This is articulation.

References

ACT. *Rigor at Risk: Reaffirming Quality in the High School Core Curriculum*. 2007. http://www.act.org/research/policymakers/pdf/rigor_summary.pdf.

Adelman, Clifford. *Answers in the Tool Box: Academic Intensity, Attendance Patterns, and Bachelor's Degree Attainment*. Washington, D.C.: U.S. Department of Education, 1999.

Assouline, Susan G., and Nicholas Colangelo. "Social-Emotional Development of Gifted Adolescents." In *The Handbook of Secondary Gifted Education*, edited by Felicia A. Dixon and Sidney M. Moon, pp. 65–82. Waco, Tex.: Prufrock Press, 2006.

Assouline, Susan, and Ann Lupkowski-Shoplik. *Developing Math Talent: A Guide for Educating Gifted and Advanced Learners in Math.* Waco, Tex.: Prufrock Press, 2005.

Benbow, Camilla P., and David Lubinski, eds. *Intellectual Talent: Psychometric and Social Issues.* Baltimore: Johns Hopkins Press, 1996.

Benbow, Camilla P., and Julian C. Stanley. *Academic Precocity: Aspects of Its Development.* Baltimore: Johns Hopkins Press, 1983.

Blackwell, Lisa S., Kali H. Trzesniewski, and Carol Sorich Dweck. "Implicit Theories of Intelligence Predict Achievement across an Adolescent Transition: A Longitudinal Study and an Intervention." *Child Development* 78 (2007): 246–63.

Bressoud, David M. "Is the Sky Still Falling?" *Notices of the AMS* 56 (2009): 20–25.

Carnevale, Anthony P., and Donna M. Desrochers. *Connecting Education Standards and Employment: Course-Taking Patterns of Young Workers.* Washington, D.C.: Achieve/American Diploma Project, 2002.

Checkley, Kathy. *Priorities in Practice: The Essentials of Mathematics, K–6.* Alexandria, Va.: ASCD, 2006.

Colangelo, Nicholas, Susan G. Assouline, and Miraca U. M. Gross, eds. *A Nation Deceived: How Schools Hold Back America's Brightest Students.* Iowa City, Iowa: The Connie Belin and Jacqueline N. Blank International Center for Gifted Education and Talent Development, 2004.

Council of Chief State School Officers (CCSSO). "Common Core Standards Initiative." 2009. http://www.ccsso.org/federal_programs/13286.cfm.

Eccles, Jacquelynne S. "Schools, Academic Motivation, and Stage-Environment Fit." *In Handbook of Adolescent Psychology,* edited by Richard M. Lerner and Laurence D. Steinberg, 2nd ed., pp. 125–53. New York: Wiley, 2004.

Eccles, Jacquelynne S., Sarah Lord, and Carol Midgley. "What Are We Doing to Adolescents? The Impact of Educational Contexts on Early Adolescents." *American Journal of Education* 99 (1991): 521–42.

Elder, Glen H. *Adolescent Socialization and Personality Development.* Oxford, UK: Rand McNally, 1968.

Goldsmith, Lynn T., and Ilene Kantrov. *Guiding Curriculum Decisions for Middle-Grades Mathematics.* Portsmouth, N.H.: Heinemann, 2001.

Gutman, Leslie Morrison, and Carol Midgley. "The Role of Protective Factors in Supporting the Academic Achievement of Poor African American Students during the Middle School Transition." *Journal of Youth and Adolescence* 29 (2000): 223–48.

Harter, Susan. "The Development of Self-Representations." In *Handbook of Child Psychology,* vol. 3, edited by William Damon and Nancy Eisenberg, 5th ed., pp. 553–617. New York: Wiley, 1998.

Kher, Neelam, William H. Schmidt, Richard T. Houang, and Z. Zou. "High School Mathematics Trajectories: Connecting Opportunities to Learn with Student Performance." Paper presented at the annual meeting of the American Educational Research Association, Chicago, April 9–13, 2007.

Klein, Felix. *Elementary Mathematics from an Advanced Standpoint: Arithmetic, Algebra, Analysis.* Translated by E. R. Hedrick and C. A. Noble. Reprint of the 1932 translation. Mineola, N.Y.: Dover Publications, 2004.

Lowenthal, Marjorie Fisk, Majda Thurnher, and David Chiriboga. *Four Stages of Life.* San Francisco: Jossey-Bass, 1975.

Midgley, Carol, Harriet Feldlaufer, and Jacquelynne S. Eccles. "Student/Teacher Relations and Attitudes toward Mathematics before and after the Transition to Junior High School." *Child Development* 60 (1989): 981–92.

National Council of Teachers of Mathematics (NCTM). *Principles and Standards for School Mathematics.* Reston, Va.: NCTM, 2000.

———. *Curriculum Focal Points for Prekindergarten through Grade 8 Mathematics: A Quest for Coherence.* Reston, Va.: NCTM, 2006.

National Mathematics Advisory Panel. *Foundations for Success: The Final Report of the National Mathematics Advisory Panel.* Washington, D.C.: U.S. Department of Education, 2008.

National Middle School Association (NMSA) and National Association for Gifted Children (NAGC). Meeting the Needs of High-Ability and High-Potential Learners in the Middle Grades. NMSA and NAGC joint position statement. 2005. http://www.nmsa .org/AboutNMSA/PositionStatements/tabid/84/Default.aspx.

RAND Mathematics Study Panel. "Mathematical Proficiency for All Students: Toward a Strategic Research and Development Program in Mathematics Education." Santa Monica, Calif.: RAND, 2003. http://www.rand.org/pubs/monograph_reports/ MR1643.

Rose, Heather, and Julian Betts. *Math Matters: The Link between High School Curriculum, College Graduation, and Earnings.* San Francisco: Public Policy Institute of California, 2001.

Rothery, Thomas G. "High School Mathematics: Why the Rush?" *Mathematics Teacher* 102, no. 5 (2008): 324–25.

Schmidt, William H. "A Vision for Mathematics." *Educational Leadership* 61, no. 5 (2004): 6–11.

Schmidt, William H., Curtis C. McKnight, Leland S. Cogan, Pamela M. Jakwerth, and Richard T. Houang. *Facing the Consequences: Using TIMSS for a Closer Look at U.S. Mathematics and Science Education.* Dordrecht, The Netherlands: Kluwer, 1999.

Schmidt, William H., Hsing Chi Wang, and Curtis C. McKnight. "Curriculum Coherence: An Examination of U.S. Mathematics and Science Content Standards from an International Perspective." *Journal of Curriculum Studies* 37, no. 5 (2005): 525–59.

Schmoker, Mike. *The Results Fieldbook.* Alexandria, Va.: ASCD, 2001.

Schriever, S. W., and C. J. Maker. "Enrichment and Acceleration: An Overview and New Directions." In *Handbook of Gifted Education*, edited by Nicholas Colangelo and G. A. Davis, pp. 113–25. Boston: Allyn & Bacon, 1997.

Sheffield, Linda Jensen. "Serving the Needs of the Mathematically Promising." *In Developing Mathematically Promising Students,* edited by Linda Jensen Sheffield, pp. 43–55. Reston, Va.: National Council of Teachers of Mathematics, 1999.

Silver, Harvey, and Richard Strong. *Strategies for Teaching Middle School Mathematics.* Ho Ho Kus, N.J.: Thoughtful Education Press, 2003.

Simmons, Roberta G., and Dale A. Blyth. *Moving into Adolescence: The Impact of Pubertal Change and School Context.* Hawthorne, N.Y.: Aldine de Gruyter, 1987.

Stanley, Julian. "Identifying and Nurturing the Intellectually Gifted." In *Educating the Gifted: Acceleration and Enrichment,* edited by W. C. George, S. J. Cohn, and Julian C. Stanley, pp. 172–80. Baltimore: Johns Hopkins University Press, 1979.

Trends in International Mathematics and Science Study (TIMSS). "TIMSS 2007 Results." Washington, D.C.: National Center for Education Statistics, U.S. Department of Education, 2008. http://nces.ed.gov/pubs2009/2009001.pdf.

Watt, Helen M. G. "Development of Adolescents' Self-Perceptions, Values, and Task Perceptions according to Gender and Domain in 7th through 11th-Grade Australian Students." *Child Development* 75 (2004): 1556–74.

Wigfield, Allan, Jacquelynne S. Eccles, Douglas J. MacIver, David Reuman, and Carol Midgley. "Transitions at Early Adolescence: Changes in Children's Domain-Specific Self-Perceptions and General Self-Esteem across the Transition to Junior High School." *Developmental Psychology* 27 (1991): 552–65.

Wigfield, Allan, Jacquelynne S. Eccles, and Paul Pintrich. "Development between the Ages of 11 and 25." In *Handbook of Educational Psychology,* edited by David Berliner and R. Calfee, pp. 148–85. New York: Macmillan, 1996.

Middle School Geometry: A Case Study

John Benson

◆ A high-level geometry course for gifted middle school students can provide continual exposure to challenging material.

◆ The choice of mathematics courses for gifted students in middle school can have a domino effect on the availability of their choices in high school.

◆ A middle school program with a good gender balance can translate to higher-level math classes with a comparable gender distribution.

◆ Geometry at the middle school level encourages habits of mind that are useful across disciplines. These habits of mind include conjecturing, justifying, and generalizing.

How can educators ensure that they present appropriately challenging curriculum to mathematically talented middle school students? Undoubtedly, there are many answers to this question, but this chapter presents one approach that has been extremely successful for many years. Evanston Township High School in Evanston, Illinois, has had considerable success in preparing students for science, technology, engineering, and mathematics (STEM) careers. A large part of our success can be attributed to the students' elementary and middle school mathematics experiences. We have seen that engaging our most able students in honors algebra as soon as they are ready—usually in seventh grade

The author extends special thanks to Genevieve Becicka, Iowa Center for Research by Undergraduates (ICRU) Scholar at the Belin-Blank International Center for Gifted Education and Talent Development, University of Iowa, for her assistance in the preparation of this chapter.

but sometimes earlier—and then teaching them honors-level high school geometry the following year have been instrumental in getting our most mathematically able students ready for the challenges that lie ahead as well as providing an experience that keeps them excited about mathematics. Geometry enables us to provide them with continual exposure to challenging problems while consistently engaging them in important, interesting tasks.

Policy and Administrative Issues

Middle school is a key period in students' education when it comes to making choices. Prior to middle school, students have not had many choices to make but have instead studied the subjects that they were told to, in the designated order. After middle school, they will have to make many choices about levels of classes and concentrations of study. Choices made by mathematically gifted and talented students at the middle school level can have a domino effect on the availability of choices in both high school (Evan, Gray, and Olchefske 2006) and college (Horn and Nuñez, 2000; Horowitz 2005). If our country intends to prepare its most able students in mathematics and science, we must engage them at the middle school level in something that they find challenging as well as enjoyable and worthwhile (NCTM 2000). We also need to empower them at this time so that they will not be intimidated later by the highest levels of calculus or physics (Business-Higher Education Forum 2005). Impressions made at this age will last a long time, and we must insist on placing them in an environment that will stimulate their interest (Sheffield 1999a) and enhance their abilities (Johnson 1994).

Geometry is the perfect subject because it connects to visual, verbal, and numerical aspects of thinking (NCTM 2000). It lends itself to creativity, and in a geometry class it is rarely the same few students who always have the key idea for solving a problem. Because the problems tend to be unique, they provide a better representation of the sorts of tasks that students will need to be able to do in advanced work. Geometry consists of many problems and few exercises. Consequently, instruction in geometry usually emphasizes teaching students what to do when they don't know what to do (Lenchner 1983). That will serve them well in later work (Carnevale and Desrochers 2003).

Mathematically gifted middle school students are ready for investigations and puzzles (Yolles 2003). During elementary school, mastery of certain skills is a necessary component of the mathematics curriculum (Swanson and Sachse-Lee 2000). Because mastery involves repetition and practice, mathematically talented elementary students may disengage from the subject (Assouline and Lupkowski-Shoplik 2005; Lupkowski and Assouline 1992). This is not to say that their teachers emphasize drill and repetition at the expense of understanding concepts and the underlying reasons that the algorithms work. Teachers are dedicated to helping students understand the important ideas. It is just that much of the work is not particularly visual but rather abstract and consequently does not lend itself to a problem-solving approach as readily as geometry does. It is also true that elementary school students must master certain skills or they will be unable to continue being successful (National Mathematics Advisory Panel 2008). An example of a way in which this can be accomplished with middle school students is through a geometry course—a course that is less about particular skills and more about a way of thinking about problems, and that is connected to their experience with tactile objects (Wheatley 1983).

At Evanston Township High School, I am one of several teachers who teach sections of honors-level geometry each year to gifted eighth graders. Many of the students whom I teach are hesitant to draw a picture or to continue working on a problem if they don't know how to solve it at first glance or believe that they cannot solve it in less than ten minutes. Geometry requires them to overcome all of that reluctance and offers new methods to promote their curiosity. They learn quickly that a diagram is essential to most problems and that sometimes it is necessary to draw and redraw to get a look at the problem. Once they get started on a problem, some of them will persist.

Some of our insights into the effectiveness of our course come from parents. Each year, several parents use parent-teacher conferences to disclose the impact of the course on their children. For example, at the spring conferences, Mark's parents shared the information that geometry is the first subject that Mark works on when he gets home. They explained that sometimes he is not able to solve all of the problems, so he moves on to other things, but later he comes back to the problems he has not yet solved. Sometimes he takes another look in the morning when he gets up, and he may come down to breakfast excitedly telling his parents about a problem that he has just solved. They also indicated that this is the first time that Mark has worked like this on math.

This is not an isolated story. It and others like it offer evidence that our class is developing important habits of mind that will carry our students through life. I think that it is the particular nature of geometry that enables us to engage students in the way that Mark has become engaged.

Mark, along with many other students in class, likes to arrive early so that he can try to solve one of the hands-on geometric puzzles set out in the classroom for investigation. The objective might be to take off a ring, reassemble the pieces into a cube, slide the pieces around so that the numbers or colors are in a particular order, take the pieces apart, or put them together. I find that the students' interest in solving these puzzles is highly correlated with their interest in solving the geometry puzzles that we set for them to try to solve each day (Waxman, Robinson, and Mukhopadhyay 1996). Mathematics educators recognize that there are number theory puzzles and algebra puzzles that are as challenging as geometry puzzles, but the physical aspect of geometry seems to be a better fit for many students at this age, and consequently gives access to a larger group (Bell 2003). The students are attracted to the puzzles that they can hold in their hands and manipulate. Three-dimensional hands-on puzzles are the perfect preamble to the two-dimensional pictures that accompany problems to be worked on in class (NCTM 2000).

Another advantage of this high-level coursework for gifted middle school students is that gender disparities are not much of an issue. Over half of the students in our program are females; they do at least as well as the male students, and most of them go on to pursue rigorous courses in math and science. The students who take our honors geometry course before they enter high school are on a track to take multivariable calculus and linear algebra during their senior year. Currently, fifteen of the thirty-five students enrolled in multivariable calculus at Evanston Township High School are females, and these are typical numbers for this course. All of these students have earned 5s on the Advanced Placement Calculus exam. This gender ratio is comparable with that of students taking the AP Calculus exam nationally, where approximately 47 percent of students are females (College Board 2008).

Another aspect of offering advanced coursework to students at this age is the opportunity to develop ways of thinking about the world that will be valuable to them across a wide variety of disciplines (Johnson 1994). Being able to take an organized approach to a problem, to build a logical structure for proving that something must be true, and to persist as necessary to solve a difficult problem are valuable skills in most fields of work (Murnane and Levy 1996). Also important in any endeavor are the ideas that there are many ways to arrive at a solution, that not all problems can be solved yet, that some problems may never lend themselves to a solution and others will be manageable once we have more knowledge, that it is useful to identify what we know and what we are trying to decide before we get very far into a problem, and that often our first instinct is wrong or needs modification (NCTM 2000). The earlier these principles are practiced, the more natural they will become in the students' work style and the more valuable they will become in his or her approach to any significant task.

It is also exciting and useful for students to experience the joy of eventually solving a problem that they have been working on for a long time—a problem that has frustrated them and that they have almost given up on but solved one day (Csikszentmihalyi, Rathunde, and Whalen 1993). The following is from a letter that I received from a former student, Jay, on his graduation from high school:

> I specifically remember the puzzle that you presented to the class at the beginning of the year. The goal was to make a three-dimensional object that was a triangle on one surface, a square on another, and a circle on another. No teacher had ever given me a puzzle to do; it was always books and assignments to stir the mind. But you took just five minutes one day to give us this challenge that lingered for months in my head. I thought about the puzzle for a few days or so, and then without any luck for a solution, it faded from my mind. But the block of wood remained on your file cabinet as a calling reminder; it became a thorn in my side. One night I had had enough. I sat down at the dining room table and was determined to solve this thing. Eventually I had it. I went downstairs, cut a dowel rod a few times, and then went to sleep that night with a different feeling in my stomach. It was not how I feel after completing a nightly assignment. It was not how I feel after getting back an A on a test. It was a feeling of real, genuine accomplishment with no grade ever to come. The next morning I walked up to you standing at the door and took the solution out of my jeans pocket. I can still hear you: "Yep!" Then, without saying a word to the class you placed your statue of Le Penseur on my desk. Everyone looked at me with wonder. And then, you told them that I had solved the puzzle.

Such experiences are life changing. Jay has gone on to try his skill at acting. I believe that sometime, somewhere, he will call on his experiences in geometry during his formative years to gain a better understanding of how to perform, and as a result he will be more able to communicate important ideas and emotions to audiences. Such is the power of geometry. It is inherently visual *and* verbal. It is not uncommon for students to disagree about something verbally and settle the disagreement by drawing a picture or building a model to demonstrate their point of view. This is intellectually much healthier than simply asking an authority for the right answer.

Examples of the Impact of Our Program

Perhaps the most important aspect of the class is that it is taught from a problem-solving perspective. Problem solving is not something that is done now and again in the class; it is the way in which the course is taught. This emphasis allows all sorts of opportunities for creativity. The teachers of the course encourage a variety of solutions and often ask questions like the following:

- "Did any of you do this a different way?"

- "Can you also answer a question that we did not ask?"

- "Can you generalize this result?"

The effect is a mathematics course that takes students to the next level of understanding and challenge, and they love it.

Another significant aspect of our course is its emphasis on having students work on problems that they have not seen before as they learn new material. We believe that this strategy is easier to implement with young geometry students than with young algebra students, partly because of the visual nature of geometry, partly because of the belief system of the teachers of the class, and partly because of the collaboration that takes place among the teachers. We believe that it is appropriate to give students a problem to work on that involves the concept that we want them to learn, allow them time to work, encourage them to collaborate, and then discuss their ideas as a group (Sheffield 1999b). Through the discussion of the problem, a new theorem will often emerge, and learning will take place. I like to call this process "teaching by walking around." The formal instruction takes place during the discussion of the problem, and the students are often the ones who have discovered, or uncovered, the new theorem or concept that we hope they will learn. This is a constructive activity; we find that it greatly enhances their understanding of concepts and their enjoyment of the class, and it empowers them to continue.

On the first day of class, after taking a minimum of time to pass out textbooks, assignment sheets, and a list of expectations, I begin instruction by asking the students to "work on" a problem. I try not to ask them to "solve" the problem, because I want to avoid implying that they will be able to solve it. Most of the students will not be able to solve most of the problems most of the time. They will all be able to work on the problems and make progress. This level of engagement enables them to understand the discussion that follows, because we are then talking about *their* problem instead of *my* problem. They want to know if they have done it correctly, or what they could have done to solve the problem and are more concerned about the mathematics than they are with copying down notes on what the teacher is saying. The first problem is the following:

How many squares are there in the figure?

I hand the students a copy of the diagram and give them time to work on the problem. As they work, I circulate among them and look and listen. There are usually several initial answers as well as several initial responses. Most students just write a number at the top of the page, but others show evidence of a strategy, outlining or writing several numbers that they add. When it appears that many students have an answer, I encourage them to compare their answers with their neighbors and discuss their thinking. Sometimes a few students are confused about the difference between a rectangle and a square and consequently get answers that differ considerably. This confusion usually is resolved quickly, leaving two answers, eight squares and nine squares. And then the fun—and the instruction—begins. Notice that the students are now stakeholders in the outcome. They have a reported answer. They are eager to learn if their answer is correct or not. They are paying attention.

I then make a point about how essential it is for us to agree on a definition of *square*. If one student thinks that the statement "A square is a rectangle" defines a square, then that student may solve the problem with perfect logic but will get a different answer from the two possibilities identified above—eight squares and nine squares. Consequently, it is essential that we agree on the meaning of words so that we are always talking about the same thing. And sometimes words have different meanings in a mathematical context than they do in casual conversation. For example, many towns have a town square, and my grandmother used to make peanut butter squares. The town square is often round, and the peanut butter squares were actually rectangular prisms. These comments often inspire laughter, but they make an important point that is one of the main objectives of the first day of class.

I then go on to a more specific example of a word used differently in different contexts—the word *line*. I refer to goal lines, foul lines, and fifty-yard *lines*, none of which are actually lines but rectangles meant to represent *line segments* or *rays*. This allows me to make those geometric terms and their notations clear, again in a context that invites laughter and consideration of situations that actually are part of the real world for many of the students.

Then we return to the problem at hand, and I solicit ideas for a definition of a square. We usually settle on four right angles and four congruent sides, with a side comment on my part that the actual definition of a square will not include all those conditions, because some of them can be inferred from others, and we want a definition to be minimal. Thus, I introduce another theme of our course: we preview important ideas in an informal way—concepts that we are not yet ready to formalize, because the students are not ready to internalize them, but which become very important to the understanding of mathematics eventually. We try to preview important ideas as much as possible in the belief that encountering something formally for the first time makes it a lot more difficult to grasp than if it has been touched on informally several times prior to its formal introduction. Many of our problems are written with the objective of embedding an important idea that has not yet been formally presented, so that students will have thought about it before they encounter it formally.

This practice also underscores the importance of having veteran teachers in daily contact with teachers who are new to the course. It is sometimes difficult for new teachers to understand why certain problems are being used, or to see the connections with later ideas, until they have taught the course from beginning to end. A veteran teacher can help a new teacher understand the importance of asking certain questions after students have solved a problem, so that these big ideas can be fleshed out early. A novice may find it very difficult to anticipate where the tough spots are likely to occur or to decide what ideas to preview and when and where to preview them; hence, the collaboration among teachers is essential to making the course as effective as it can be.

After clarifying the definition of *square*, my class then returns to the question, and I ask someone to identify the squares that he or she has counted. Sometimes students forget the large square itself, but it is more likely that they overlook the one in the middle on the left. This leads us to a discussion of the question, "How do you know that there isn't another square that you just have not seen yet?" We then arrive at the idea that we need a systematic approach that does not allow for oversights like this. Usually two suggestions emerge. The most popular one is to count all the small squares, the medium ones, and the large ones. A second approach is to count all the squares with a vertex at the upper left-hand corner, and then move to the next vertex and count all of the squares that have not yet been counted. Using these approaches, we decide that there must be nine squares in all.

And then for the final "lesson" of this problem, I ask the students how they know that any of these shapes is a square. How do they know that the angles are right angles or that the sides are congruent? I show them the optical illusion at the right to demonstrate the fallacy of jumping to conclusions based on what the picture looks like.

Which of the two line segments is longer? Students who have not seen this configuration before invariably select the vertical one. In fact, the segments are the same length. Returning to the problem of the squares, I ask them how they would tell a 90° angle from a 90.01° angle, even with a protractor. These questions lead to a discussion of what things can be assumed from a diagram (the relative positions of points) and what things cannot be assumed from the diagram (anything that has to do with measure). I insist that the correct answer to the problem that I gave them is that we do not have enough information to solve the problem.

I have presented this discussion as though it takes place in one continuous period, but in fact it often extends over a couple of days. It serves many purposes in addition to the mathematical ones, and I point these out to the students as well. I then let them know that I will give them problems that will teach them mathematics, and that is where the learning will take place. I let them know that the problems that I intend to give them will not usually send them out for practice but will instead put them on the field where the mathematical game is played. Consequently, I will often give them problems that I expect them to get wrong. Getting things wrong is necessary to learning something new. Sometimes they will see a problem through to the end and will figure out the difficulties. We will collectively celebrate such moments. They need to understand that I am not going to show them how to do problems and that I am going to react to their attempts to solve the problems that I pose. I call these problems "openers," not because they open the class, but because they open the mind. The plan that I have in mind is that they will work on the problems by themselves, then discuss them with their neighbors, collectively come to some conclusion, and share their observations and ideas with the rest of the class. Learning happens best after some frustration and perseverance, and I will try to frustrate them and expect tenacity in trying to solve the problems.

It has been my repeated experience that this approach works very well with insightful middle school students and that the students whom I teach find it unusual. They are used to having their math teacher show them how to do a problem and then give them a worksheet that offers more problems of the same kind for them to solve for practice. These students love puzzles and challenges and are engaged by the idea that they are expected to figure things out. Many are a bit concerned that they will not be able to learn this way, but that concern usually vanishes in the first few weeks, after they find out how much fun it is to be "solving puzzles" in class.

Below are a few more examples of how this method plays out in our geometry classrooms. We give students the first problem below after they have been proving that triangles are congruent by using SAS, SSS, and ASA. It is intended to demonstrate the occasional need for introducing a line segment into a diagram where none is shown.

Given: $\odot O$

$\overline{GO}$ bisects $\overline{FH}$

Prove: $\angle FGO \cong \angle HGO$

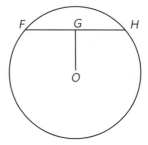

Students typically inspect the problem, mark the diagram, and then stare at the problem for a while. Some start writing down what is given. As soon as I see that writing the given is becoming a widespread approach, I stop the discussion and try to convince them that writing down the given when they have no notion of how the rest of the proof will work out is a little bit like starting up a car, and driving off without any idea of how to get to the destination. I try to convince them that the steps of a proof need to come in a logical, sequential order and that they cannot know when they will need the facts that are given until they know the entire proof. This is a hard lesson to learn, and starting now is critical. The analogy of planning a trip before setting out seems to make sense to them. They laugh at my notion that we should get in the car and start driving, perhaps eventually arriving in Red Bud, Illinois!

But at this point it is unlikely that anyone has solved the problem. So I keep walking around and watching and listening. Inevitably, some student lightly draws segments from O to F and from O to H. When I see this I usually softly say, "Good idea," as I walk past the student. By the time I get to the other side of the room, many students are gathering around the student to see what the good idea was. This collaboration honors the clever student whose insight allowed her to solve the problem and enables her to teach her idea to the class. Word spreads, and then someone asks if it is "OK to draw something." The teachable moment has arrived, and I seize the chance. I have the student demonstrate what she has done, and I ask the students whether they think it is allowable and why or why not. The class has already previewed the idea in an earlier problem asking if two identified points are collinear even if the line is not drawn, so someone in the class is usually ready to claim that there must be a line through O and F and a line through O and H, and therefore we are allowed to draw in the segments on our diagram. This opportunity allows me to suggest that perhaps the first statement in the proof should be a statement that we are drawing the line segments and that we are allowed to do so because two points uniquely determine a segment. This discussion also invites consideration of why it is a good idea to draw line segments in this situation. The problem creates a need for the technique. Drawing segments is the strategy that the students need to solve the problem. This is a powerful lesson in how mathematics develops.

I also take the opportunity to warn against arbitrarily drawing lots of lines, because they will tend to complicate the diagram, and I also ask the students whether they should be allowed to draw a perpendicular to a line through a point or to draw a parallel to a line through a point. Everyone thinks that we should be able to do both. These notions create a very interesting situation: we justified the initial move with a postulate, so why not postulate the other two as well? I encourage the students to hold that thought, since eventually it will become a very big idea, but we are not quite ready to deal with it yet. Eventually, of course, we can prove the perpendicular existence and uniqueness with an indirect proof and minimum distances, but we will have to decide on the parallel postulate. Once again, the strategy of asking students a leading question and exploring it as a class leads to a desired result as well as to some deep mathematics that they will encounter later in the course.

Another challenging proof that I ask my students to write once led to one of the most exciting moments in my teaching career. I was about to give students their first proof without an accompanying diagram. I knew from experience that they would be likely to draw special cases of what was in fact a general situation and thus could be misled by their diagrams. (For example, when given a problem involving an isosceles triangle, students often draw an equilateral triangle, so their diagram exhibits properties that a non-equilateral isosceles triangle does not have.) After much thought, I wrote what I believed was the perfect problem for what I hoped to achieve. Other benefits of my problem were that it had two solutions, one of which used a theorem recently learned by my students, and that it also reviewed the strategy of introducing line segments. I was pleased with my problem and presented it confidently to the class the next day:

> **Prove:** If two circles intersect at two points, the segment joining the intersection points is perpendicular to the segment connecting the centers of the circles.

As I expected, my students did not know how to start, but by that time of the year, they had become skilled in using each other as resources. Soon nearly everyone had two congruent circles drawn on his or her paper and was starting to try to write the proof. I saw this as a teachable moment. I pointed out that many students had drawn congruent circles and asked where in the problem it said the circles were congruent. I proceeded to draw two intersecting congruent circles and two intersecting non-congruent circles side by side, as below:

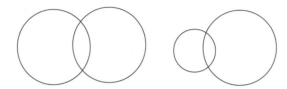

I then asked, "What next?" The students suggested that I start drawing radii and segments. It soon became difficult for us to continue the conversation unless we labeled points on the segments that we had drawn. So, another important part of the process had emerged from our need to communicate about mathematics, and we labeled our diagram, arriving at something like the following:

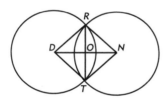 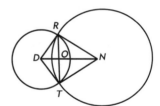

This exploration led to a discussion of which triangles look congruent on the left (triangles *ROD, RON, TON,* and *TOD*) and which ones look congruent on the right (triangles *RON* and *TON* and triangles *ROD* and *TOD*), and so I was able to make my point about general diagrams. This gave me the opportunity to emphasize how important it is for them to draw the most general diagram they can when they have the task of drawing the diagram as part of the problem.

I then sent them back to work and started walking around again to see which approach they would take. I noticed that many of them were trying to write a proof without establishing what the conditions of the problems were, and this situation gave me yet another teachable moment: no one can solve a problem until there is a problem to be solved. Because this is a proof problem, it is necessary to indicate what is given and what is to be proved. I carefully worked with them until we agreed on the specific details, and then I asked them to resume work on the problem. I was walking around, observing their progress and noticing which students were using perpendicular bisector theorems and which ones were using congruent triangles, when I came to Phil, who was sitting with his arms folded, a diagram in front of him but no proof, and the words "Not true" written on his paper. I looked at his diagram and saw the following:

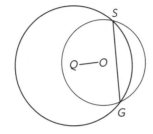

Given : ⊙O, ⊙Q

Prove: $\overline{OQ} \perp \overline{SG}$

I was amazed and delighted. I ran over to my cabinet and took my model of Rodin's *The Thinker,* which I keep there for such occasions, and placed it on Phil's desk, and then I invited him to share his drawing with the rest of the class. The result was that students learned an even more important lesson than the one I had planned—namely, that a diagram not only has to be general but that the person writing the proof needs to consider all possible consequences of the given information.

I think that one of reasons that our program is successful with talented middle school students is that we are providing them with a completely new set of experiences. They have not experienced proof before. No other topic that I teach naturally lends itself to such a wide variety of approaches and makes virtually every problem a new challenge.

One example of how we manage this problem-solving approach will illustrate our overall approach to engaging gifted eighth-grade students in challenging, worthwhile problems. When we are working on similar triangles and the students have become comfortable in identifying similar triangles and solving proportions, we have them solve several similar triangle problems that are really about the altitude to the hypotenuse theorem (which holds in part that the altitude to the hypotenuse of a right triangle forms two similar triangles that are both similar to the original triangle). One such example follows:

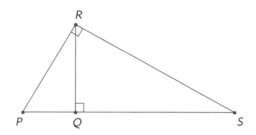

Given: $\overline{RQ} \perp \overline{PS},\ \overline{PR} \perp \overline{RS}$

Prove: $RQ^2 = PQ \cdot QS$

After demonstrating that triangles QRS and QPR are similar, students can say that $RQ/QS = PQ/RQ$, so $RQ^2 = PQ \cdot QS$. We also ask them to solve numerical problems that relate to the altitude to the hypotenuse theorem, like the following:

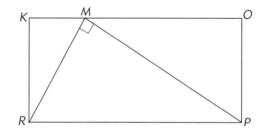

$KOPR$ is a rectangle,

$\overline{RM} \perp \overline{PM},$

$OM = 9,$ and

$RP = 13.$

Find $KR.$

Find any other lengths that you can.

To solve this problem, students must recognize that all three triangles in the diagram are similar, and they must set up the proportions properly and solve them. Having previously figured out several problems like this on their own, they are prepared for the similar triangles involved in the altitude to the hypotenuse theorem and ready to address the theorem formally.

After our students have established this theorem, we tease them by telling them that they finally have enough knowledge to prove the Pythagorean theorem and that as soon as someone provides a proof, they can use it. Invariably, someone comes to class the next day with a similarity proof based on the altitude to the hypotenuse theorem—a proof that is usually very much like the classic one. The class debates the advisability of renaming the Pythagorean theorem after the student who proved it, but we decide that we ought to stick with the familiar name so that others will understand what we are doing. I then make a big show out of how important the Pythagorean theorem is by putting a sum of money in an envelope in my desk. (This year it was $20.) I inform the students that if there is ever an entire class period from that day forward during which we do not use the Pythagorean theorem at least once, the first student who calls it to my attention will get the money in the envelope. If a student claims that we did not use the Pythagorean theorem that day and we did, that student will have to add a quarter to the envelope. This deal makes quite an impact on them, and it ensures that we continually review the Pythagorean theorem. (I have lost the money on occasion but usually not until May and sometimes not at all.)

It is also rewarding to have the students work on numerical problems where finding the answer is not the end of the story. Consider the problem below:

ABDC is a parallelogram,

$m\angle EAB = 50°$,

$m\angle BEA = 60°$, and

$m\angle BDE = 30°$.

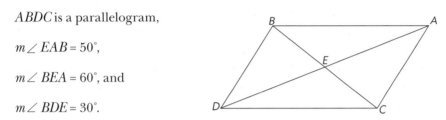

Find the measures of all of the angles.

This problem appears to present an ordinary situation about parallel lines and the angles they form until students take a close look at the answer. As it happens, $\triangle BED$ turns out to have two $30°$ angles and so must be isosceles. That makes the parallelogram a rectangle, and consequently the vertex angles are all right angles. This contradiction means that the parallelogram is overdetermined. It is usually the case that a few students in class will get that far, especially with a little prodding. Next comes the important part. If the parallelogram is overdetermined, then which of the given pieces of information should we delete so that it is still possible to determine all the angles of the parallelogram? It becomes clear that if we ignore any one of the three givens, we are not able to determine the measures of the remaining angles. So, a fairly simple problem leads to an open-ended question about what it takes to determine a shape. Students also learn that they have to check their work—not just for careless errors or arithmetic errors, but also for inconsistencies in the problem itself. Again, they are learning valuable lessons about how to do mathematics.

I should also confess that this problem, like so many other good problems, turned out to be so valuable only as the result of our general approach of challenging students to think about their work and not just plow through it. I wish I could take credit for deliberately creating this interesting problem that led to important mathematics, but I was actually just writing a problem that would quickly review the relationships between the angles of a parallelogram. In fact, this is a problem that I made up on the spot at the end of class one day. However, one of my students noticed the two thirty-degree angles and established that $\triangle BED$ must be isosceles and determined that the figure was impossible. It was then that I pulled out my statue, and it was then that I realized I had a very good problem on my hands.

It is situations like this one that motivate me to advocate geometry as a path for advanced middle school students. They are doing much more than learning some theorems about mathematics as they forge through the material. They are, in fact, learning important problem-solving skills and developing lifelong habits of thought and inquiry that will enable them to continue excelling in mathematics for years to come.

The problems that I have shared so far are problems that we do during class time. As I said earlier, I give the students a problem and walk around while they work on it. They initially work alone and then collaborate and compare results and methods. This structure not only empowers them, but it is a very efficient way for me to manage class time. At the end of this process, rarely does a student still have a question that turns out to be just the result of a copying error or a miscalculation, because their friends have cleared up those kinds of errors before they get to the rest of the class. We spend our class time talking about important issues. One of the attributes of a class based on problem solving, especially in geometry, is its emphasis on metacognition. Because the students have already spent considerable time and effort trying to solve a problem, the discussion that surrounds it tends to be more about how the student realized that a particular strategy was appropriate and what to do when you don't know what to do than about an algorithm for solving all problems like this one. I believe that this learning environment is much easier to create and maintain in geometry than in any other mathematics course because of the visual nature of the subject. Looking at a picture in a different way makes the problem seem like another problem. There is a strong logical component as well as a visual and verbal component to the problems, so problem solving becomes an emphasis in a course designed for gifted students.

One thing that we realized early in the development of this course was that the homework and tests that we gave our students had to reflect the level of work that we expected from them in class. If we asked our students to solve challenging problems in class and then sent them home with routine problems to do, they would soon learn that they did not have to pay much attention to the problems in class. Likewise, if our assessments of their progress did not reflect the level of challenge involved in the classroom problems, students would soon lower their standards to do as little as possible to get good grades. The problem below is an excellent example of the sort of homework problem that we ask our students to work on:

The medians to the legs of a

right triangle have lengths

$2\sqrt{13}$ and $\sqrt{73}$.

Find the length of the hypotenuse.

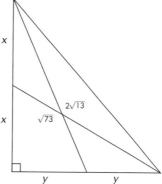

Students rather quickly draw and label the diagram as shown, but then the trouble begins. It takes some work to get them to the point where it seems natural to write a quadratic equation to represent this situation. Then many of them do not square the coefficients and end up with incorrect equations. But even if the algebra is done correctly, working with the resulting equations can be challenging:

$$x^2 + 4y^2 = 73$$
$$4x^2 + y^2 = 52$$

Some students will see that this is a system of quadratics that can be solved by using either substitution or linear combinations to learn that $x = 3$ and $y = 4$ provide a solution since x and y are both positive. This problem not only gives us a chance to review some fundamental ideas in algebra but also allows us to be creative. If we add the two equations, the sum is $5x^2 + 5y^2 = 125$. Adding the equations is a logical thing to do if one notices that the coefficients are the same numbers reversed. Dividing by 5 gives us $x^2 + y^2 = 25$. Now we can go back to the diagram and connect the midpoints of the legs, as shown below.

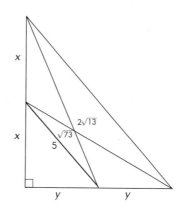

The segment connecting the midpoints is a *midline* of the triangle, and we know that it has length 5 because of the preceding equation, $x^2 + y^2 = 25$. So our answer is that the length of the hypotenuse of our original triangle is 10, and we did not need to find the value of x or y. It is not uncommon in more advanced courses to think of a quantity as a linear combination of other variables and use that fact to establish a length or other measure. It is uncommon to encounter such problems in algebra 1. Geometry is a natural place to introduce these ideas and also provides an opportunity to experience some new ways to think about algebra.

The problem below illustrates yet another important aspect of our approach to the class. This question is an "opener"—a problem that we have students work on in class.

> **Prove:** If the bisector of an angle of a triangle passes through the midpoint of the triangle's opposite side, it is also perpendicular to that side.

The diagram and setup are both fairly easy, as shown below.

Given: $\overline{AM}$ bisects $\angle BAC$

M is the midpoint of $\overline{CB}$

Prove: $\overline{AM} \perp \overline{CB}$

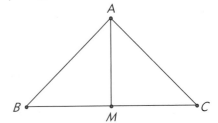

When I give my students this problem, they have not yet seen the angle bisector theorem. I was under the impression that the solution to this problem required that theorem, and I wanted them to have the experience of thinking that it was a fairly easy problem and then being unable to solve it. After they had worked on it for while, I planned to tell them that they would soon learn a theorem that would enable them to solve it. And so we would have another example of a problem that they would be able to solve when they knew more mathematics. This strategy of presenting them with problems that they cannot yet solve has a dramatic impact on the class. It makes them more skeptical, and it helps them to understand that mathematics is a story that is unfolding daily, before their eyes.

The only flaw in my plan for this problem was that it *can* be solved without the angle bisector theorem, and two years ago one of my students did exactly that, by using a creative method that had been presented for a different problem. He extended $\overline{AM}$ to a point P so that $\overline{AM} \cong \overline{PM}$. He then connected B and P and C to create a parallelogram. He knew it was a parallelogram because the diagonals bisected each other. But if a diagonal is also an angle bisector, then the parallelogram must be a rhombus, and rhombi have perpendicular diagonals. Once again I was amazed. I am not sure that I would ever have thought of this solution, because I was convinced that any solution would depend on the angle bisector theorem. And so, once again, a student made a contribution to the class's knowledge of geometry. This contribution would not have been possible if the students had not been challenged to work problems on their own before someone told them how to solve them.

Consider another problem that I offer to students in the same spirit as the last one, except that this one has a twist:

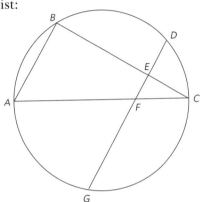

$\overline{AC}$ is a diameter of the circle,

$AB = 12$,

$m\overset{\frown}{DC} = 40°$,

$m\overset{\frown}{AG} = 80°$, and

$\overline{AB} \parallel \overline{DG}$.

Find the diameter of the circle and the measures of all the arcs.

Find any other measure that you can. Can you determine EF?

The interesting part of the question comes up when students are asked to determine the length of $\overline{CE}$. They have no trouble determining that $\triangle ABC$ and $\triangle EFC$ are 30-60-90 triangles and obtaining the lengths of all sides of $\triangle ABC$. They then get stuck, however, and there are often several interesting conjectures about the length of $\overline{EC}$ and the measure of the arcs that correspond to them. Some students conjecture that the ratio of EC to BE should be 1:2 because $m\overset{\frown}{DC} : m\overset{\frown}{BC} = 1:2$. This conjecture seems reasonable, but we do not have a proof, so we open Geometer's Sketchpad and make a sketch:

$m\overset{\frown}{AB}$ on $\odot BI = 60.10°$

$m\overset{\frown}{DC}$ on $\odot BI = 40.01°$

$EC = 2.70$cm

$EB = 6.22$cm

$\dfrac{EB}{EC} = 2.30$

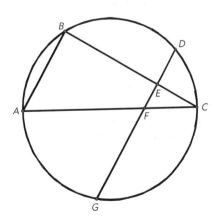

The calculations performed by Geometer's Sketchpad make it evident that the ratio of the arcs is different from the ratio of the sides. This year, one of my students, Joey, solved the problem by using trigonometry. Joey discovered that $DC = 24 \sin 20°$, and $EC = DC \cos 40°$ while $DE = DC \sin 40°$, so after two quick computations, the missing pieces were in place.

Another important aspect of the course that students find interesting is the concept that there are several different ways to solve a problem. In fact, gaining and appreciating this flexibility are such major parts of the class that we often ask our students to solve the same problem in two different ways on a test. The following problem provides an excellent example of this idea:

Find the volume of the truncated cylinder.

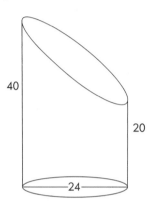

A favorite approach of mine is to make a copy of the drawing and turn it over on top of the original, making one cylinder with height 60. The volume then is $\dfrac{\pi \cdot 12^2 \cdot 60}{2} = 4320\pi$. Some students make it into a 20-foot cylinder and half of another 20-foot cylinder. Some students make a horizontal cut at the 30-foot mark, and fold down the top half to make a cylinder with a height of 30 feet. Other strategies are to make a vertical cut and paste the half cylinders together to make one big half cylinder 60 feet tall.

The following problem can be done in at least twelve different ways. See how many you can find.

$\overline{ST} \parallel \overline{PQ}, \ \overline{PQ} \parallel \overline{RM} \parallel \overline{WN}; \ ST = 8, \ SQ = 5, \ TP = 13, \ RS = 20$

$\overline{SQ} \perp \overline{QP}; \ \overline{RW} \parallel \overline{SQ}; \ \overline{MN} \parallel \overline{TP}; \ \overline{RS} \parallel \overline{MT} \parallel \overline{NP} \parallel \overline{QW}$

Find the volume of the solid in at least three different ways.

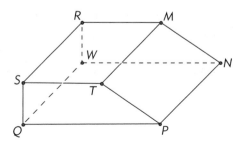

This time, we ask students for at least three solutions, but we get many more than three. We then find it useful to discuss whether there are advantages to one of the methods over another. We also emphasize that there may be some problems that lend themselves more to certain methods than to others, so being aware of many methods is important.

Conclusion

These examples offer a glimpse of the kind of work that we have been doing with our high-ability middle school students for the last twenty years. On the basis of feedback from parents and students in the course, as well as from former students when they are seniors in high school, we are confident that many students have benefitted greatly from our class. We have taught many students who have come back years later, telling us that they have entered professions where mathematics is vital. This is largely because we challenge them, we respect their intellect, and we teach in a style that helps them become better at doing mathematics.

Talented students in middle school are intellectually at just the right point to learn geometry, and geometry is the perfect course for this stage in their development. Because the visual aspect of the subject is so central to understanding it, it appeals to a different, more concrete aspect of their intelligence than algebra. The strong emphasis on justification helps to integrate getting answers with knowing how to get them. Geometry allows students considerable flexibility in their approach to a problem, and so it allows a teaching approach that is much broader than any that they have encountered up to this point. Geometry can be taught in a manner that takes the students to the next level of mathematical understanding and expertise, integrating their love of puzzles with their emerging ability to express their thoughts. My high school coach frequently repeated the adage "The way you practice is the way you play." I believe that the way that a student learns mathematics is the way that he or she will do mathematics and that geometry is the best way to develop appropriate mathematical habits.

References

Bell, Clare V. "Learning Geometric Concepts through Ceramic Tile Design." *Mathematics Teaching in the Middle School* 9 (November 2003): 134–40.

Business-Higher Education Forum. *A Commitment to America's Future: Responding to the Crisis in Mathematics and Science Education.* Washington, D.C.: American Council on Education, 2005.

Carnevale, Anthony P., and Donna M. Desrochers. *Standards for What? The Economic and Demographic Roots of Standards Based Reform.* Princeton, N.J.: Educational Testing Service, 2003.

Csikszentmihalyi, Mihaly, Kevin Rathunde, and Samuel Whalen. *Talented Teenagers: The Roots of Success and Failure.* Cambridge: Cambridge University Press, 1993.

College Board. *Program Summary Report.* Princeton, N.J.: College Board, 2008. http://professionals.collegeboard.com/profdownload/ap-data-2008-Program-Summary-Report.pdf.

Evan, Aimee, Tracy Gray, and Joseph Olchefske. *The Gateway to Student Success in Mathematics and Science.* Washington, D.C.: American Institutes for Research, 2006.

Horn, Laura, and Anne-Marie Nuñez. *Mapping the Road to College: First-Generation Students' Math Track, Planning Strategies, and Context of Support* (NCES 2000-153). Washington, D.C.: U.S. Department of Education, 2000.

Horowitz, Jordon. *Inside High School Reform: Making the Changes That Matter.* San Francisco: WestEd, 2005.

Johnson, Dana T. "Mathematics Curriculum for the Gifted." In *Comprehensive Curriculum for Gifted Learners,* 2nd ed., edited by Joyce VanTassel-Baska, pp. 231–61. Boston: Allyn & Bacon, 1994.

Lenchner, George. *Creative Problem Solving in School Mathematics.* Boston: Houghton Mifflin, 1983.

Lupkowski, Ann E., and Susan G. Assouline. *Jane and Johnny Love Math: Recognizing and Encouraging Mathematical Talent in Elementary Students.* Unionville, N.Y.: Trillium Press, 1992.

Murnane, Richard J., and Frank Levy. *Teaching the New Basic Skills: Principles for Educating Children to Thrive in a Changing Economy.* Glencoe, Ill.: Free Press, 1996.

National Council of Teachers of Mathematics (NCTM). *Principles and Standards for School Mathematics.* Reston, Va.: NCTM, 2000. http://nctm.org/fullstandards/document/default.asp.

National Mathematics Advisory Panel. *Foundations for Success: The Final Report of the National Mathematics Advisory Panel.* Washington, D.C.: U.S. Department of Education, 2008.

Sheffield, Linda Jensen, ed. *Developing Mathematically Promising Students.* Reston, Va.: National Council of Teachers of Mathematics, 1999a.

Sheffield, Linda Jensen. "Serving the Needs of the Mathematically Promising." In *Developing Mathematically Promising Students,* edited by Linda Jensen Sheffield, pp. 43–55. Reston, Va.: National Council of Teachers of Mathematics, 1999b.

Swanson, H. Lee, and Carole M. Sachse-Lee. "A Meta-analysis of Single-Subject-Design Intervention Research for Students with LD." *Journal of Learning Disabilities* 33 (March-April 2000): 114–36.

Waxman, Barbara, Nancy M. Robinson, and Swapna Mukhopadhyay. *Teachers Nurturing Math-Talented Young Children.* Storrs, Conn.: National Research Center on the Gifted and Talented, University of Connecticut; Washington, D.C.: U.S. Department of Education, Office of Educational Research and Improvement, Educational Resources Information Center, 1996.

Wheatley, Grayson H. "A Mathematics Curriculum for the Gifted and Talented." *Gifted Child Quarterly* 27 (Spring 1983): 77–80.

Yolles, Arlene. "Using Friday Puzzlers to Discover Arithmetic Sequences." *Mathematics Teaching in the Middle School* 9 (November 2003): 180–85.

CHAPTER

8

Equity

Max Warshauer, Terry McCabe, M. Alejandra Sorto, Sharon Strickland, Hiroko Warshauer, and Alex White

◆ All students should have opportunities to grow and develop, and equity means that this fundamental idea also applies to students who are gifted in mathematics.

◆ A set of guiding principles allows teachers to address the needs of all students in a variety of ways and create classrooms that provide all students with exciting learning opportunities in mathematics. Teachers should enable students to think deeply about seemingly simple ideas and processes, explore rich problems, develop a growth mindset, and gain early access to algebraic thinking.

◆ The needs of gifted students can be addressed outside the classroom in cost-effective ways; the key is to recognize that this effort is necessary and will benefit other students as well.

We use the word *equity* to mean the opportunity for all students to develop their mathematical abilities to their full potential. Equity is not the same as equality, in the sense of equality of services or resources. Although a physically challenged student may need the use of a wheelchair, equity does not imply that every student should have access to a wheelchair. Indeed, using a

The authors acknowledge the special contributions of Joanetta Ellis, principal of Fossum Middle School in McAllen, Texas, and Sam Baethge, retired high school teacher from Austin, Texas. Valuable insights were also shared by three Texas middle school teachers—Amy Warshauer from Austin, Sandra Saenz from McAllen, and Amanda Voigt from San Marcos—about their teaching and how they have provided opportunities for gifted students in mathematics.

wheelchair would deprive some students of necessary physical exercise. In the same way, equity for gifted students does not imply equality with others in educational environment. It does, however, imply equality of opportunity—every gifted child should have the same possibility as any other child of developing his or her capabilities to the full extent.

This point about equity versus equality brings up another distinct but related issue: equity is often associated with the education of students from disadvantaged backgrounds or whose families belong to groups that are underrepresented in science, technology, engineering, and mathematics (STEM) professions. As the National Mathematics Advisory Panel (NMP 2008) notes, "Unfortunately, most children from low-income backgrounds enter school with far less knowledge than peers from middle-income backgrounds, and the achievement gap in mathematical knowledge progressively widens throughout their Pre K–12 years" (p. xviii). In short, members of certain groups do not have the same opportunities as their peers.

Although equity for these students is an important issue, it is likewise important to recognize that gifted students, of whatever background, require certain resources to develop their abilities, simply by virtue of being gifted in the field of mathematics. Every student should have the opportunity to learn something new every school day.

We discuss both of these issues: the neglect of the growth of gifted students in general, and the additional neglect to which gifted students in certain groups (such as women, minorities, and economically disadvantaged students) are further subjected. We first describe elements of the kind of classroom that will equitably serve a gifted population. We next discuss some problems that arise in constructing such an environment, and we suggest some possible solutions. Finally, we address specific issues arising in identifying and serving gifted students in resource-poor communities.

Gifted education is a special branch of general education, so it should not be surprising that many of the points that we raise apply to students of all levels of ability and achievement. We have attempted to shape our remarks to emphasize their special significance for gifted students.

Likewise, many of the points that we make are valid at all levels of education and not just the middle school level. Again, we have tried to emphasize that the middle school years are critical. As the National Math Panel asserts, "The sharp falloff in mathematics achievement in the U.S. begins as students reach late middle school, where, for more and more students, algebra course work begins" (NMP 2008, p. xiii). International studies also show that middle school is precisely the time when the mathematics performance of many groups of students exhibits a precipitous decline (Schmidt et al. 2007; NCES 2000).

A Vision of a Middle-Grades Mathematics Classroom

Designing classroom learning environments that meet the mathematical needs of all students, including promising learners, is a daunting task for teachers but one that they confront daily (Chval and Davis 2008). Our concept of an ideal middle-grades mathematics learning environment rests on four fundamental principles, which we elaborate in this section. In some ways, these principles apply to any classroom and to work with any student. We stress specific ways in which they apply to the gifted student.

Principle 1: "Think deeply of simple things"—Arnold Ross

"Think deeply of simple things" was the often-repeated advice of scholar, teacher, and mathematician Arnold Ross and became the motto of the Ross Mathematics Program, a summer program that Ross founded for gifted precollege students at Ohio State University in 1957. Studies of gifted students point to the importance of creating a teaching and learning environment that nurtures their talents (Tomlinson et al. 2003). A classroom where every student is challenged academically, and, in particular, where gifted students are provided with opportunities to think deeply and creatively about problems and their solutions, helps students to become effective learners (Dixon et al. 2004). One danger in teaching is to stress procedures while neglecting the simple ideas that explain why they work and what they accomplish. To the average student, the study of mathematics as a set of procedures can seem complicated and mysterious. To the gifted student, this approach can render mathematics flat and lifeless— something to be merely tolerated while favoring more attractive and creative mental endeavors.

Teaching sometimes becomes so focused on mastering procedures that the simple underlying concepts are neglected. This hurts all students. Teachers often use warm-up problems to begin a mathematics class to ensure that the students are prepared for the standardized state assessment. When these problems are routine review and not clearly related to the main content of the day's lesson, the more proficient student may find the process boring and fail to engage in the important work still ahead. These students are not challenged.

According to the National Research Council, "The primary goal of advanced study in any discipline should be for students to achieve a deep conceptual understanding of the discipline's content and unifying concepts," and "schools and school districts must find ways to integrate advanced study with the rest of their program by means of a coherent plan extending from middle school through the last years of secondary school" (NRC 2002, pp. 197–98). In a later report (NRC 2005), the National Research Council recommended that the mathematics curriculum consist of a coherent plan to connect mathematical knowledge

157

organized around the foundational ideas of mathematics. Teachers need to create a classroom culture in which there is an expectation that all students will learn to think deeply about the mathematics.

A program such as the Texas State Honors Summer Math Camp (HSMC) (http://www.txstate.edu/mathworks/camps/hsmc.html) offers one model for this. In 2001, this program received the Texas Star Award for Closing the Gaps, and in 2008 it earned the Siemens Albert Hoser Founder's Award for its contributions to developing talented students in mathematics. Like the Ross Mathematics Program at Ohio State (http://www.math.ohio-state.edu/ross/) and the Program in Mathematics for Young Scientists (PROMYS) at Boston University (http://www.promys.org/), the Texas State summer program follows the Ross model of teaching students to "think deeply of simple things." Students explore numerical problems, make conjectures, and then justify their answers with proofs. The problems are given with instructions to "prove or disprove and salvage if possible." This places the burden on the students themselves to decide what is important, without simply giving them a procedure to follow.

Of course, there are other models. To build on prior knowledge, teachers need to recognize when students already know some of the curriculum (Page 2000). Amy Warshauer, a sixth-grade teacher at a magnet middle school in central Texas, suggests that a change in the culture of the classroom is necessary: "Before teaching how to do something, ask the students how they would do it.... The students usually will understand how to work through a problem after they are shown how, but it is even more exciting to see if they can do it on their own or working with their classmates. This allows them to share with others (and me) new ways of looking at and solving problems" (personal communication, March, 21, 2009). That is, this teacher assumes that the students can figure out how to do a problem, and then teaches only what needs to be taught. The technique can be used with all students, but acquires special meaning with gifted students: it acknowledges and uses their own contributions and makes the learning their own.

Many special needs of gifted students are different from those of more general students only in degree. Researchers and observers of classrooms have pointed out that all students must find the activity or task worthwhile and challenging. All students need a classroom environment that guides them to probe deeply, to risk making mistakes, and to take the task to a new level (Freiman 2008; NCTM 2000). Routine problems that superficially address concepts or provide little challenge or new knowledge for the students result in their disengagement from learning (Sheffield 1999). The classroom difficulty is that a problem that challenges the average student may be routine for the gifted student.

Consequently, we must be sure that the intellectual "ceiling" of our teaching is high enough that the gifted student isn't forced to stoop. One key is differentiated instruction: the art of offering problems or environments that are at once meaningful to the average student and challenging to the gifted student. Chval and Davis (2008) provide ideas for successful differentiation in a middle school classroom, particularly for the gifted students, and Page (2000) addresses professional development needed to prepare and support teachers in implementing differentiation in their classroom practices.

When presented with the question, "How do you differentiate your instruction for these gifted students?" Sandra Saenz, a seventh-grade math teacher from McAllen, Texas, in the Rio Grande Valley, responded, "One way I differentiate instruction is by assigning students to groups by ability level (low, middle, high). They are assigned a basic problem and an algebra problem based on the same concept. As I assess them through observation and conversation, I am able to pinpoint those students capable of higher achievement. When they present their problems, the presenter(s) are usually those students that understood both the basic material and the algebra. To those students that are ready I assign algebra-based problems from their textbook" (personal communication, March 22, 2009).

Differentiation can occur in the areas of curriculum, practice, and assessment. It allows teaching practices that support students' participation, engagement, and mathematical learning at their own level. It also allows for assessment that gives students genuine feedback about their learning, while offering teachers feedback that informs their instruction (Winebrenner 2000).

Unfortunately, differentiating instruction can be very difficult, given the numerous demands on a teacher's time. The most challenging aspect of teaching in such a learning environment might well be how to orchestrate curriculum that engages all the students in the classroom. This leads to our second principle of an equitable education for mathematically promising students.

Principle 2: Challenge students with rich problems that encourage deep exploration

Problems that can be modified, extended, and differentiated can give all students opportunities for growth. Even struggling students need to engage in solving interesting problems that promote understanding and may require additional time and practice. For high-performing students, the need is greater still. Allowing students time to explore rich problems is critical to their developing the confidence to tackle new problems in the future. By discussing their solutions with one another, students will gain new insights and a much better understanding of their own ideas.

Amanda Voigt, who teaches seventh and eighth grades at a middle school in San Marcos, Texas, uses the routine task of adding and subtracting fractions as an opportunity to differentiate her teaching. While most of Voigt's students work on numerical problems, she poses questions about adding and subtracting fractions with algebraic expressions to those students who are up to the challenge. This task gives her students an opportunity to extend their understanding of the process of operating with numerical fractions while weaving in algebra to generalize and extend the problem.

Other examples involve stretching or adding to the curriculum. For example, middle school students can explore problems involving graph theory, game theory, or combinatorics—topics not usually covered in their textbooks. The challenge is to find open-ended problems that can be investigated at multiple levels.

Successful experiences with such problems require that both the teacher and the students believe that through hard work any student can progress towards a solution. Too often mathematical problems are presented as puzzles that the gifted students "get" and the rest "don't get." It is our task as teachers to nurture and develop all students' abilities through hard work and careful training. Our third principle provides the key.

Principle 3: More progress is possible if students develop a growth mindset

As social psychologist Carol Dweck (2006) elegantly observed, teachers' views of intelligence can lead to dramatically different outcomes of instruction. The National Math Panel summarized this idea:

> Children's goals and beliefs about learning are related to their mathematics performance. Experimental studies have demonstrated that changing children's beliefs from a focus on ability to a focus on effort increases their engagement in mathematics learning, which in turn improves mathematics outcomes: When children believe that their efforts to learn make them "smarter," they show greater persistence in mathematics learning. Related research demonstrates that the engagement and sense of efficacy of African-American and Hispanic students in mathematical learning contexts not only tends to be lower than that of white and Asian students but also that it can be significantly increased. Teachers and other educational leaders should consistently help students and parents to understand that an increased emphasis on the importance of effort is related to improved mathematics performance. This is a critical point, because much of the public's self-evident resignation about mathematics education (together with the common tendencies to dismiss weak achievement and to give up early) seems rooted in the erroneous idea that success is largely a matter of inherent talent or ability, not effort. (NMP 2008, pp. xx)

The view that mathematical ability is something that can be developed through hard work is what Dweck (2006) calls a "growth mindset." People with this view are more likely to persist when given a difficult problem and therefore have the potential to make significant contributions. People who view mathematical ability as being static have what Dweck calls a "fixed mindset." They are much more likely to give up when faced with a difficult problem since they will conclude that they just don't have the ability to solve it.

In an interesting study of the mindset of gifted students, Assouline and colleagues (2006) reported on the factors to which gifted girls and boys attributed school success and failure, including success and failure in mathematics. Both boys and girls usually ascribed failure to effort—not ability—an outcome supporting their having what Dweck would term a "growth mindset." However, an important difference between the boys and girls in this sample of gifted students emerged in the factors to which they attributed success. More boys than girls attributed success to ability. These results would seem to indicate that more boys than girls had, in some sense, a fixed mindset, raising an important question: What is the impact of having a fixed mindset regarding success and a growth mindset regarding failure? Alternatively, the results may have had less to do with what the boys believed that it takes to succeed at mathematics and more to do with their desire to project an image of cool detachment toward the outside world. In their minds, to blame failure on a lack of effort may mean that they did not place enough value on the activity to succeed, and hence the failure reflects more negatively on the activity than on them. The critical issue is whether students with a fixed mindset related to success tend to give up more easily when confronted with a task that pushes them to the limits of their ability, or whether other variables that are equally important to understand and address determine one's persistence. More research in this area might prove fruitful.

It is important to stress that giving gifted students more difficult material—material with which they must struggle—is not inequitable. Indeed, it ensures equity for this group of students because it gives them the environment that they need to develop their abilities to the fullest. If gifted students are more likely to have growth mindsets than fixed mindsets, as Assouline and colleagues (2006) found, then it is very important for teachers to have growth mindsets when thinking about their students. Even the most promising students have significant room for growth and should be put in situations in which they must work hard to achieve that growth. Students who find that all the mathematics that they are given is easy are at risk of turning their minds to other, more intriguing intellectual endeavors. If they continue studying mathematics, at some point they will inevitably come to a time and place where hard work is necessary. They should learn this lesson when they are younger, or they will be discouraged when they are older.

Two questions arise: What level of mathematical content is appropriate, and how does one provide the appropriate level of challenge for all students, including the gifted student? For the most part, the actual content topics are of secondary importance to the three principles articulated so far. However, there is overwhelming evidence that one mathematical strand is essential: algebra (NMP 2008).

If students do not receive an early introduction to the use of variables to model problems, there is a risk that they will not develop the mathematical fluency to tackle difficult problems. Such a gap can result in their losing confidence later on in their ability to solve problems, since they will not have the basic tools to express themselves mathematically or generalize specific examples. Algebraic thinking provides much more than a powerful tool for solving problems; it provides a language for describing patterns and relationships. Its importance is at the heart of our fourth principle.

Principle 4: Early access to algebraic thinking is critical for all students

The National Math Panel reports, "Students who complete Algebra II are more than twice as likely to graduate from college compared to students with less mathematical preparation" (NMP 2008, p. xiii). Algebraic reasoning offers a key to thinking deeply about mathematical problems. The earlier students can use variables, the easier it will be for them to communicate and organize their mathematical thoughts. If students are not introduced to algebraic concepts when young, they often develop a fear of mathematics, thinking that abstract concepts, variables, and algebra are beyond their abilities. In fact, many students have never been given a chance to develop their potential.

Algebra means much more than simply using variables as unknowns. Saul (2008) provides examples of the many facets of algebra. Briefly, the use and understanding of variables on the middle school level allows for the generalization of arithmetic. As Hazlewood, Stouffer, and Warshauer (1989) suggest, algebraic thinking can be taught effectively to young students just as music can be taught to them successfully by use of the Suzuki method (Suzuki 1983).

Although all students should receive a thorough and early introduction to algebra, such an introduction is especially important for students with high potential in mathematics. These students can be stifled if they must wait until ninth grade to experience algebra. A delay in this critical development restricts their progress in ways that may be difficult for them to overcome.

Usiskin (2000) describes levels of mathematical talent. Level 1 allows students to achieve the basic mathematics education in arithmetic that the majority of U.S. students attain by tenth grade, if not earlier. Level 2 permits students to complete "honors" classes in algebra (the work that most students do in high school). Usiskin's levels of talent continue all the way to level 7—the Fields medalist sort of talent. Usiskin points out that high school is not the only time when students can do mathematics associated with talent at level 2. To get to each new level of talent requires additional energy and effort. So a student wishing to get to level 3 not only needs to have talent at level 2, but also needs to exert more effort. Usiskin warns that because students need more and more energy for each new level, the longer they remain at one level, the less likely they are to continue to the next. The key is to begin doing mathematics when young—to learn the language of mathematics and algebra just as one learns to read. This is particularly important for the gifted, since each new level represents a challenge that requires more energy than the preceding levels.

The question of how to weave the simple ideas of variables and algebra into the curriculum is not a simple one. One approach is to encourage students with problems that are so elementary that they can be easily worked without variables. Although this approach is valuable as a first step, it is not powerful enough to generate the interest and excitement that come from using variables to solve problems that are not easily approached without them. This takes us back to our fundamental principle that all students need to be engaged in working on rich problems, not just routine calculations.

Fulfilling the Vision: The Challenge

We have described some of the ways in which we can support the learning of gifted middle school students. Why aren't these supports more commonly in place? Unfortunately, there are numerous obstacles. Some of these are structural. Recently, the No Child Left Behind Act (NCLB 2001) has focused the nation on addressing the needs of students who are having difficulty in meeting minimal standards. Although this is a worthy goal, one result—probably unintended—is that teachers are judged by how successful they are in bringing every student up to a minimal standard, rather than by how successful they are in raising the level of mathematics for every student. In a key report from the Fordham Institute, Duffet, Farkas, and Loveless (2008) examined data from the National Assessment of Educational Progress (NAEP) and showed that this rewards structure for schools and teachers has resulted in an erosion of the quality of education for gifted students.

Another structural problem stems from the evaluation of schools and teachers. It is difficult to find methods of evaluation that measure the progress of all students. One way to do so is to use a "growth model" that measures the increase in each student's performance. In 1991, William Sanders proposed such a system: the Tennessee Value-Added Assessment System (TVAAS; see

Sanders and Horn [1998]). This system tracks student performance over time. In analyzing the research findings from TVAAS, Sanders and Horn [1997, p. 252] point to research that indicates a pattern of higher-scoring students making disproportionately lower gains than average and lower-scoring students. Research indicates that there may be multiple reasons that the needs of the gifted are not being met, including a lack of challenging materials and accelerated course offerings, as well as a concentration of instruction on average or below-average students.

Another problem in working with gifted students, and a problem with significant implications for equity, is that of identification. How do we recognize which students need more challenging problems? Sandra Saenz describes her work with middle school students in McAllen: "I can recognize these students that are able to do more because these are students that are able to have a mathematical conversation with you. They get it. They are at a higher level. They think abstractly. They have a good handle on the basics. They use the vocabulary easily. Math comes naturally. They apply what they've learned with the basics to algebra. They have lots of tools in their tool belt and use them at the right time. They are problem solvers" (personal communication, March 22, 2009).

These comments aptly characterize the work of gifted students. Perhaps more important, they give us clues about how to identify them. Saenz used multiple ways to identify the gifts of students. Reliance on one test or one criterion will not show the various ways in which mathematical talent can reveal itself. This is particularly true of students in schools with limited resources that must be allocated for the mastery of basic skills. In such a context, the gifts that students exhibit in the classroom, in varied and subtle ways, can easily be overlooked.

Indeed, the efforts of the teachers on the classroom level are central to our success in serving gifted students. With all the demands on teachers' time and attention, providing special care for gifted students can easily fall to the bottom of the list. Equitable education for gifted students requires training, support structures, and incentives for teachers, along with the time, tools, and desire to create a positive and challenging learning environment.

In addition, teachers' evaluations of their students must place equal emphasis on all students if we truly want equity in our teaching. It must no longer be acceptable to say, "This student is gifted and will reach a high level no matter what we do." Rather, we need to say, "This student is promising, and it is critical that we nurture and develop the abilities of all of our students." In particular, teachers need to understand the special challenge of providing rich problems that nurture the creativity and imagination of all students. As teachers learn to address the special needs of their gifted students, they will simultaneously create an environment that will offer additional stimulation to all of their students—an environment where students are not afraid of failure but share in the joy of mathematical exploration and discovery.

Doubly at Risk: The Gifted Student in a Resource-Poor Environment

An uncomfortable fact remains for us to examine: in many schools and communities, students who are gifted do not receive the same opportunities as similar students in more affluent schools and communities. These typically underrepresented students (including, but not limited to, women, minorities, rural and some urban students, and economically disadvantaged students) often find themselves in school contexts where there are few resources to encourage the discovery or development of their mathematical gifts.

Consider, for example, the students in Texas who are selected each year to compete on the state's American Regions Math League (ARML) team in a national math competition. The thirty-two to forty-five students who compose this team come predominantly from only a handful of schools in the Houston, Dallas, and Austin areas. According to Sam Baethge, head of the ARML team from Texas, "Over the past five years, the team has been approximately 88 percent boys, 12 percent girls; and is 57 percent Asian American, 42 percent European American, and 1 percent Hispanic. Over the past fifteen years, only one or two students on this team have come from the Rio Grande Valley [a heavily Hispanic area of Texas]" (personal communication, March 15, 2009).

In addition to their regular mathematics classes, the schools that are the source of many of the Texas ARML team members provide special classes for advanced students. A well-funded school might be able to afford such special classes, expenses related to sending students to competitions, or teachers to oversee student math clubs outside of classroom time. In certain environments, the parents of these students might have extra free time to work with students, volunteer at school, or coordinate trips related to mathematics.

These sorts of resources are not available everywhere. In many locations across the United States, schools are doing well if they can fill teaching positions without resorting to under-qualified teachers (for example, non-mathematics majors or teachers without the standard certifications) and can meet the minimum needs of staffing, textbooks, and basic materials. In these schools, finding specialized teachers to work with gifted students and finding the money to pay them to teach extra, elective-style courses would be a luxury. For rural or inner-city schools, filling teacher positions can be a difficult task. To require those schools to add extra staff and offer courses especially for gifted students (aside from fairly common honors-style courses) can seem impossible. Yet, talented students live in and grow up in communities without these resources. What can be done to help students and families in communities with fewer resources?

Fortunately, mathematics education for gifted students is not as expensive as training programs for gifted athletes and musicians. Mathematics does not require large fields for practice, expensive musical instruments, workout machinery, or large band halls. The basics of mathematics instruction are readily available in most schools—a room to learn in, some paper, books, pencils, calculators, and possibly computers. With the exception of computer software and specialized textbooks, the tools of mathematics are reasonably inexpensive and well within most budgets. Money begins to be a larger problem when personnel issues become factors. Some suggestions follow for creating a gifted program without much additional money:

1. Analyze the current school schedule. If a school makes use of a special time each day (or every few days in a block schedule) for homeroom or study hall, talented mathematics students could be assigned to the classroom of a particular teacher—say, from the math department—where students could spend that time working on interesting problems, contest preparation, or a general enrichment curriculum. In San Marcos, Texas, additional time each day is devoted to homeroom and tutorials. During this time, some students attend a class where they prepare for MATHCOUNTS competitions. This approach requires creative scheduling but offers promise as a way to engage talented students constructively while the rest of the school continues to use the same time in regularly scheduled homeroom activities. It is important to look for time in the schedule to offer a challenging elective course. Assuming that such an extra course offers even thirty minutes of instruction daily, students will receive two-and-a-half extra hours a week, or ten hours a month. In a school that offers six six-week units, thirty minutes daily adds ninety extra hours for students to develop their talents in mathematics.

2. Look for volunteers. If the school cannot find time or staff for a modified homeroom or elective period, it may be possible to find community members who are willing to work with students. This strategy requires an adult volunteer and space for students to work beyond the school day (or during lunch or some other available time). Mathematics teachers are obvious candidates as volunteers. They are already at the school, know the students, and have access to classroom resources

such as computers, pencils, and copiers. If teachers are unavailable, community leaders can sometimes help. Volunteers sometimes come from church and civic organizations or are retired seniors, parents, or members of the business community. Meetings can also be planned creatively, such as brown-bag lunch days where everyone meets at a special table or room, or weekend sessions.

3. Keep parents informed. Some families may be able to volunteer time or space. An available parent might host weekly meetings of a math club. Prepare a newsletter or an e-mail list that notifies parents of competition dates and special activities. This newsletter can also include samples of competition-style problems that the family can try at home and links to web resources and materials. A family might not have the means to volunteer time, space, or goods to a program, but might be able to fit in extra at-home learning opportunities.

4. Create a summer math club or camp. Sometimes a school has re-sources that are available during the summer but not during the year, making a summer math camp or club possible. A summer math club might be similar to an after-school club held during the school year. A camp could take the form of a one- to six-week day program offering interested students either enrichment or an accelerated curriculum.

5. Consider outside funding. Many local, state, and national organiza-tions, as well as private foundations and local businesses, offer money for schools to develop and run extra educational programs. To be successful in obtaining funding, conduct research to see what sort of program might fit your school's needs and then write a proposal high-lighting those needs and detailing a coherent plan of action for using the funds. Questions to consider are what students your program will serve, how you will locate those students, how you will advertise the program, what resources you can offer (space, materials, etc.), and what resources you will need. Consider ways to credit the donors publicly for their support. You might be able to solicit volunteers to research and write the proposals.

6. Think outside the school. If there is a local university that offers a teacher preparation program, maybe an arrangement could be made for these preservice teachers to do internships with gifted mathemat-ics students at the school, either during regular school hours or out-side of them. Similarly, professors of mathematics or education might

be able to coordinate their work with the school. Many university educators are in constant need of opportunities to work with students and teachers for research or curriculum design. A possible arrangement might be for professors to have access to relevant data from the school in exchange for helping the school's math program, or even generating such data from their work with the gifted students.

7. Explore the possibility of launching a "math circle" that brings together university faculty to work with middle and high school students on interesting math problems. This could be particularly effective for schools that are located in close proximity to a university.

Conclusion

Gifted students of mathematics compose a group of students with special needs that are often neglected. It is not a question of elitism to insist on serving this group but rather a question of equity. Meeting the needs of students in this group is vitally important if our country is to be competitive in the twenty-first century. This problem can be addressed in multiple ways, ranging from in-school adjustments of expectations for what students can learn, to early algebra, to creative ways of using local resources.

As we have seen, the needs of gifted learners often closely parallel those of other learners. In fact, the issues of equity—both the problems and the solutions—for this group of students are not really different in quality from similar issues for other groups of students. So it is perhaps no surprise that schools making an effort to address the needs of their gifted students often raise the level of learning for all their students.

The most important step in solving any problem is to realize that it is a problem. Then, as Pólya (1945) suggests, we need to make a plan, carry out that plan, and continually check to be sure that what we are doing is effective. By using the same ideas that mathematicians use in problem solving, we can provide a rich learning environment that will develop our next generation of students in math and science, enabling them to be competitive with the best students anywhere.

References

Assouline, Susan G., Nicholas Colangelo, Damien Ihrig, and Leslie Forstadt. "Attributional Choices for Academic Success and Failure by Intellectually Gifted Students." *Gifted Child Quarterly* 50, no. 4 (2006): 283–94.

Chval, Kathryn B., and Jane A. Davis. "The Gifted Student." *Mathematics Teaching in the Middle School* 14 (December 2008): 267–74.

Dixon, Felicia A., Kimberly Prater, Heidi Vine, Mary Jo Wark, Tasha Williams, Tim Hanchon, and Carolyn Shobe. "Teaching to Their Thinking: A Strategy to Meet the Critical-Thinking Needs of Gifted Students." *Journal for the Education of the Gifted* 28, no. 1 (2004): 56–76.

Dweck, Carol. *Mindset: The New Psychology of Success.* New York: Random House, 2006.

Duffet, Ann, Steve Farkas, and Tom Loveless. *High-Achieving Students in the Era of No Child Left Behind.* Washington, D.C.: Thomas B. Fordham Institute, 2008. http://www.edexcellence.net/doc/20080618_high_achievers.pdf.

Freiman, Viktor. "Problems to Discover and to Boost Mathematical Talent in Early Grades: A Challenging Situations Approach." In *Creativity, Giftedness, and Talent Development in Mathematics,* edited by Bharath Sriraman, pp. 155–84. Missoula, Mont.: Information Age Publishing, 2008.

Hazlewood, Donald G., Sandy Stouffer, and Max Warshauer. "Suzuki Meets Pólya: Teaching Mathematics to Young Pupils." *The Arithmetic Teacher* 37 (November 1989): 8–10.

National Center for Education Statistics (NCES). *Pursuing Excellence: Comparisons of International Eighth-Grade Mathematics and Science Achievement from a U.S. Perspective, 1995 and 1999.* NCES 2001-028. Washington, D.C.: U.S. Department of Education, 2000.

National Council of Teachers of Mathematics (NCTM). *Principles and Standards for School Mathematics.* Reston, Va.: NCTM, 2000.

National Mathematics Advisory Panel (National Math Panel; NMP). *Foundations for Success: The Final Report of the National Mathematics Advisory Panel.* Washington, D.C.: U.S. Department of Education, 2008. http://www.ed.gov/about/bdscomm/list/mathpanel/report/finalreport.pdf

National Research Council. *How Students Learn: History, Mathematics, and Science in the Classroom.* Committee on How People Learn: A Targeted Report for Teachers. Edited by M. Suzanne Donovan and John D. Branford. Washington, D.C.: National Academies Press, 2005.

———. *Learning and Understanding: Improving Advanced Study of Mathematics and Science in U.S. High Schools.* Edited by Jerry P. Gollub, Meryl Berthenthal, Jay Labov, and Phillip Curtis. Washington, D.C.: National Academies Press, 2002.

No Child Left Behind Act of 2001. Public Law 107-110. 107th Cong., 1st sess. 8 January 2002.

Page, Sandra W. "When Changes for the Gifted Spur Differentiation for All." *Educational Leadership* 58, no. 1 (2000): 62–65.

Pólya, George. *How to Solve It.* Princeton, N.J.: Princeton University Press, 1945.

Sanders, William L., and Sandra Horn. "The Tennessee Value-Added Assessment System (TVAAS): Mixed-Model Methodology in Educational Assessment." *Journal of Personnel Evaluation in Education* 8 (1994): 299–311.

Sanders, William L., and Sandra P. Horn. "Research Findings from the Tennessee Value-Added Assessment System (TVAAS) Database: Implications for Educational Evaluation and Research." *Journal of Personnel Evaluation in Education* 12 (1998): 247–56.

Saul, Mark. "Algebra: The Mathematics and the Pedagogy." In *Algebra and Algebraic Thinking in School Mathematics,* Seventieth Yearbook of the National Council of Teachers of Mathematics (NCTM), edited by Carole E. Greenes, pp. 63–79. Reston, Va.: NCTM, 2008.

Schmidt, William H., Maria Teresa Tatto, Kiril Bankov, Sigrid Blömeke, Tenoch Cedillo, Leland Cogan, Shin Il Han, Richard Houang, Feng Jui Hsieh, Lynne Paine, Marcella Santillan, and John Schwille. *The Preparation Gap: Teacher Education for Middle School Mathematics in Six Countries.* East Lansing, Mich.: Center for Research in Mathematics and Science Education, Michigan State University, 2007. http://usteds.msu.edu/MT21Report.pdf.

Sheffield, Linda Jensen. "Serving the Needs of the Mathematically Promising." In *Developing Mathematically Promising Students,* edited by Linda Jensen Sheffield, pp. 43–56. Reston, Va.: National Council of Teachers of Mathematics, 1999.

Suzuki, Shinichi. *Nurtured by Love: The Classic Approach to Talent Education.* Miami: Warner Bros. Publishing, 1983.

Tomlinson, Carol Ann, Catherine Brighton, Holly Hertberg, Carolyn M. Callahan, Tonya R. Moon, Kay Brimijoin, Lynda A. Conover, and Timothy Reynolds. "Differentiating Instruction in Response to Student Readiness, Interest, and Learning Profile in Academically Diverse Classrooms: A Review of Literature." *Journal for the Education of the Gifted* 27, no. 2–3 (2003): 119–45.

Usiskin, Zalman. "The Development into the Mathematically Talented." *Journal of Secondary Gifted Education* 11, no. 3 (2000): 152–62.

Winebrenner, Susan. "Gifted Students Need an Education, Too." *Educational Leadership* 58, no. 1 (2000): 52–56.

CHAPTER

9

Inspiring and Developing Student Interest: Several Examples from Foreign Schools

Alexander Karp

◆ International models vary greatly. We can learn from them, but not simply by copying other countries' practices.

◆ Work with gifted students is fully successful only if it is based on effective and challenging mathematical work with all students. The system of working with the gifted should be *open* to everybody.

◆ Successful international programs are *systematic, engaging, substantive,* and include *varied* problems and activities.

◆ Knowledge about mathematics, as well as a love for it, must be built gradually, even when working with gifted students. Different countries have developed different approaches to this task.

This chapter describes several examples of work with gifted middle school students outside the United States. Work of this kind is greatly varied and multifaceted, and there is no room in this short chapter to provide anything close to an exhaustive description of such work around the whole world or even in several countries. Many forms and techniques of teaching, as well as many countries whose systems of mathematics education deservedly attract attention, must be

The author wishes to express his gratitude to Miriam Amit, Anthony Gardiner, and Iosif Heifez for their help in writing this article.

left out of the discussion altogether. Other treatments of foreign approaches to working with gifted students may be found, for example, in works by Sheffield (1999), Karp and Vogeli (2003), and Barbeau and Taylor (2009), which also provide bibliographies on the subject. Here we will focus on just a few examples whose analyses we believe to be particularly important for today's American educator.

When examining international examples, we must keep in mind the many differences that exist between foreign and American schools, beginning with the different numbers of years allotted to the education of students and, in certain cases, the absence of the very notion of a "middle school." Generally speaking, we cannot expect to replicate directly experiences from other countries: the cultural-historical and social differences are usually simply too great. Nonetheless, analyzing foreign approaches leads us to look at American education in new ways, which in turn enrich us with new ideas.

International experiences in working with the gifted have been examined numerous times in the United States. One example is the work of the Russian psychologist Krutetskii (1976). The characteristics of mathematically gifted students identified by Krutetskii are mentioned in virtually every article on this topic. Not infrequently, however, significant aspects of the experience being analyzed are not adequately appreciated. Thus, researchers do not always note the fact that Krutetskii himself always discussed work with gifted students under the assumption that general education for all students was also at a sufficiently high level. For example, Krutetskii explicitly criticized Thorndike, who believed that the study of various sections of algebra, which had been successfully implemented in Soviet public schools on a large scale, was accessible only to sufficiently gifted students.[1]

The interaction between gifted education and general education is a topic that deserves particular attention today. It is this aspect of the examples examined below that is worthy of scrutiny. In selecting them, we have aimed to underscore several characteristics of work with mathematically promising middle school students that appear to be of particular importance. Specifically, education of the gifted must be *open, systematic and substantive, varied,* and *engaging.* Let us explain what these terms mean.

The cohort of mathematically promising students must not be thought of as being predetermined once and for all. Examples of brilliant mathemati-

---

1. Krutetskii characterizes Thorndike's conception as being "extremely mechanistic and permeated with fatalistic ideas on the innateness of ability" (Krutetskii 1976, p. 37). Later, after listing two groups of algebraic abilities defined by Thorndike, he writes, "It is quite apparent that all the 'abilities' in the second group and some in the first are not abilities at all, but typical learned skills" (p. 38).

cians whose talents became manifest only after they reached a certain age are well known, as are instances of people who exhibited remarkable promise that failed to bear fruit in the absence of adequate support. Consequently, the education of the gifted should be constructed in a way that is as *open* as possible, with a view to encompassing more and more new students. Such education should offer students *varied* opportunities to reveal their gifts and interests. It must be constructed *systematically,* with a systematic approach to identifying and recruiting potentially gifted students and a systematic approach to providing them with education and support. At the same time, it is essential to take into account the specific characteristics of the age group that is being served: quite a lot depends on "packaging"—on the presentation of the mathematical content. In other words, instruction must be *engaging.* Attention to this aspect of instruction, however, does not mean that it must not also be *substantive:* educators can and must acquaint middle school students with genuine mathematics. They must not postpone this for later, waiting until the students get older and exposing them only to amusements and diversions for the time being.

Below we give examples of ways in which these principles can be implemented in various situations: in working with promising students as part of a larger group of average students; in more selective forms of education, such as math club sessions or specialized optional classes in one school; and in even more selective contexts—math clubs attended by students from different schools.

Example: "Equalization Problems"

Consider the following problem:

> Two bags contain 90 pay phone tokens, and the first contains 10 tokens more than the second. How many tokens are in each bag?

Certainly, this problem can be easily solved by using equations—the number of tokens in the first bag is x, the number of tokens in the second bag is y, there are $x + y$ tokens in all, $x + y = 90$, and x is 10 greater than y. All that we have to do is to solve the following system of equations: $x + y = 90$, $x - y = 10$. However, the authors of the Russian sixth-grade textbook (Dorofeev and Sharygin 2003, p. 85) in which this problem appears suggest a completely different approach:

> If 10 tokens were removed from the first bag, then 80 tokens would be left in both bags, and moreover they would be evenly distributed between them. Therefore, each of the bags (including the second bag) would contain 40 tokens. Since initially the second bag contained 10 tokens fewer than the first, the first bag initially contained 40 + 10 = 50 tokens. Thus, the answer is: 50 and 40.

The solution given is virtually oral and does not require command of algebraic symbolism. However, it presupposes an ability to pursue a line of reasoning. Such an ability, of course, must be cultivated and developed. The textbook does this by offering several problems in a similar manner. Moreover, it also offers students more difficult problems. Thus, the problem just analyzed leads naturally to a problem in which not just two, but three objects must be "equalized":

> There are 47 books on three shelves. The middle shelf has 4 books fewer than the top shelf and 2 books more than the bottom shelf. How many books are on the top shelf? (Dorofeev and Sharygin 2003, p. 85)

We have cited two problems whose solutions are provided in the textbook. The problems that must be solved by the students are divided into two parts, A (easier problems) and B (more difficult problems). This section of the textbook is intended for all students, without any division between more and less gifted groups. However, the choice of problems for independent solution is left to the teacher's discretion. For example, certain students might not be required to solve the more difficult problems (although these problems, solved by other students, will still be discussed in front of the entire class). This section is followed by another, titled "For Those Who Are Interested," which the teacher is not required to cover in class; it is meant to be read by interested students or used by the teacher in one-on-one work with such students. Here the idea of "equalization" is applied to more difficult situations. For example, this idea is used to solve the following problem:

> Three textbooks and 5 notebooks cost 95 rubles, while 1 textbook and 2 notebooks cost 33 rubles. How much does a notebook cost?

The proposed solution consists in "equalizing" the numbers of textbooks in the first and second cases. To do so, problems solvers must multiply the numbers of textbooks and notebooks in the second case by 3, deriving the fact that the cost of 3 textbooks and 6 notebooks is 99 rubles. After this, it is obvious that one notebook costs 4 rubles.

Examining the example in greater detail

The example just cited deserves to be examined from several different angles. The first striking thing about it is that the textbook's authors make no mention of gifted students per se. Gifted students are not the ones—or more precisely, not the only ones—whom the authors address. The textbook is addressed to all students. Interesting and *substantitive* mathematical problem solving is *open* to everybody.

We note in connection with this example that in analyzing many years of data about the winners of Leningrad Mathematical Olympiads (see Karp

2003), we have repeatedly come across sudden increases in numbers of winners at one or another school in the city. Such jumps were invariably explained by the arrival of a new teacher at the school who was capable of structuring work with the students in a new way. Consequently, the Olympiads—which are usually viewed as a means for selecting gifted students (although in Leningrad they were initially conceived not as a means for selecting students but as a way of getting students involved in mathematics)—in effect merely registered the emergence of giftedness, which had taken place, as might be supposed, thanks to the teacher. "Development into the next level of talent" (Usiskin 2000) involves, at its initial stage, working with all students and viewing them all as potentially gifted. Such work entails offering all students the possibility of gaining at least a marginally adequate notion of how mathematicians think and operate.

The example above also reflects a specific organizational and methodological approach, and this is the second point that deserves our attention. We see here an approach that is *systematic:* we are presented not just with the solution to a single problem, but with the methodical unfolding of a mathematical concept. Furthermore, from working with all students, the textbook moves on to differentiated work, in which students may work on different problems or on the same problem in different ways—for example, *actively,* by solving it independently, or *passively,* by being exposed to someone else's solution. This stage is followed by another, at which, as we have seen, further differentiation occurs—some students will be interested in reading the special section, whereas others will not be (despite the textbook's efforts and presumably the efforts of the teacher), and they will consequently be allowed not to read it. The textbook underscores the importance of interest, and this is consistent with Ridge and Renzulli's (1981) approach, long known to American researchers, in which interest or "commitment to the subject" constitutes one of the characteristics of talent. The authors of the textbook assume that more advanced students will, generally speaking, prefer to examine the section being covered in greater detail and will spend more time studying it. (Note the fundamental contrast between this approach and the approach of textbooks that indicate in teachers' editions that advanced students and advanced classes may cover one or another section much faster than ordinary students.) The gradualness and smoothness of the transitions between the stages described here are worth noting again, as is the *open* nature of the groups of students that emerge in the process. A student might not solve a B-level problem in one section but might solve B-level problems in another section, or a student might be interested in some of the "For Those Who Are Interested" sections but not in others.

We stipulated above that work with the gifted must be *varied* and *engaging,* and this is a third point that deserves discussion. The problems analyzed here, naturally, look nothing like the problems that are usually solved in American classrooms, and this fact by itself attracts our attention; however, the specific methodological construction of the section described above may well be challenged. Indeed, the section begins by identifying a certain technique for solving problems, this technique is then examined on the basis of several examples, and then students are given a series of problems that can be solved by using this technique. Can this be considered an instance of genuine problem solving, fit for developing potentially gifted students, or does it offer nothing more than routine exercises, based on the memorization of a technique and its replication?

The Russian psychologist Kalmykova (1981) strongly objected to drawing an excessively sharp distinction between productive creative activity and replication as an activity that is supposedly based exclusively on rote memorization. In keeping with her viewpoint, it is more appropriate to think about a kind of continuous spectrum with replication that is indeed based entirely on rote memorization on one end and the most vivid examples of independent creativity on the other, with various situations that contain different proportions of creative activity and replication in the middle. Consequently, the desire to develop students' creative abilities by no means implies the rejection of repetition and replication: everything depends on the specific dosage of creative and replicative elements in the problems presented to the students, and on the differences between the problems that are united in one section by one idea. An endless series of completely identical tasks is undoubtedly harmful for mathematical development, but the usefulness of a problem set in which every problem is fundamentally different from every other is also open to question—all students, including gifted ones, need an opportunity to become familiar with a new idea. Excessive haste can push them away. By contrast, the well-balanced set of assignments found in this textbook, which includes a fair amount of repetition but also allows students to go through a smooth and gradual development, helps to keep students engaged and interested.

The sample problems above are also interesting because they suggest a source from which nonstandard and engaging mathematical topics and assignments for the mathematically gifted can be drawn. Once, schools used to devote a great deal of attention to solving word problems, by using arithmetic, rather than algebraic, methods, similar to the ones employed in the solutions of the problems described above. An enormous number of intricate arithmetic techniques were subsequently deemed—in our view, quite rightly—to be useless and merely serving to clutter the school curriculum, which was already crammed with sufficient content (Smith and Reeve 1927). This does not mean, however, that the modern course in mathematics must have no place for arithmetic solutions. It has been noted in the literature that many difficulties in the study of algebra may be explained by shortcomings in the teaching and studying of arithmetic. Arithmetic gives students an ability to develop their reasoning without relying heavily on algebraic symbolism, which is often a source of difficulty for students.

It is not arithmetic alone that is the issue, however. The history of mathematics and the history of mathematics education are replete with examples of substantive theories, deep problems, interesting and clever reasoning techniques, and so on, which over time have faded from the interests of professional mathematicians and become inappropriate for the general—and inevitably brief—school course in mathematics. This heritage of the past, however, may be exceptionally useful in working with potentially gifted students, whom it is vital to expose to accessible examples of genuine mathematics. As we can see, Russian mathematics educators are making use of this heritage. Other countries also have traditions of putting this heritage to use; for example, a classic instance of such a use and presentation of the heritage of the past—although one aimed not at middle school students, but at older ones—is found in Rademacher and Toeplitz (1966).

Continuing the Work in School

The next stage of work with mathematically promising students might take the form of math clubs (or "math circles") and optional classes organized by the school. These are extracurricular activities in which not all students take part, but only those who are interested. Continuing our description of the Russian experience, let us focus on several more examples.

Sheinina and Solovieva (2005) offer brief descriptions of thirty such optional classes for fifth and sixth graders (ages 10–12). The classes last for an hour and a half or two hours and take place at least twice a month. They are for the most part devoted to problem solving, but the problems are presented in different ways to be both varied and engaging. For example, in one class, the students first solved a problem about the age of the hero of one of their favorite fairy tales, then solved the problem in a "standard" mathematical formulation, and finally solved a word problem from an ancient book, with the problem accordingly formulated in verse. In addition to problem solving, each class also includes some discussion of an item from the history of mathematics—for example, biographies of Archimedes, Descartes, Newton, Sofia Kovalevskaya, and others.

A more advanced program than the one just described might take the form of optional classes—in other words, classes selected by students with particular interests in mathematics. In this case, the students study specific sections of mathematics in a more *systematic* fashion. An example of what the curriculum for such classes might look like may be found in a manual by Nikol'skaya (1991), which offers the following topics for grades 7 and 8:

- Number systems
- Prime and composite numbers
- Geometric constructions
- Special points in a triangle
- Sets of numbers
- The coordinate method
- The elements of mathematical logic
- Geometric transformations of the plane

Each section consists mainly of problem sets, prefaced by brief theoretical introductions and examples.

Of course, the work of such an optional class requires that its students participate in it from the very beginning; that is, from the beginning of the school year or the semester. However, for students who have never taken such classes, it is relatively easy to begin doing so—the topics covered by the various classes are not presented in any kind of rigid order, which makes the classes quite *open*.

An example from the United Kingdom

The books in the British series "Extension Mathematics" (Gardiner 2007) represent an example of a similar approach, which is also aimed at entire classes of schoolchildren. The author points out that the books may be used with students of various ages, but it is evident that he regards children between the ages of 11 and 14 as his principal target audience. The books are not aimed at rare individual "exceptional" schoolchildren—but rather at a sizable cohort, large enough to fill a special class at a school, which would use such a book as a textbook. The author notes that the "material here seeks to encourage pupils not just to grind out answers but to think and to talk about elementary techniques" (Gardiner 2007, Alpha, p. 4). This goal is accomplished through problem solving, and the books effectively consist of problem sets on different topics.

The sections of each book in this series typically begin with special introductory assignments that the author deliberately asks teachers to give to their students to solve individually or in groups—teachers are not to analyze and solve them in front of the whole class as examples. The problems "should be used to bring out—and to correct—misconceptions and errors, so that every member of the class understands how to approach such problems and so that all pupils emerge from the discussion with a clear idea of what is expected in that section" (Gardiner 2007, Beta, p. 7).

An example of such an assignment is the problem that opens the section "Calculating Angles":

In quadrilateral *ABCD* the sizes of three angles are given (see fig. 9.1).
a) Work out the size of the angles marked *w* and *x*. Justify your answers.

b) What can you prove about △*ABC*?

c) Can you calculate the sizes of the angles marked *y* and *z*? (p. 40)

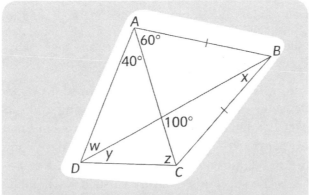

Fig. 9.1. Quadrilateral *ABCD* from a sample problem on calculating angles, from Gardiner (2007, p. 40)

Note that the problem is formulated in an "open" fashion: the students are not told to "prove that △*ABC* is an equilateral triangle," but simply asked, "What can you prove about △*ABC*?" They are not told to "calculate the sizes of the angles," but simply asked, "Can you calculate the sizes of the angles marked *y* and *z*?" This seemingly slight change heightens the exploratory aspect of the assignment.

The assignments in the book are divided into three levels: "Tasters," which are seen as being accessible to all students in the class; "Core Items," which cover the entire program but are possibly not appropriate for all students; and "Extension Items," which "push Core ideas slightly further" (p. 6).

Drawing some conclusions

The issues of *openness* and of large-scale applicability arise here once more. "Giftedness" is often thought of as a special and thus rare occurrence. Yet, in the examples just cited of material not intended for use with all students but specifically with those who are gifted and interested, we once again observe a concern for many students rather than a search for one or two exceptional ones. Gardiner (2007), who for many years was responsible for working with the UK team at the International Mathematics Olympiads and thus handled the most mathematically gifted students in the country, nonetheless takes a skeptical stance toward the prevalent view that the main problem consists in discovering talent in some miraculous fashion, after which nothing more remains to be done except to provide certain materials for its use in displaying itself. Talent does not come "ready-made": it is formed and manifested gradually in the process of study. Consequently, it requires gradual, multiple-stage work that demands time and labor from both students and teachers. As Gardiner (2007, Teacher's Book, p. 14) writes,

> Most pupils need time to absorb new ideas and methods, and to identify and overcome basic mistakes. So effective provision for able pupils cannot be based on occasional activities, talks, or visits—no matter how remarkable they may be. Long-term progress depends on consistent, day-by-day provision.

Such *systematic* work is built first and foremost around problems, and the selection of problems on various topics, with interesting and substantive formulations that inspire students to investigate them—problems that are not isolated from one another but comprise some unified and developing theory—is particularly important. Children come to such classes not to be entertained but to work, and it is the substantive nature of such work, including its successes and its discoveries, that is its main interest and attraction. At the same time, as we have seen in the example of the Russian math circles described above, classes are supposed to have room for interesting stories, games, and other forms of activity that will attract middle school students and help them to sustain their interest in mathematics during the initial stages. One must not forget that interest in "pure" mathematical activity also comes gradually and is formed in the course of study.

Going outside the School: An Example from Israel

Work with gifted students inside the school can and must be supported by independent (or family-supported) reading on the part of the students. Although the mathematical literature for middle school students is much smaller than the mathematical literature for high school students, it does exist. Nonetheless, such independent work clearly cannot be a substitute for working with a more experienced and professional mentor and interacting with other interested and gifted students. To organize such work within the framework of a single school is often impossible; thus, it requires other organizational frameworks that encompass a broader audience.

One example of such an educational framework is the Israeli program Kidumatica, which appeared more than ten years ago under the auspices of Ben Gurion University in Beer-Sheva. Each year, the first organizational stage of this program consists in establishing contact with potentially interested students. To this end, the program operates through the schools, asking them to submit lists of students between the ages of 10 and 14 who might be interested in participating. Subsequently, invitations to apply to the program are sent out to all of these students. About 800 students usually apply (note that those who do not apply in one year may apply in subsequent years—the program is *open*, and students can join it at later stages). They are asked to solve several problem sets, and their solutions are used to select the 200–250 future participants in the program.

The problems that prospective participants are given vary and cannot be characterized either as standard classroom problems, which test how well students have assimilated what they have been taught and their command of certain algorithms, or as standard Olympiad problems or puzzles. They include problems that require students to explain or to prove something, and—even more frequently—problems that require students to examine different cases, go over all possible variants, and so on. Lacking the means to admit all interested students and recognizing the inevitable mistakes of any method of selection at this stage, the faculty aims to select students who appear to be disposed to prolonged, *systematic* work (and subsequently, the faculty members do everything possible to dispel the notion that a problem will either be solved in one minute or will not be solved at all).

The selected students attend weekly two-and-a-half-hour classes. These classes are extremely *varied*. Every five weeks, the students participate in program-wide events—games, contests, Olympiads. The other classes may be arranged as mini-courses (four weeks each), in which students study some small area of mathematical theory and use it to solve problems. These courses might be entirely devoted to solving sets of interconnected problems and discussing their solutions, or they might be devoted to difficult exploratory problems (this approach becomes more popular in the higher grades).

During their first year in the program, the students are assigned to groups on the basis of their classes in ordinary schools; in subsequent years, the groups are reshaped mainly in accordance with students' levels of achievement, so that one and the same group might contain students from different classes.

The program is very successful. Among its graduates are many highly accomplished students and graduates of Israel's leading universities. Although mathematics Olympiads are not a precise measure of achievement, it is noteworthy that prior to the creation of Kidumatica, almost no students from the geographical region that this program serves were among the winners of the country's mathematics Olympiads. Since its inception, however, Israel's team at the international Olympiad in mathematics has regularly included two or even three of its graduates.

Two Case Studies

It is not possible in this chapter to describe the most selective Russian mathematics clubs (or "circles"; see Fomin, Genkin, and Itenberg [1996]), which constitute a vital component of work with gifted students in the Russian system, some of whose other components have been discussed above. Nor have we addressed other highly selective forms of education, such as specialized schools for the mathematically gifted, which students in Russia also have the option of attending beginning at age 13. However, those who go through such selective education are precisely the ones who usually become well known. To examine the examples that we have previously analyzed from a different angle, we will now shift the focus of our analysis from the educational framework to the students who received their education in it, and offer two case studies of individuals who came in contact with the system of selective gifted education.

Case study of D

D's father was a college mathematics teacher. Therefore, D started becoming acquainted with mathematics at home, from about the age of seven. In sixth grade, he began attending the city math circle (his school did not have one). The circle's sessions were devoted to solving problems that were, as he recalls it, more entertaining than difficult. Everything changed during the spring of that year, after D's successful performance at the city mathematics Olympiad. D was invited at once to two very strong math circles, where the children solved very difficult problems and a fair amount of attention was devoted to studying non-school mathematics. D attended both circles for some time and then concentrated on one of them. To this experience were added mathematics summer camps, in which a math circle's participants studied mathematics daily for a month. In eighth grade, D entered one of the city's strongest mathematics schools, where the mathematics curriculum was much more advanced than that at ordinary schools and contained twice as many classes. D remained at this school until graduation, combining his studies there with participation in various city mathematics circles. D was a winner at Olympiads of the highest level. Currently, he is an associate professor in the mathematics department of one of Russia's most prestigious universities.

Case study of I

I was always a very good student in school, but she never attended any mathematics circles before sixth grade. In sixth grade, she performed very successfully at the city mathematics Olympiad and was invited to the selective city-level mathematics circle. She recalls the meetings of the circle as being incredibly boring. "They would write problems on the board, then for over an hour everyone would sit silently and try to solve them. Then those who had solved something would talk about their solutions in a very boring way. Then we would be sent home or, if there was still time, we would be given new problems. The teacher never told us about anything, and the group never did anything collectively." After several sessions, despite her parents' objections, I quit the mathematics circle and never again participated in a mathematics circle or a mathematics Olympiad. Currently, she has a doctorate in biology and works in the biology department of the same university as D.

In Lieu of a Conclusion: What Can Be Learned?

The two case studies above demonstrate how differently students may develop within one and the same system while very similar methods are in use. Of course, a great deal has to do with individual differences, but probably it would be wrong to ignore the seemingly minor differences in teaching styles in circles and in the students' education at home and in school before they joined selective mathematics circles.

In talking about the education of the gifted, we must always find a certain balance between two extremes: the education must be serious and substantive, yet at the same time entertaining; it must be open and offer new opportunities to those who were previously outside the system, yet at the same time clearly include an element of selectivity. To recognize the variety of the existing possibilities is the first thing that can be learned from studying foreign experience.

It is natural to see D's case as proof of the success of this system of working with gifted students: the education that D received in mathematics circles, in summer camps, and at the mathematics school was indeed deep and multifaceted and obviously exerted a great influence on him.

We have not addressed the details of working with the strongest students. The concrete methods for working with them, as well as the problems and other materials used in working with them, are becoming increasingly available in English (beginning with Fomin, Genkin, and Itenberg [1996]) and can be put to use anywhere (and indeed have already been used for a long time).

It is important to understand, however, that success in working with D was achieved in part because he had entered the system of mathematics circles at a certain age, because he was sufficiently mathematically developed to perform well in the Olympiad, and so on. It may be said that in D, the system received a kind of bonus—a kind of return on its investment in making the mathematics circles sufficiently popular, and in ensuring that in the previous generation, D's parents had been sufficiently well prepared to help in his initial development. This fact alone should make it worth our while to think about how foreign approaches might help us to improve the mathematics education of promising students whose achievements are far below D's level.

Our starting point must be a widely recognized fact: by comparison with foreign mathematics education, general mathematics education in the United States often falls short. It tends to be both less substantive and less systematic (Schmidt 1999). Although NCTM (2000, p. 52) has recognized that "problem solving is not only a goal of learning mathematics but also a major means of doing so," an examination of numerous textbooks reveals that this principle is still far from being put into practice. Moreover, one often comes across a kind of imitation of problem solving, reasoning, and proving, in which assertions that are completely obvious to the student are proved at length and with all kinds of references, while any assertions that have the least bit of substance to them figure as axioms. Such an approach can only kill interest in genuine reasoning and proving. All students are capable of learning about far more substantive problems than the ones to which they are exposed today. This is possible—children in other countries do it!

We have mentioned the importance of gradualness in working with school-children, and in particular, the usefulness of presenting the same topic at different levels of difficulty. How many American middle school teachers are capable of selecting problems at two, three, or four levels of difficulty, while taking into account the variety of their students' abilities and interests? Is this skill something that is taught in the process of teacher education? Are teachers equipped with the necessary materials for this and with an adequate variety of supplementary manuals? Publicizing the literature that already exists in the United States and abroad would constitute an important step toward improvement—as would the translation of certain materials into English (and as we indicated above, much has already been done in this respect). Renewed involvement with the use of various classic materials (problems) would be most valuable; their use abroad has been discussed above.

Extracurricular activities must also be varied. It has long been noted that U.S. students are often convinced that a problem will be either solved in a minute or not solved at all (Schoenfeld 1985). Consequently, the foreign experience of working on "long" problems—and of a general orientation toward such work—is highly useful. It is likewise necessary to plan out the work of newly appearing programs in the long term: serious results are linked to changes in students' psychology, and these do not happen overnight. Consequently, both administrators and those who support various programs in mathematics stand to benefit from becoming acquainted with foreign approaches and from recognizing the fact that perhaps the most important results appear only over time and that it is naive to expect to see them immediately.

The pedagogical and the mathematical elements of working with schoolchildren are often treated as two separate things in everyday discourse. It is not unusual to hear statements like, "She is a good mathematician but does not know how to teach," or, "He works really well with children but does not know the subject." A common assumption is that pedagogical and mathematical elements of working with schoolchildren are skills that are learned separately as well. But the pedagogical and the mathematical must converge into one. Teachers must know how to solve pedagogical problems through mathematics, and conversely, they must be able to select adequate pedagogical means to achieve a better understanding of mathematics. These skills, of course, are important in working with all students, but in addition, without them it is impossible to identify and develop the mathematically promising ones. Examples of such work (both American and foreign) must become widely known.

This in turn leads to what is perhaps the most important thing that can be learned by analyzing other countries' experiences: public attention to working with the gifted is essential. Working with the gifted must be perceived not as standing apart from working with other children (if not directly opposed to it), but as a kind of indicator—however narrow it might be—of the state of working with children in general. The state of working with the mathematically promising must be widely, regularly, and comprehensively discussed: this will help to create new and valuable traditions and to sustain the ones that already exist.

References

Barbeau, Edward J., and Peter J. Taylor, eds. *Challenging Mathematics in and beyond the Classroom: The 16th ICMI Study* (New ICMI Study Series). New York: Springer, 2009.

Dorofeev, G., and I. Sharygin, eds. *Matematika 6. Chast' I. Uchebnik.* [Mathematics 6. Part I. Textbook]. Moscow: Drofa, Prosveschenie, 2003.

Fomin, Dmitri, Sergey Genkin, and Ilia Itenberg. *Mathematical Circles: (Russian Experience).* Translated by Mark Saul. Providence, R.I. : American Mathematical Society, 1996.

Gardiner, Tony. *Extension Mathematics.* Alpha, Beta, Gamma, Teacher's Book. Oxford, UK: Oxford University Press, 2007.

Kalmykova, Z.I. *Produktivnoe myschlenie kak osnova obuchaemosti* [Productive Thinking as the Foundation of the Ability to Learn]. Moscow: Pedagogika, 1981.

Karp, Alexander. "Thirty Years After: The Lives of Former Winners of Mathematical Olympiads." *Roeper Review* 25, no. 2 (2003), 83–87.

Karp, Alexander, and Bruce R. Vogeli. "Other Nations' Approaches to Providing for Talented Students." In *Activating Mathematical Talent* (NCSM Monograph Series, 1), edited by Bruce R. Vogeli and Alexander Karp, pp. 28–36. Golden, Colo.: NCSM–Houghton Mifflin Company School Division, 2003.

Krutetskii, V. A. *The Psychology of Mathematical Abilities in Schoolchildren.* Translated by J. Teller. Chicago: University of Chicago Press, 1976.

National Council of Teachers of Mathematics (NCTM). *Principles and Standards for School Mathematics.* Reston: Va.: NCTM, 2000.

Nikol'skaya, I., ed. *Fakul'tativnyi kurs po matematike.* 7–9 klassy [Optional Class in Mathematics, Grades 7–9]. Moscow: Prosveschenie, 1991.

Rademacher, Hans, and Otto Toeplitz. *The Enjoyment of Math.* Princeton, N.J.: Princeton University Press, 1966.

Ridge, H. Laurence, and Joseph S. Renzulli. "Teaching Mathematics to the Talented and Gifted." In *The Mathematical Education of Exceptional Children and Youth,* edited by Vincent J. Glennon, pp. 191–266. Reston, Va.: National Council of Teachers of Mathematics, 1981.

Schmidt, William H. *Facing the Consequences: Using TIMSS for a Closer Look at United States Mathematics Education.* Dordrecht, The Netherlands: Kluwer Academic Publishers, 1999.

Schoenfeld, Alan H. *Mathematical Problem Solving.* New York: Academic Press, 1985.

Sheffield, Linda Jensen, ed. *Developing Mathematically Promising Students.* Reston, Va.: National Council of Teachers of Mathematics, 1999.

Sheinina, O., and G. Solovieva. *Matematika. Zaniatiya shkol'nogo kruzhka.* 5–6 klassy [Mathematics. Lessons for the School Circle, Grades 5–6]. Moscow: NTS ENAS, 2005.

Smith, David Eugene, and William David Reeve. *The Teaching of Junior High School Mathematics.* Boston: Ginn and Company, 1927.

Usiskin, Zalman. "The Development into the Mathematically Talented." *Journal of Secondary Gifted Education* 11, no. 3 (2000): 152–62.

Afterword

As editors, we now take advantage of the opportunity to have the last word about mathematically promising middle school students. Our focus is the future. What's next?

We hope that this publication—a joint venture of the National Council of Teachers of Mathematics (NCTM), the National Association for Gifted Children (NAGC), and National Middle School Association—will be the first in a series of collaborative endeavors. Perhaps another collaboration might be a joint statement from the three organizations that can guide educators and parents in the development of district policies about mathematics education that support gifted students and educators working with them. Each district will have slightly different ways of addressing and advocating for some of the most important issues, but a joint position paper that includes suggestions for appropriate identification, support, and development, as well as best practices for instruction, would be a welcome resource.

We hope, too, that mathematicians and educators will likewise undertake joint ventures in providing mathematical resources for gifted children in middle schools. Mathematics is endowed with a structure that can be perceived on the most elementary levels and which endures as the student's mathematical horizons expand. The tradition of examining elementary mathematics from an advanced standpoint deserves continued attention.

We have much to learn about the kind of classroom environment and professional development that teachers of mathematically talented students need. These are other areas of research that are missing from the current research landscape.

Activities outside the classroom encourage students to think outside the box and help their talents to blossom. We need to think of ways to expand access to such programs for all students and to get support from families and communities—not just from educators.

The search for equity is an ongoing process. Gifted and talented students in every school and every community need opportunities for continuous progress.

We need to lift the ceiling for all these students, a process that will require funding for researchers and counselors, as well as instructional materials to support promising students—especially those from communities of poverty or historically underserved groups.

Currently, there is much discussion about the status of U.S. students in relation to students in other countries. Indeed, so much has been said about work with students in Asian cultures that we did not even include this area of the world in the chapter about international models and issues. We have much to learn from this rapidly developing part of the world.

Reciprocally, we hope that student progress in the United States will be seen as a source of inspiration for other countries. We have good reason to be proud of the American approach to education. We are good at fostering creativity. We have deep experience in general enrichment. Perhaps most important, we are flexible: we find ways to let students who are "late bloomers" blossom to their fullest. America is the land of the second chance.

We hope that other cultures will see the benefits of some of our approaches. An exchange of contrasting views will allow students—wherever they may be—to benefit from a global perspective on education. Cross-cultural research that looks broadly at both curriculum and instructional practices would be internationally beneficial.

We conclude with the suggestion that the deeper purpose of this book is not simply to provide an overview, but to open up a dialogue among the many stakeholders for effectively working with mathematically promising middle school students.